SPIRITUAL HEALING *of the* MIND *and* BODY

SPIRITUAL HEALING *of the* MIND *and* BODY

PAUL F. GORMAN

REDONDO BEACH
CALIFORNIA

SPIRITUAL HEALING OF THE MIND AND BODY

FIRST PAPERBACK EDITION 2015

ISBN-13: 978-0692358061

ISBN-10: 0692358064

Published by Vine Press, Redondo Beach, California

Set in Tramuntana 1 Text Pro 10.5/13.5

Printed by CreateSpace

Available worldwide from Amazon and all other book stores

www.miracleself.com

Edited by M.L. and W.U.

With deep gratitude for your loving, devoted and invaluable work on this, and every text.

Rise in conscious awareness—this is the entire secret.

As conscious awareness rises, detaching from and
leaving behind false belief, ever greater degrees of heaven
become visible through the unconditioned mind.

"As in heaven so on earth."

The earth and all its people, creatures and conditions
are witnessed unconditioned, whole and harmonious,
love and union of all emerging through the fog of false sense.

Indeed, "As in heaven so on earth" emerges as the one
reality. The bondage of false, material sense is dispelled,
and the unconditioned experience of man, earth and
universe is experienced harmonious, peaceful and free, in love.

Paul F. Gorman

Other Books by Paul F. Gorman

The Miracle Self

The Giving Self

The Impersonal Self

The Way of Awakening

Satisfied with God Alone

The 7 Spiritual Steps To Solving Any Problem

Opening The Windows of Heaven

The Fully Manifest Self

Only God Is

That Which You Seek

www.miracleself.com

CONTENTS

One

Spiritual Being

The deep truth of being, body and world has been taught and demonstrated for over 4000 years. The few of each generation who can hear it get up and walk free on earth and beyond, but the majority cannot hear, and remain in the prison of belief.

Truth has been given to humanity by the greatest illumined beings who have walked the earth including Gautama the Buddha, Jesus the Christ, Nanak, Mohammed, Shankara, Lao Tzu, Rumi, Fakhruddin 'Iraqi, Maimonides, St. Francis, Brother Lawrence, Meister Eckhart, Jacob Boehme and many others, to the more contemporary mystics and their teachings, particularly Mary Baker Eddy's *Christian Science,* Joel S. Goldsmith's *Infinite Way,* and today's *Miracle Self.*

That truth is this: life (mind, body and universe) is *principle*—the great principle itself. As principle it is as clearly demonstrable as any principle is when *it itself* is realized and lived. We cannot expect principle to adjust itself for our benefit (can you imagine the chaos of such an arrangement?); rather we must discover and adhere to *it* if we wish to benefit by it. When and as, and by the degree we do, we have the boundless freedom of that principle for the benefit of not only ourselves but the world.

In this very way, the principle of truth—God, spirit—must first be discovered and adhered to. The way is "straight and narrow" as is the way of any principle. The truth of being is wonderfully clear and succinct, yet if we veer off its definite path we lose it. It is only as we stay in truth that we *have* the infinity and omnipresence of God throughout our experience—just as we have the infinity and omnipresence of math as we stay in the principle of math.

"Where the spirit of the Lord is [where the principle of truth is as individual being], there is liberty"—where the presence of true spiritual consciousness is, there is harmony, health, plenty, freedom and peace.

Only the very few throughout history have caught and were able to demonstrate the great truth that man is a spiritual being living in a spiritual universe, not a physical being living in a material universe. Still today, only the very few truly awaken and live the life of spiritual harmony, freedom and purpose in all their ways. Why? Because the straight and narrow way of the great truth principle has not been understood. Those who have understood and adhered to truth have what is termed the "healing consciousness." Their selfless works benefit many thousands or tens of thousands of people searching for healing and then ongoing health, wholeness and vitality of body.

As spiritual being, every person is infinite, eternal, divine being, forever free in truth, perfect and purposeful in the one presence: God. But because truth is unknown and mostly unwanted by the masses, and still misunderstood by even most on the "spiritual path" today, the world has long suffered illness, disease, injury, poverty, starvation, prejudice and injustice along with an inability to heal or be healed spiritually. Yet health, wholeness and vitality of body; plus safety, security, abundance, union and justice; and the healing of any and every mental, bodily and world discord; and then (as the individual and collective race lift into a greater living awareness of truthful, spiritual identity) even the avoidance of all human disease and suffering are—to the spiritually illumined—as natural as the living of any principle.

It is time to be clear about what healing is. Today, collective spiritual awareness has risen and significantly expanded to the height and receptivity that enables truth to not only be heard but accepted and received. This significant acceptance and receptivity enables individuals who are seeking truth to finally rest from the multitude of false beliefs about God, being, body and world, open their awareness to God itself, and experience the health, harmony, abundance and peace of truthful living. In this spiritually rested and receptive state the body heals naturally. But we must understand what the body actually is before spiritual healing can be experienced, first individually and then collectively.

HEALING IS NOT WHAT IT IS BELIEVED TO BE

Spiritually healing the body of any illness, disease, injury, dysfunction or deterioration is not what it seems to be, nor does it take place "where" the problem seems to be. The misunderstanding about what the body is, and what the multiple problems are that sooner or later affect it, are the major reasons so many spiritual students fail to heal. Much false belief about the body and its healing must be dissolved before the experience can be yours—and that of others who will soon come to you for the experience.

Be prepared for all false belief to be dissolved in you by opening yourself to receive the healing message contained in these pages. Don't question the message, but simply trust, accept and receive it (as you can any true spiritual message), and let it take root and blossom in the silence of your being.

I will assume you are not a "beginner" on the spiritual path. We are to immediately discover the mystical (yet one hundred percent practical) truth of the body and the "image and likeness" of the one body as what we call the human body. Keep constantly in mind what you are about to discover. This is certainly not truth a "beginner" can receive and understand, but a spiritually receptive individual certainly can and must. You are to hear the spiritual—Christ and Buddha—secret of healing and sustained health, wholeness, vitality and purpose of body.

Please make sure you are rested and still, spacious and receptive as you absorb the message. Expel or ignore or forget about all collective belief about God, spirit and truth, and about being, body and world. This is important. Everything we have known of God, if it isn't perfectly and tangibly evident and demonstrable in experience, is nothing more than accepted false belief. That is shocking to hear for many, but it is true. As soon as God is actually known and tangibly experienced, all formation is witnessed as that *of* God because God and formation are one. "I and the Father are one." God is fully evident, fully manifested, fully tangible and visible, fully demonstrated right here as the *truth*—the good, harmony, completeness and peace—of experience (formation).

So let us realize always that if truth is not *evident,* it is not because truth is not present. God, truth, is everywhere and equally fully present, fully manifested and demonstrated, visible and tangible. More than fully present, God *is,* and besides that one *is,* there is none else. *All* is God, period. Therefore, all is the omnipresence of God. If truth is not evident, the only reason is that we have not yet lifted high enough in the *awareness* of God-as-all to see it, to experience it as all formation. We have not yet lifted out of the belief of truth, to truth itself. Make no mistake that when truth itself is lived, it is fully and perfectly evident as the tangibility of everyday life in all formation and all ways.

Drop and forget all the ideas you have about the body—all the collective belief and concept you have about what the body is and what it is not. Also drop every belief you have about God—about what God is and what God is not. It is only when we are empty of the personal self and all it believes it knows about God and the body that we are open and receptive to experience the freedom of truth itself. Only when we have sufficiently emptied ourselves of "our self" are we open and ready for truth itself to take root and become evident as the very life-form we experience as "us," "our body" and "our world."

THE PHYSICAL BODY SENSE

The body believed to be "human" and "physical"—believed to exist as an entity and reality in and of its own self—is one hundred percent illusory or false sense. Hear that deeply: the experience of the physical body, the idea of body, the belief in and of the physical body we experience and name "human" is illusory sense. We have a corporeal *sense* of that which is entirely incorporeal—that which is one hundred percent God or spirit. Therefore, all the effort we make towards its health and healing, its beauty, its vitality, its use and its purpose is equally one hundred percent false or illusory.

You would do well to make an indelible note of this. That "one hundred percent" is most important to realize. We have to, from this hour, drop the whole idea of what body is. We also have to be willing to drop our pampering of the body, and the methods we have been using to maintain its health, vitality, youthfulness and beauty. The *truth* of the body is entirely different from the *belief* we have had of it, therefore the experience of the body we have lived with until now—both its health, strength and vitality *and* its ill-health, pain and suffering.

As truth rises in awareness and we begin to awaken and live by the experience of God instead of humanity and physicality as our reality, we experience the form of God as a healthy, strong and vital body. The body becomes free of all false (non-God) experience. It heals of its illness, disease, injury and degeneration and becomes immune to future problems, or quickly able to witness any problem, no matter how "serious," as being the nothingness it is in truth.

Two

ONLY GOD IS

Let us begin to understand that *only God is*. We have heard this a thousand times throughout the *Miracle Self* and of course another thousand times throughout each of the teachings of Joel S. Goldsmith and Mary Baker Eddy. Centuries before these, we heard it from Jesus, Gautama, Shankara, Lao Tzu, Meister Eckhart and many others. Only God is and besides God "there is none other."

God is oneness: the one infinitude and omnipresence of spirit—goodness and wholeness without opposite. The whole macro is present as every micro experience; the whole of God—which is the only—is present at, and as, every point of itself simultaneously. Therefore, wherever your awareness is, whatever you are observing and whatever the form observed, there is the whole of God as the experience, and the awareness you are aware with.

God is one and is not, nor ever can be, partial or fragmented, separated from the whole. It is impossible to have only a part of God, a fragment, a portion (like a portion of cake). Is it possible to have a separate, singular entity among an infinity of other separate, singular entities? No! God is one and forever whole. God is the infinite and omnipresent oneness of all, and in the infinitude and omnipresence of oneness there cannot be anything "else." Indeed there is not. Only *God is*; only *oneness is*.

Everything of the infinitude is that oneness and the whole of that oneness existing fully as each place of awareness, each moment of awareness, and each object of that place and moment. Anywhere you go in the whole of the infinitude, there you find the whole of oneness, the whole of God. The whole of the infinitude exists right here as you and as that which you are observing or experiencing. Therefore, keep in mind that only God is, that there is nothing else but God, spirit and truth, I, consciousness, incorporeality—whatever you wish to name it. Only *that* is, only *God* is, only *oneness* is. Nothing else is or ever can be. Therefore, all of the infinitude is that one and one*ness* and nothing else.

The *whole* is present at every point of itself simultaneously. Nothing "else" is present anywhere in the entirety of the infinitude because only the infinitude of *one* is. There is nothing different, nothing less, nothing separate from the whole, the oneness, the omnipresence of God—spirit and truth *being* the whole of itself as you, me, all. Take this literally: the whole of God, the whole of omnipresence, the whole of the infinitude is present at every point of itself at the same time and is the *only*.

Keep *oneness* in mind. God—the infinitude, omnipresence, spirit, being, mind, body, world and universe and everything everywhere of it—is *oneness,* not separateness. Oneness is not divided into unfathomable separateness, each "part" separate and finite, a separate and loose entity which is "part" of the one, collective whole. No, oneness cannot have and does not have (even as temporal or momentary experience) a collective group of beings, bodies and objects. Oneness exists as—and only and wholly as—the entirety of itself, at every point of itself at the same time. Therefore, you are that oneness, I am that oneness, and all is that oneness. There is none else but pure and entire oneness to be or to have.

Oneness . . . oneness. Only oneness is. Because only oneness is, there is only one body. Oneness does not have an infinite number of "separate" bodies, all finite, all consisting of a "part" of the infinite, all separate entities living in a large universe of other separate and different entities. Oneness does not even have two bodies. Oneness has just one body, and that one body is the infinitude of *consciousness* with no matter in it whatsoever, no mentality, no physicality, no objectivity and no locality.

Let us hear it again: the whole of the infinite exists at every point of itself at the same time. Therefore, the one body exists at every point of the infinite at the same time. In fact, *the one body is the infinite existing at and as every point of itself simultaneously—that one being consciousness itself.*

Only consciousness is; only oneness is.

Only oneness is body, *the one body of consciousness.*

God is all; therefore, *God* is the body, the one body of omnipresent one*ness*—not "bodies," not plural. Forget the idea of plural "bodies" for this moment. Forget any "number" apart from one. God is one and oneness, not a myriad, divided "number" of itself. God is one, God is oneness, and because God is *all,* only one is, only oneness is, that one being *consciousness.*

WHAT IS GOD? WHAT IS THE BODY?

What is the truth of being and body, the truth we call God? What is the closest we can come to understanding what God is, therefore what all is, therefore what being-body-universe is?

Before we can understand this, we have to lift out of the idea of a "local" body, a "personal" body, a "physical" body, "your" body versus "mine," versus all the other, personal, locally-existing bodies populating the universe and world—not only the human body but every animal, insect, plant, flower and fruit body; every "he, she or it" body, whether animate or inanimate; every planet and sun body. Forget these accepted beliefs about the body of any form. They are all beliefs and the concepts about those beliefs. None of them is truth because only God itself is truth.

In truth, all embodied experience (every being, body and thing, everywhere) is perfect, good, true and free—and evidenced as being so—when we stop believing appearance to be something in and of its own self; when we understand the truth of God being the only, therefore the truth of being, body and world as being *God, one* and *omnipresent.*

So for this moment, keep your awareness in the *is* of God alone being all. *Only God is,* and God is *one,* which means that *only oneness is.* Oneness is God—the infinity and omnipresence of being, mind, body and universe. Infinite and omnipresent *oneness* is the only existence, the only presence. You can understand, therefore, that infinite and omnipresent *oneness* is the only body there can be, and indeed is. *Infinite and omnipresent oneness is what God is, therefore what the body is.*

The next question is, what is God, what is oneness? If we understand this, we quickly understand the body. God is *consciousness.* Therefore, consciousness is the one and the only existence and the one and only formation of existence. As the one and only, consciousness is the one and only *body.* There is no "other" type or version of body. Consciousness is the only; therefore, consciousness is the only body. Your body is consciousness. Your experience of body is an experience of consciousness. Your body is not what you have thought it is: physical, fleshly, finite, local, a body of organs and functions; height and weight, size and girth; born, growing, maturing then aging, deteriorating and finally dying, with many pleasurable, fun, creative and fulfilling experiences along the way and many not so pleasurable or creative—many suffering, painful, ill and maybe diseased experiences along the way. Most importantly, your body is not you, and you are not your body.

Body is consciousness and consciousness lives eternally, in perfect and harmonious oneness. Let us hear again: *only God is.* God is one; therefore, only *one is.* And God—oneness—is *consciousness.* Consciousness is *the one and only existence.* Consciousness is *the* oneness, *the* infinity, *the* omnipresence, *the* spirit and truth—*the* incorporeal, infinite, omnipresent one body. In consciousness, in God, in one and oneness, in infinity and omnipresence, in incorporeality, there is no shape, no form, no object, no amount, no age, no number, no place, no locality, no name. Nothing other than God, *oneness* exists. Therefore nothing but oneness is detectable, present, and experienceable in God, in oneness, in consciousness.

Because God is consciousness, and consciousness is one—the oneness of existence—your consciousness is the *one* consciousness. Consciousness embodies the whole of God at every point of itself at the same time. Therefore, you embody the whole of God at every point of your consciousness at the same time. Why is this true? Because God, the infinite omnipresence, exists at every place of itself at the same time. The whole of God, the whole of the infinite, the whole of omnipresence exists at every point of itself at the same time. And God, the infinite, the omnipresent, is *consciousness*. Therefore, consciousness embodies God, *is* God, at every point of itself simultaneously. The whole of God exists simultaneously at and as every point of consciousness. Nothing is separate or apart from you in truth; nothing is different from you because "you" are that one presence, that one being and mind which is consciousness itself. There is none "else." There is not, and indeed cannot be, any "other" being, mind, body, thing, place or condition in oneness, in God. How could there be? All is God, oneness, omnipresence—all, all, all!—and God cannot finitize or localize or personalize itself.

God is one and omnipresent. God is consciousness, consciousness is God, consciousness is *one,* consciousness is omnipresent *all.* Therefore, wherever you place your awareness in the infinitude of consciousness, there is the whole of God, the whole of omnipresence, fully existent, fully perfect—*the one, the only* fully whole and complete.

Oneness *is* consciousness. Oneness is and has all that consciousness is and has, fully existent as itself alone, fully whole and perfect at every point or place of itself simultaneously.

Oneness is consciousness; consciousness is oneness. Therefore, *consciousness* is the only body, *oneness* is the only body. Your body is the body of *consciousness,* the body of *oneness,* the body of *om-*

nipresence. Your body is the body of the entire universe you are conscious of, and everything everywhere in it and of it.

DROP THE PERSONAL AND PHYSICAL SENSE OF BODY

From now forwards begin to drop the personal and physical sense of the body. You do not exist in the physical body because you are consciousness. Consciousness cannot fit into anything. Consciousness exists as the whole of itself at every point and form. Your body is in you (in your consciousness) and is just one of the infinite forms (bodies) of experience in your consciousness.

Begin to realize that the whole of consciousness is your body—the one and omnipresent body of consciousness. And because consciousness is infinite and omnipresent, it embodies everything of your universal experience—everything.

You can look right out into your world, right up into the sky and up into the universe and everything included in it and realize that everything you're observing—experiencing—is the whole of God, oneness, being everything everywhere. You're observing God, oneness, in a magnified way—the micro of oneness observed as your macro experience. Every subject and object is God, omnipresent as every form of your experience. It doesn't matter what belief believes about the subjects and objects, amounts and activities, animate and inanimate forms being observed. The truth is that every form and detail of experience—despite what belief believes—is the whole of God because none but the whole is. Omnipresence is the only presence, no matter what is being observed—human, animal, vegetable, amount, activity, place or condition.

Forget belief and forget about believing you have to understand how mind experiences oneness as multiplicity. All that is necessary to know is that mind forms. Only God is; therefore, mind is nothing but the presence and power of God—simply experienced as a macro multiplicity of formation (our universal experience). Each and every form of experience is the whole and omnipresence of God. Everything God is and has, form also is and has. "The earth is the Lord's, and the fullness thereof.... The earth is full of the goodness of God." What appears to be God *and* mind *and* form are not three different conditions of being, but *one.* "I and the Father are one"—*one* omnipresence of being, not two, not separate, not different.

What you observe as every detail and moment of your experience—no matter what the subject or object of your observation is, and no matter whether it seems as if the "it" of your observation is mind, body, world or universe or any detail thereof—is the omnipresence of God, consciousness, oneness. It is a facet or aspect of your one body of being because God, consciousness, oneness is the only body, the one body—the one embodiment of being (which includes everything of the macro of experience). *Everything* about you is your macro experience of oneness, God, consciousness. That *everything* (consciousness) is your true body.

In other words, the whole universe is your body, the whole world and every person, thing and place in it. The whole of everything everywhere is the one body of consciousness. But the one body of consciousness is experienced at our current, "human" degree of awareness as seemingly multitudinous, separate and different bodies, forms, names, qualities, natures, amounts, shapes, weights, colors, fragrances. Experience is illusory until its truth is known, that truth being God, consciousness, oneness. "Judge not according to the appearance."

The first major step in spiritual healing—a very necessary step—is to realize that *consciousness* is your body. Consciousness is your one embodiment of being, body, mind and world. Consciousness is the truth of all, the body of Christ, the body of Buddha, the body of God, the body of spirit and truth, the one body of one*ness.*

Three

Consciousness Is Body

There is only oneness; therefore, there is only one true body. Consciousness is that body. Anything and everything of your consciousness—your experience—is that one. There is no other.

Consciousness is my body. Everything everywhere of my experience—despite the way it appears to be, and despite the collective belief about what it is or is not—is my one body of consciousness, my all-in-all one body of being, the whole of God being every detail and moment of everything about "me."

Only God is, only consciousness is, only *oneness* is. Therefore everything of my experience is that oneness, despite the way it appears to be or act, despite what name, quality or condition it appears to consist of, and despite what belief believes it is or is not. Ignore belief; turn right away from belief! Belief is what the scriptures of the world term "the devil." All belief is false awareness or accepted false idea—the "devil," the "tempter."

You can easily see the truth of this when you examine any belief in the light of truth. For instance, belief has, since the beginning of time, believed that the body is physical, personal and local. It believes that cause and effect, time and space are real. It believes in locality, separateness, difference. It believes that human and world experience are separate and different from God. It observes the whole macro of experience and everything everywhere in it and of it, and believes it to be reality. It sees "me here" and the rest of the world "out there"—a tree, flower, fruit, a human body, an animal body, an insect body, a home, a cloud, the breeze, the sunshine, main street, the stores and the market and all the produce, product, staff and customers in the stores and market.

All of this belief believes to be separate and different, animate or inanimate, here or there, mine versus his, hers or theirs, me versus him, her or it, harmonious or disharmonious, plentiful or lacking, fair or unfair, satisfying or unsatisfying, happy or unhappy, successful or unsuccessful. Belief itself *is* the entire pairs of opposites. All belief is false. Why? *Only God is,* and God is one and one*ness,* not multiplicity, not separate, not different, not God "and" me, he, she or it, but *all God, all one,* all the *one consciousness* being all of experience.

MIND FORMS ONE INTO "MANY"

You see how mind forms oneness into an infinite variety of individual forms, bodies, shapes, colors, amounts, activities, places and conditions. Mind forms the "many members" described in 1 Corinthians 12:12—"For as the body is one, and hath many members, and all the members of that one body, being many, are one body."

Spiritual illumination (and the discernment that comes with it) lifts us into the reality of God as one and all, the all in all of experience. God—which is omnipresent oneness—is the reality, the substance, quality, character, form, amount and activity of all. The "all" of experience is the all of mind formation. But mind formation does not, and cannot, change the oneness of God as being the very presence of that "all." God is the *only is,* and nothing can change that truth, lessen it, make it separate or different.

With this truth alight in you, you see that all form *is* and *has* all that God is and has. You see that because all form is and has all that God is and has, all form is infinite, omnipresent, harmonious, whole and complete and cannot be less—not even a grain less.

God *is,* and is omnipresent *as,* every moment, subject and object of experience. The one whole is the only presence, the only substance, the only life, the only body, the only existence—the one *whole,* indivisible and inseparable from its wholeness.

All is *the whole of oneness,* therefore is the one *body,* there being no other presence, substance, life or form that body can be. *Only* God is. And because God is consciousness, it is *consciousness* that I am, have and experience as the body of me. And because consciousness is infinite and omnipresent, my body is infinity and omnipresence, not the local, finite, physical, personal and limited body I have believed it to be.

I am the infinite and omnipresent body of consciousness existing individually and purposefully as the *whole universal* experience of "me." *That* is my body.

You are the infinite and omnipresent body of consciousness existing individually and purposefully as the whole universal experience of "you." *That* is your body.

KEEP YOUR AWARENESS ONE

Keep your moment-by-moment awareness lifted into oneness, into God, into consciousness. Keep aware that consciousness *is* God, the whole one and only existence and formation. And because consciousness is omnipresent, indivisible and inseparable—forever fully existent as the whole of itself as each point and body of experience—consciousness is what my body is, what your body is, and what all bodies are.

God is, and is fully embodied as and throughout consciousness—which is my body. My body is universal, not finite and local, not separate from all "other" bodies. All bodies of experience are the one body seeming to be many.

My body is the one infinite and omnipresent body of self, the one life, the one substance, the one existence embodied, the one presence, the one form and the one activity of experience. Consciousness embodied in experience is what I am.

Let us hear it again. The whole of God is, and is fully embodied as and throughout—and is all that is in—my consciousness. We can take the "my" out: the whole of God is fully embodied as and throughout consciousness.

The only presence there is, is consciousness, God. The only life there is, is consciousness, God. And because God is indivisible and inseparable, my consciousness is the one consciousness of which I am an individual and unique expression. I am an individual expression of the whole of consciousness living its whole and perfect, purposeful and fulfilled existence as me, as I.

I am the body of consciousness; therefore, everything everywhere of my consciousness is the one embodiment of me—every person, animal, plant, insect, object, place, amount and activity; every body of space, the air filling that space, the sun and moon, the stars, the hills and mountains, the rivers and oceans, the valleys and glades.

Everything I see, hear, taste, touch and smell, and everything I can think, is all consciousness "happening" as "me."

I am awakening to the truth of being: that consciousness is the one, that consciousness is God, and that because God is all, consciousness is the one body of me.

I am awakening to the truth that I am individual and unique God-being. I am being and having an individual experience of consciousness, which means I am being and having an individual experience of the one body.

I am awakening to the truth of the one body, that being consciousness, which includes everything everywhere I experience in and as my consciousness—everything.

I am consciousness. I am the body of consciousness. My body is consciousness, all-inclusive, self-embodied and omnipresent consciousness. Whatever he, she or it is "in" your consciousness, is the presence, form and life of consciousness itself, and whatever has presented itself to you is your consciousness being aware of itself as form.

Mind is simply being your formed experience of oneness, of God. But remember—remember!—mind does not, nor can it, *change* God into something less or different. All is God; nothing other than God exists, and nothing can change God being all of itself as all of experience!

All formation is the very presence of God itself, therefore the very presence of infinity and omnipresence itself. Form is never limited or lacking except experientially when we insist on believing it is different and separate from God. Then *in experience* we have to suffer the limit or lack of our belief (because belief is experience). But when we know that all is God, we evidence and have the freedom, the infinity and omnipresence of all good form being unconditionally and immediately available to us. We are *being* the truth (infinity and omnipresence) of all form when we live the truth of consciousness being our all-in-all body of experience.

Anything at all you can name, anything at all you observe, anything at all you feel, you sense, is not "in here or out there, different and separate from you," but is you—the conscious self—experiencing as much of its infinity and omnipresence as it is *aware of,* and as much of the nature and quality of true self as it is aware of.

You experience what you "know to be true" of yourself, and I experience what I "know to be true" of myself. The more we are awake to our truthful identity and our truthful embodiment of being—that being the oneness and omnipresence of God, consciousness—the more we experience harmony, happiness, peace, life, love, abundance, purpose and satisfaction filling and animating our lives.

I AM THE BODY OF CONSCIOUSNESS

I am consciousness, and because consciousness is all, I am the body of consciousness. There is nothing about me other than consciousness. I am consciousness.

Only God is. God is one alone, and that one is consciousness. Therefore, my consciousness is God which is the entirety of me—my being, mind, body, world and universe including everything everywhere in it and of it.

There is none other than God, spirit, consciousness; therefore, there is nothing I am or my mind-body-world is but consciousness. There is nothing about any person, thing, place, activity, amount or condition other than consciousness.

My consciousness is the oneness and truth—the God—of my universe of person, thing, place, activity, amount and condition.

My consciousness is the oneness that is I, the oneness that is individual and unique me, the oneness that is earth (experience) as it is in heaven (pure consciousness).

Begin to realize that the whole of the you that you are is—from the deepest "inner" part to the farthest "outer" place—*consciousness.* Because consciousness is what God is—the one and the only ("I am the Lord, and besides me there is none other")—the you you are, including everything everywhere of you, is that one presence, substance, being, mind, body, world and universe of God. "I am that I am." All beings are that. We simply have an objective *sense* of that which is pure consciousness, a corporeal *sense* of that which is one hundred percent incorporeal.

Everything of being, including everything of experience, is not what it seems to be, but is consciousness, oneness, God. The experience of mind, body, world and universe is simply an objective sense of consciousness, oneness, God. The objective sense gives us the experience of a multiplicity of different and separate beings, substances, forms, weights, colors, amounts, categories, natures, characters, qualities and conditions. In its purity, this is a wondrous and true experience of being! It is only if or when we believe multiplicity of its own self to be real that we fall foul of that "different-and-separate-from-God" belief. There is no "he, she or it" different or separate from God. There is no form, thing, activity, amount, condition or place different or separate from God. All is God, the one, the only. All being is consciousness, all body is consciousness; all substance, material, shape, weight, activity, amount and condition is consciousness; all presence, life, nature and character is consciousness because "besides me (God, consciousness, oneness, spirit and truth) there is none else."

All the names we give to experience, all the different and varied details and categories, weights and measures, places and conditions, activities and qualities, circumstances and "facts" are nothing other than differently *sensed* experiences of the *one* and *omnipresent* experience which is God—consciousness.

Four

Body Is Non-Local

I am consciousness. The whole of my being is that of consciousness. The whole of my mind, body, world and universe is consciousness.

Because consciousness is non-local, and because I am consciousness, I am non-local. There is nothing local about me, my mind, body, world or universe.

If personal sense is believed, everything of being seems to be local. Yet all is, in fact, consciousness, therefore non-local.

God is the one, the only, and that one and only is consciousness. God is the infinite and the omnipresent—the non-local consciousness, the one reality of all; therefore I am that and all is that.

Because only God is and because God is consciousness (which is non-local), there is nothing local, nothing finite, nothing objective and nothing personal even though material belief believes there is. There is no God, no truth, whatsoever to belief. Only God is; therefore, only consciousness is, and because consciousness is infinite and omnipresent—not material, finite, locally and personally present—being, body, world and universe are non-local.

I am the infinity and omnipresence of being. My body is the infinity and omnipresence of body. There is nothing local about my being or body. Indeed, there is nothing local about anything of my entire experience—mind, body, world and universe and everything everywhere in it and of it.

God is one, therefore being and body are one. As oneness is experienced through mind, I experience a multiplicity of form because God is mind is form. Form, therefore body, is one. All form, therefore all body, is and has all that oneness (God) has.

I am and have the one body, the only body in existence, the body that is the one being, substance and form (God) experienced uniquely and individually as "me"—but always one, always of God, consciousness, infinity and omnipresence with nothing local about it whatsoever.

My body—being consciousness, the one omnipresence, the one life—is never separate from the whole of consciousness, never divided, never different, never sliced into portions: one being "John" over there, another being "Mary" over here, another being an animal, another an insect, another a plant, another a fruit, another a cloud, another a rain drop, another a dollar, another a blade of grass, a flower, a color or a fragrance.

No! These "different" beings and forms are simply oneness experienced as mind's multiplicity of form. Mind forms oneness into a multiplicity of experience. But mind's formation does not, and cannot, change God into something less than God is, something different, something separate, divided, finite, local and personal. God *is*, period. Nothing but God is. Therefore, you can understand that God *is* mind, and because mind forms (mind *is* formation), mind is the infinite variety of formation we call bodily, worldly and universal "experience"—but all and forever God, always the wholeness and completeness of God, consciousness, infinity and omnipresence.

In actuality, in truth, in literal and practical terms here, now and forever, only God is. God is one, God is one*ness,* God is the one and only life, the one and only substance, the one and only presence, the one and only form, the one and only body—the *one body*—that being consciousness. Therefore, you understand that body is incorporeal not corporeal, spirit not matter, God not human. Corporeality, matter and humanity are nothing but *sense* believed to be and accepted as being real.

I am consciousness, my body is consciousness—the whole omnipresence of consciousness. You are consciousness, your body is consciousness—the whole omnipresence of consciousness.

The *whole of consciousness* is your body and mine—the one truthful body. We simply have a corporeal *sense* of the incorporeal body, a material or physical *sense* of the body which is one hundred percent spirit and spiritual.

This truth is given in the statement "The earth is the Lord's, and the fullness thereof." In scripture, *the Lord* refers to *the mind.* "The earth is the Lord's" refers to form being the mind's. The *earth* is mind's formation of oneness, God, consciousness. As you realize that nothing changes or lessens God, nor can, you see that form is God, simply objectively experienced. In contemporary interpretation we have "The earth is the Lord's, and the fullness thereof" as meaning the earth is mind's form, and the fullness of mind which is the fullness of God.

Each and every form—including the form we call the "physical body"—is the omnipresence of God because nothing but the omnipresence of God exists. All is and has all that God is and has. Nothing is different from or less than the fullness of God—the infinity and omnipresence that is God.

The earth—the body—is the Lord's (mind's) and the fullness thereof. The body, being mind's formation of oneness, is itself oneness, and *has* all that oneness has. You and I experience "the body" because it is the mind's formation of individual body at what has been called the "human" degree of awareness. This is easy to understand when we catch the truth that God is mind is form. Each of the infinite degrees of mind—one of the infinite number of "mansions in my Father's house"—is, and experiences, its own formation. At its own level, and if believed to be a reality in and of its own self, any particular degree of mind is believed to be reality. In fact, all formation, despite its degree, is and has all that God is and has. The particular form or degree of form doesn't matter. What matters is knowing that all form and all degrees are actually, despite appearance, God "and the fullness thereof." And because God is consciousness which is infinite and omnipresent, all form including the body is consciousness, therefore is infinite and omnipresent.

"The earth is the Lord's and the fullness thereof" means that the earth (all formation) is one and oneness—one being, one body, one life, one substance, one presence. And because oneness (God) is consciousness, the earth, inclusive of its infinite variety of formation, is also consciousness, "and the fullness thereof." The whole of consciousness (the whole of God) is fully present, fully existent and fully formed; finished, manifested and demonstrated at and as each place of experience (consciousness) simultaneously.

ALL IS ONE

All is God—one. God is indivisible and inseparable. Therefore *all* is indivisible and inseparable. Nothing is divided, nothing is separate from anything else, nothing is different. There is just God, therefore just the indivisible and inseparable one being, one body, one substance, one life. Consciousness is that being, body, substance and life. Consciousness is who you are, what you are, what you're made of, what every grain and form of your universal experience is. Consciousness is every organ and function. The physical form you have been led to believe is your body is not the truth of body but just the *sense* of body. Consciousness is body (because consciousness is the only), and consciousness is the *whole* of your universal experience, not a finite, physical, local, personal, separate-and-different-from-all-other-bodies body.

Look as far as you can throughout your experience this minute. What do you see? When I look into my experience, I see inside the room in which I sit to write these words. I see everything in the cabana, and the walls, door and window. As I look through the window, I see our house and garden. I observe these formations and realize that they are a part or an aspect of my one body—the body of consciousness. They are not "outside" of and "separate" from me; they are "in" me—one as, and an aspect of, the one consciousness of me. The grass, trees, flowers, colors and fragrance in the garden, the birds and the bird song are also "in" me, forms of my one body—an aspect or experience of my one body.

My one true body is consciousness—infinite, omnipresent and non-local. And because there is no such thing as "unembodied" consciousness, consciousness is the totality of the embodiment of my being. That embodiment is my true body and yours.

We can observe anything, anywhere and realize that he, she or it is "in" and part of the one body of consciousness that is what we are. All is happening and is observed "in" consciousness, and is consciousness itself. And because all is consciousness, all is omnipresent God. All is the whole of God, fully existent, fully manifested and already demonstrated despite the way it appears to be to material belief. All is God; therefore, all is the whole of life, the whole of good, the whole of harmony, peace and joy, the whole of infinity. Everything everywhere throughout my universe is the omnipresence of spirit. It is all happening "in" and as my consciousness, which is my true embodiment of being (my true body).

Everything everywhere is my one body of consciousness, therefore good, therefore free, therefore life itself, peace itself. All is in harmony with everything else of my bodily experience because the only bodily experience, the only bodily object and aspect, place and condition, activity and amount, is the whole of oneness itself, and oneness (God) cannot be disharmonious with itself. All in and of oneness is oneness itself, God itself, the one life, one love, one harmony everywhere present. What could argue with what? What could be disharmonious, unloving, ill, diseased, poor or unhappy with what? There is only one "what" and it is God—the omnipresence of itself as all.

ONE CANNOT DISAGREE WITH ITSELF

One cannot disagree with itself by being disharmonious, ill, limited or lacking. One is *one, self-inclusive, all-inclusive, omnipresent form* and nothing other. The whole of oneness exists everywhere throughout infinity at the same time because infinity *is* oneness—and not only oneness but the omnipresence of oneness. Oneness *is* omnipresence; omnipresence *is* oneness. Once you have and live by the consciousness of oneness, you have all because oneness is all. There is no more to have. If you had all the good the world has in it but had not oneness you would have nothing. If you have oneness, you not only have all the good the world has in it, but infinitely more than the world has ever before seen.

To have oneness, you must realize the non-locality of truth. Good is non-local because good is God and God is non-local. God is omnipresence not local presence; God is omni-form not local form; God is incorporeal not corporeal. This understanding—along with the realization of oneness being all there is, therefore forever whole and self-complete, unable to be discordant, ill, diseased or in lack—is the key. The oneness of true (God) life, love, wealth, harmony, peace and fulfillment cannot be in disagreement or discord with itself. All is God, good itself, oneness and none other. It would require two different entities, aspects or elements of being to create a possible misalignment, disagreement, discord, illness or disharmony. But God is *one;* therefore, *all* is one and *of* oneness. Oneness cannot have illness "there" and health "here" because "there" and "here" are not two, but one and forever self-complete and perfect. What seems to be two different forms of being are actually one—the whole of God *being* all. Nothing is disharmonious, nothing is ill, nothing is over- or under-satisfied, nothing is lacking or limited, different or separate in actuality. All is God; and nothing of God—good, life, love, harmony and fulfillment—is lacking anywhere, at any time; nothing of the perfection of form is lacking, nor can it be.

Whatever I observe throughout my body of consciousness, and whatever the subject or object appears to be—this physical body of flesh, bones, blood, organs and functions; another human or animal body; a house, a garden, tree, or flower, a fluffy white cloud floating in a blue sky or an angry grey cloud threatening in a dark sky; a road, automobile, gas station or store; a table, chair, lamp, book or the words in the book—it is all actually, despite appearance, God or consciousness.

All is consciousness, and because I observe or experience it, I observe and experience "my" consciousness. And because consciousness is body, I am forever observing and experiencing aspects, forms, activities, amounts, places and conditions of my very own body—the one body individually experienced as "mine."

In this way, you understand that all is consciousness, and because consciousness is God, you experience *God* everywhere as *all* because there is nothing but God.

God is consciousness; and because God is all, I am consciousness; and all "in" my consciousness is itself consciousness.

Consciousness is one and omnipresent; therefore, everything everywhere that I observe, and everything I experience, is the oneness and omnipresence of consciousness, God.

Because I am consciousness, and because consciousness is the only presence and form—that presence and form being omnipresent, not locally or personally present—my body is the omnipresence of consciousness, not the seeming local and personal presence of a physical form.

The physical sense of body exists in me (in my consciousness) just as everything else in my experience exists in me. I do not exist in the physical sense of body, nor does everything of my multitudinous experience exist outside of or separate from me. I am consciousness; my true body is the entirety of my consciousness in and as which all exists.

The whole of God (infinity and omnipresence) exists in and as my consciousness. This knowledge is the secret of all in my experience—including the health and vitality of the physical sense of body—becoming whole, healthy and vital.

Only God is, and God is one and omnipresent; therefore, only the one body is. All the bodies in experience are simply individual experiences of the one and omnipresent body which is consciousness.

Consciousness is body, body is consciousness.

LIFT OUT OF AND BEYOND PERSONAL SENSE

The first thing we must do is lift away from, or out of and beyond, the personal and local sense of being and body. Personal and local sense (belief) is the killer—the one actual problem with anything of experience.

There is only one being, one life, one actual sense, one actual experience, one truth: God. Yet we have believed a personal, local, finite sense of our oneness, our infinity and our omnipresence. It is that *belief* in a personal, local, finite sense that causes experience and everything in and of experience to seem to consist of both good *and* bad.

Belief *is* the pairs of opposites; belief *is* good and bad; belief *is* the experience of separation and difference from God. As soon as you have a belief, you have its opposite too. Every belief has an opposite, and because belief is experience, when experience is lived full of belief instead of full of God, it is full of pairs of opposites. It is for this reason alone that human life is filled with the joy, health, love, creativity and fulfillment of good *and* the struggle, hardship, disease, poverty, pain and injustice of bad.

We collectively (humanly) believe ourselves to be personal, separate and different from God. We *believe* we are each a "me" different and separate from every other person. We *believe* we are of a certain character, height, weight, and lineage that are different and separate from every other person's. We *believe* we have a personal mind, body and life with a personal set of circumstances different and separate from every other personal life and set of circumstances. This believed personal sense *is itself* the good and bad of the pairs of opposites we experience.

Hear that deeply. Belief *is* experience. It is the personal sense of being—which is false belief—that gives us that which appears to be a real personal set of experiences or circumstances consisting of both good and bad. When something happens in our experience, we take it personally. We believe it to be happening "to" or "for" or "against" us. We then attempt to deal with it personally. The problem, whatever its name or nature, is not what it seems to be but is the *personalizing* of, or *egoistic sense* of, existence. Indeed, masters often call the personal self the *selfish self*—the self that looks out for itself but not all others, who seeks to gain the good and treasure of life for itself but not all others, who seeks the safety, security and fulfillment of the earth for itself but not all others. But there is no personal self; there is no personal experience in God. There is only the one universal being, the one infinite I experiencing itself as infinite individual self.

Being is an individual and unique experience—yes! However, each and every individual is the infinity and omnipresence of God. God is one, whole and self-complete, indivisible and inseparable. All being and all experience, inclusive of every subject and object of experience, is itself the whole of God—fully existent and present, fully formed, manifested and demonstrated. Yet, because we've believed a personal sense of self, our experience of mind, body and world is also personal, therefore limited, finite, and full of both good and bad. Belief is experience. Whatever we collectively or individually believe, *there it is* as the formation of our experience. There is nothing we can do but live with it. Believed experience is not *true* experience (which is forever good, whole and complete), but for as long as we continue to live by belief, we have no choice but to live with the forms of belief—the forms of both good and bad. The moment we lift from belief to God we have the forms of God (good) throughout our experience. The pairs of opposites dissolve and disappear, and we live in the harmony, freedom and fulfillment of God-being, untouched by the good and bad forms of belief.

Five

Healing that Succeeds, Healing that Fails

The failure in what has been called "healing" is that we have attempted to have truth heal or free or harmonize a physical, finite, local, personal body, even though we have been given this truth. Perhaps now, after hearing this, we'll go back and reread the truth books we've read all these years, and quickly discover why it has been impossible for us to evidence the true and healthy, healed, free and vital body. We've attempted to get God, which is spirit, infinity, and omnipresence, to heal a physical, finite and locally present body *which spirit does not have nor recognize.* The physical, finite, local and personal body is nothing but *sense,* not reality.

It is because there is no such *actual* physical body that all attempts to "use" God or spirit to heal it fail. That which does not actually or truthfully exist (matter) cannot be healed by that which is true and real (God or spirit). It is for this reason that there is so much failure among the spiritual communities of the world in the ability to bring forth healings. If spiritual students understood matter as being nothing but a material *sense* of spirit—a corporeal *sense* of that which is one hundred percent incorporeal—they would quickly stop attempting to use spirit to heal the physical body. There would then be quick and considerable healing around the world.

In this new light, reread any truly spiritual or mystical teaching—the writings of pure spirit and true omnipresent, all-inclusive oneness; the teachings that realize God *as* mind *as* form such as are given the world throughout the teachings of Jesus the Christ and Gautama the Buddha, and the contemporary Miracle Self and Infinite Way—and you'll be amazed at what is revealed to you with newly illumined awareness.

THE BODY IS THE ENTIRETY OF CONSCIOUSNESS

You now realize that because consciousness is body, and because consciousness is omnipresent, indivisible and inseparable, the *entirety of your consciousness* is your one body.

Individual body is not the physically-believed body you have sensed as being real. Body is consciousness, and consciousness is always the omnipresent entirety of itself. In other words, the entirety of your conscious awareness (your entire experience) is your truthful body, not just a fraction of your experience named the physical body. Consciousness is your body, your one and whole body. It doesn't matter that there are an infinite variety of experiences happening in and as your consciousness every moment: beings, bodies, objects, subjects, shapes, amounts, activities, qualities and conditions. Actually, because God is consciousness, and God is one, all-inclusive whole, your consciousness is that one embodiment (body) of being, whole and all-inclusive. You simply have (as all beings have) an individual and unique experience of the one and omnipresent whole at this degree of awareness—this degree being "one of the many mansions in my Father's house."

Now that you realize this truth, you will never again attempt to heal the physical sense of the body in and of its own self, or any physical, local problem it is experiencing, but will seek to experience a greater illumined *awareness* of the one real (spiritual) body. The more illumined our awareness is, the more that illumination becomes evident as the physical experience. In other words, the more spiritual presence you experience "happening" as you, the more *that felt-presence itself* reveals a healthy, harmonious, vital and strong physical sense of body. This is the secret of spiritual healing.

Never again attempt to bring spirit into matter, to bring the incorporeal into the corporeal, the infinite into the finite, or the omnipresent into the locally present to heal it, fix it, free it, harmonize it or satisfy it. You will never succeed because it is impossible to achieve!

What you do—and what is happening this minute for you and all students who are hearing and absorbing this truth—is realize that your consciousness, including the entirety of it (in its purity, before mind, before thought), is the one body, presence and life of God. Omnipresence itself is what you are, what I am, and what all are. There is "none else." There is not, and never can be, God *and,* oneness *and,* omnipresence *plus* another type of presence. "And" or "another" would not be God or oneness but twoness, difference and separation. Such does not exist and is not even momentarily possible in truth, in God, in oneness.

It doesn't matter what being, object, activity, place or amount is witnessed—is being experienced or is appearing. It doesn't matter what name, shape, color, fragrance is presenting itself as experience. Forget all *categories* of experience—all names and amounts, all hims and hers, all specifics. Everything of experience *in and of its own self* has no actual reality, no actual presence, no power, no ability to act upon you either positively or negatively. There is only *one*—which is God; therefore, there is only one true category.

The five senses and infinite formation of mind do not change God into something different, finite, local, personal, limited or untruthful. Nothing whatsoever changes God, nor ever can. In order for anything to change or lessen God there would first have to be a second power, and not only that, the second power would have to be greater than the power that is God. That, of course, is utterly untrue. There is *one alone*—"I am the Lord, and beside me there is none else"—therefore one power alone, one presence alone and one form alone.

Ignore that which seems to be. "Judge not by the appearance, but judge righteous judgment." Realize that all is the one power, presence and formation. All is actually, despite the way it seems to be, God, therefore infinity and omnipresence, fully present and manifested *as* each form of experience simultaneously—always one, never divided, never separate, never different, never less. And that *one* is *consciousness.* You are that one, I am that one, all is that one. Everything about you, everything *of* you—everything—is that one which is consciousness. Therefore your body is consciousness—the entirety of consciousness, *your* consciousness. Your body does not exist *in* consciousness, as a single entity among millions or billions of other entities existing *in* consciousness. Your body *is* consciousness, the one and whole of consciousness, the all-inclusive *one body* of you.

AWAKEN! ILLUMINE AWARENESS!

With this realization, your entire purpose is not to attempt to "use" spirit to heal a physical ill (which is impossible) but to allow your awareness to become spiritually illumined. With spiritual illumination come the *forms* of spiritual health and harmony. Illumined awareness and illumined (healed) form are one.

Never again focus on a "particular place or condition of disease" and attempt to spiritually heal it. Normally, in desiring to heal the body, the student or "spiritual practitioner" takes "the illness or disease or injury into consciousness" and hopes that spiritual awareness, meditation and silence will heal it. This is why healing has not "worked." It is impossible to have spirit heal matter. Why? There is no matter. What has been named *matter* is just a *sense* of spirit, not a real (spiritual) entity or material or substance.

But now, in realizing that consciousness is the body, and that the "individual physical body" is just a miniscule grain of the whole of the bodily experience (which is the infinity of consciousness), you ignore the name and category of illness, disease or injury, and where it seems to exist, and you turn your attention fully to spirit itself. You fill your awareness with God as God for God to God. You empty yourself of the human sense and fill yourself with spiritual sense. Then you rest and relax and let spirit flood your senses with itself, as itself and for itself alone until you feel the very presence of spirit as your every faculty; until the peace and light and warmth and freedom of spirit so fills you that you would say it is living you rather than your "humanity" living you. *This illumined state quickly evidences itself as the healed and healthy bodily form.*

Oh, I hope you are catching this! The whole of your consciousness and everything in it and of it, infinitely, as far as you can see, hear, taste, touch, smell and think is your body, is *the* body of you, the *one* body, the *real* body of you.

No describable one aspect of conscious experience, or place of experience, or form or activity of experience—including what we have believed about our physical body—is the individual's true body. Rather, God is body; the whole of consciousness is the one body, and because the whole exists at and as each point of individual awareness, each individual's body is the whole of consciousness. Illness and disease (and every discordant experience that can happen to or in the body) are just forms of low spiritual awareness. They are forms of the "fog" or "dark" that exists as our lack of God awareness—our belief that we are and the world is something other than and different from God. With this knowledge you see that "healing" of the body is the dissipating or dissolving of the fog or dark of false awareness—the illuminating of awareness. Just as the morning sunlight dissolves the dark of earth, spiritual illumination dissolves the dark of false belief and healing is experienced.

As soon as we have a higher and purer awareness of God as the truth of our being—as consciousness being our all-inclusive and true reality and one body—healing of all form including the "physical body" is infallible. Consciousness and form (body) are one;

therefore, as a greater degree of consciousness is realized, the forms of experience are witnessed as more truthful, more healthy and vital, more peaceful and harmonious—and often miraculously so.

REALIZE ONENESS

The very first step in achieving spiritual illumination is to realize oneness, not to separate, not to divide, not to categorize, not to think of the body as being physical, walking around the "outer" earth on legs, powered by internal organs and functions, all operated by a brain. No, the body is the whole of consciousness and consciousness is oneness—in fact, the omnipresence of oneness. You will be amazed at the miracle of healing that is often experienced just with the lifted awareness of oneness (omnipresent oneness) being your body—the whole of consciousness being the body of you, and the body you have.

You will be amazed at the transformation and healing you experience, not only throughout the physical sense of body, but throughout your entire body—your body of consciousness. As soon as you lift out of the personal, finite and local sense and realize that the whole of your consciousness—all-inclusive of its universal experience of form, activity, amount, place, and condition—is all the same *one body of consciousness* (your true body), you are released from false belief and are free in truth. "Know the truth, and that very truth will set you free."

Consciousness is my body.
Consciousness is every body.
Consciousness is infinitely all.

Indeed you will be amazed at how quickly the truth and miracle of oneness becomes tangibly evident as your health, strength and vitality, your harmony and peace, your abundance of life in all its formation, as soon as you lift into the realization of *consciousness* being the body of you rather than the false belief that you are a mental being with a physical body living in a material world.

For this moment, your only concern is to lift away from the personal sense—all personal sense—into God sense, which is the recognition that "I am consciousness and besides me there is none else."

I, God, is consciousness, and because I is the only—infinity and omnipresence—there is none other than I, than God, than consciousness.

And because consciousness is one—inseparable and indivisible—the body of me is not a local, finite, temporal, physical entity, but infinite and omnipresent, forever whole as one. No person, thing, place or condition exists outside of me or separate from me. I am the oneness of my experience, every aspect of which is one and equal as the whole of God.

I and my body are one, and because I am consciousness, my body is the body of my consciousness, forever one, forever whole, forever full of the omnipresence and goodness of God.

Belief believes that consciousness is *not* all. Belief believes in many different and separate materials, substances, powers, amounts and experiences. It believes in the physical, local and personal body and its many organs and functions. It believes in other matter called "wood" from which structures, furniture, utensils and sculptures can be made. It believes various types of "fabric" exist from which clothes, towels, curtains and coverings can be made. It believes in organic matter from which plants, leaves, berries, flowers and fruit grow. It believes in other materials such as stone, sand, brick, concrete, iron and steel. It believes in entities such as mountains and oceans, beaches and deserts, valleys and glades, forests and fields. *Ad infinitum,* belief categorizes, divides, separates, names, believing that there are an infinite variety of different life-forms, substances and materials, qualities and conditions, sizes and amounts, natures and characteristics which make up the sum of experience—all of which have their degree of either good or bad, and all of which are experienced in different *ways* and *degrees* by each individual.

But truth awareness recognizes that only God is, only consciousness is, *despite the way experience seems to be*. So the very first step in spiritual illumination is to lift out of the personal sense of self, in all its ways, into the fact that consciousness is I, that "consciousness is my body." There is no unembodied consciousness; there is only oneness, and oneness is forever embodied, manifested, tangible and visible. Therefore, there is one body and that is the body of consciousness. "I am that I am."

Take in your entire consciousness and realize its oneness, despite appearance:

The whole of my consciousness is the oneness of God, the oneness of truth, the oneness of life itself, harmony, wholeness and peace itself.

The entirety of my consciousness is fully embodied in, and as, and with, God at every place of itself simultaneously. The entirety of my body is and consists of God at every place of itself simultaneously. There is nothing of my entire body, my all-inclusive consciousness, my infinite and omnipresent consciousness, that is not God and God alone, good and good alone, life and life alone.

But in order to experience the truth of life, I have to realize that I—the whole universe of me—am consciousness. I am not a human being with a mental mind existing in a physical body. I do not have a physical family, friend, neighbor and colleague; I do not live in a material home in a certain state, country or world, suspended in a vast universe. No, I am a spiritual being, a spiritual mind and body, existing in the boundless vastness of my spiritual universe. All of me is consciousness, and because consciousness is omnipresence, all of spirit (God) is omnipresent as each place and point of "me." All of "me" is oneness, infinity and omnipresence—the very presence of God in individual expression as "me."

I, the whole of I, is consciousness, and everything everywhere of my consciousness—which embodies my sense of a local, personal body, my sense of a local, personal family, my sense of home, my sense of person, activity, amount, condition and place—is just objective *sense* of the one body of consciousness. I have a corporeal *sense* of that which is one hundred percent incorporeal, and that corporeal sense includes an infinity of different individuals, things, activities, amounts, conditions and places. But this multiplicity of sense is actually one—God, consciousness—and never different, never separate, nor ever able to be.

Lift into this truthful awareness now.

I am the one because there is none else, and that one is consciousness. Therefore, the entirety of my consciousness is that one.

I am the body of consciousness.

As you realize this, you are not thinking of a physical, local, personal body. You are embracing the entirety of your consciousness, all-inclusive consciousness—not an "inner" versus an "outer," not spirit and matter, spirit and a physical body, no, no—just spiritual I, spiritual body, spiritual consciousness, the one and oneness of all.

Can you do that, friends? Can you, from this hour, lift away and keep away as best you are able, from the belief of a personal self existing in a vast material world and infinite universe which seems to be "out there" completely separate from and different from the mental self you believe you are and the physical body you believe you have?

Lift into truth this hour. You "and" your body are consciousness, the one all-inclusive (universal) consciousness of you, the one omnipresence of you with no part or aspect of experience being personal, local, different, separate or less than the whole of consciousness, omnipresent at every point of itself at the same time.

This is what you are and what you have.

And because the body is consciousness, it is infinite, omnipotent and eternal. I am life eternal. There is no other type or category of life. There is only one life, and that is eternal. You are that, I am that, all is that. You have never been born and you have never died. You are life eternal. There is no other type or span of life you can possibly be because the only life there is is eternal life. It is only because we, as a race, have unwittingly and without question accepted the belief in a personal self with a temporal span of life that we have lived the experience of birth and death. Belief *is* experience. But life is eternal; birth and death are one hundred percent *belief,* not reality. Belief is born and belief eventually dies. Truth does neither.

NO BIRTH, NO DEATH

You have never been born, and you have never died and never will. Your life is the one life which is eternal. Only God is, and God is life which is eternal. There are not different choices or types of life span. God is the only, and God is life; therefore, because God is eternal, life is eternal.

There is no temporal existence, being, mind or body. There is no temporal world or universe. Everything everywhere is eternal because everything everywhere is God and exists only because God exists. God is one and life eternal—flawless life eternal. You, I and all are that one eternal existence. There is none else. "I am the Lord, and besides me there is none else. . . . God made all that was made, and all that was made is good [pure consciousness, flawless, eternal, infinite and omnipresent, without opposite]."

As you lift now, away from the personal sense of self with the physical sense of body and material sense of world and experience, into your truthful being and body which is consciousness, you will never again have the experience of birth and death. Consciousness is eternal; consciousness is not born and does not die. Consciousness is life eternal, mind eternal, body eternal, presence eternal, world and universe eternal. You are that, I am that, all is that.

It is time to drop the belief in a personal, physical, local, temporal sense of self and lift into all-inclusive *consciousness* as being who you are, what your body is, what your world "and" universe are, and what everything everywhere in your world "and" universe is—all being your *one body* of consciousness.

I am consciousness. I am the body of consciousness—all-inclusive, infinite and omnipresent consciousness.

The whole world and universe and everything everywhere in it and of it is my one body of consciousness.

The whole infinitude is my one body of consciousness. I have the freedom of body this very moment as I realize that I am the body of consciousness, and consciousness is infinite, omnipresent, flawless and eternal. I immediately experience my bodily infinity, bodily omnipresence, bodily flawlessness and bodily omnipresence.

I can observe anything anywhere and realize that it is my body—it may look like a person, a flower, a tree, a house, a couch, a table, a pen, a book, food; it may look like the sky, a rainbow, a cloud, an ocean or sparkles on the ocean, a mountain, snow, a clear day or a rainy day—and realize that all the multiplicity of experience is the one consciousness of me, the one body of me (God-spirit-truth) simply experienced subjectively and objectively. Whatever form my one body of consciousness is appearing to be at this moment of experience makes no difference. What it truly is and has is God, consciousness. It is the one I, the one presence and form which is God—infinity, omnipresence and eternity. *This* is what *all* of me is, and none else.

Only God, the incorporeal, is. Mentality, physicality and materiality are simply corporeal *sense* of the incorporeal. Corporeality *in and of its own self* is unreal. It is sense alone and as sense alone it is innocent and impotent. Nothing is unreal or untrue about sense itself. It is only as we introduce *belief* to sense—belief in corporeality being an entity in and of its own self—that we are plunged into finiteness, temporality and the opposing pair of good and bad within each experience. As soon as we know the truth, therefore withdraw belief, experience becomes true, boundless and free.

That truth is that God is all; therefore, I am that. And because God is consciousness, the I that I am is consciousness—all-inclusive, all-embracing consciousness, which means there is nothing local or personal, mental, physical or material about who I am and what I have. Indeed, I, my mind, my body, my world and universe and everything everywhere in me and of me is consciousness, therefore infinite, omnipresent and eternal.

ILLUMINED AWARENESS HEALS THE BODY SENSE

Let us understand that illness and disease are not the physical ailment they have been believed to be but are the ailment of *belief*. Belief is a lack of God awareness, and any and every lack of God awareness *is itself* the ailment, illness or disease of experience. As truth rises in awareness, and belief is dropped, the body experience heals. As we realize that we, our bodies and universe are consciousness, that there is no type or choice of being, body and universe but that of consciousness, then belief about the sensed me and body dissolves, and truth emerges.

As we realize *I am the being of consciousness—I am and have the body of all-inclusive consciousness, the infinite, omnipresent and eternal body of consciousness*—our awareness is illumined. We are filled with the light of truth instead of the dark of untruth (belief). Our awareness has risen from a low degree of illumination that believes in the personal self, the mental mind, physical body, and material world (all separate and apart from each other) into oneness—pure, infinite, omnipresent and eternal consciousness. We have realized that consciousness is one and omnipresent. We have realized that God is consciousness, and God is one; therefore, all is one. We have realized that *I am that, I am consciousness, and I have and am that one body that is God, that is oneness, that is consciousness.*

My consciousness is that one consciousness; therefore, I am the being, and I have and am the body, of consciousness.

Once we realize this truth—once we have de-localized our sense of being and sense of body; once we have de-localized our sense of everything everywhere and realized that all is one, infinity and omnipresence, fully present at every place of consciousness, every place of experience; once we have lifted into the conscious awareness of oneness—then all we have to do is rest from our effort and behold the miracles of life "happening" as us, our bodies and our world.

The miracle of life is omnipresent here and now and always has been. It is evidenced simply by knowing the truth and then lifting away from the personal belief of being, body and world into oneness. Once we know this truth, we can rest and behold God as all. No effort is required—mental, physical or material—because God already is. God is the finished kingdom itself; and because God is the only, infinite, omnipresent, flawless and eternal, I am that and all is that. There is nothing for "me" or "you" to do. "The earth is the Lord's, and the fullness thereof. . . . The earth is full of the goodness of God." Indeed, there is nothing for us to do other than know this truth and then rest back in it, witnessing its glory, harmony, joy and fulfillment populating and animating experience.

GOD IS SELF-MAINTAINED

God self-maintains experience. God is self-complete, self-perfect everywhere, infinitely, eternally with nothing else existent. Therefore, if I am that, and I am; if my true being is that which is consciousness, and it is; if my true mind and body is that which is consciousness, and it is, then what do I have to manage? For what am I responsible?

Only God is, and God is the whole, perfection and fulfillment of all, and *all involved* in all. Nothing "else" is; therefore, there is nothing else to manage.

All I have to manage is the ceaseless knowing of this truth (the one truth) and then rest, beholding the management and government of God as all. And because God is fully present at and as every place and point of me—*being* the very presence, persons, activities, shapes, amounts, conditions and places of my entire universal experience—not one aspect of my experience requires my management or government. Then I have and I witness the good, the life, the perfection, the harmony, the freedom and the fulfillment of God as the fullness and fulfillment of me—of my mind, body, world and everything in and of my world—all being one, consciousness, the miracle of God being all.

Watch the miracle that quickly fills your life as you realize the oneness of you and rest in it, receptive and open to that which is (instead of anxious and cautious about that which is not).

Devote every moment to being *consciously aware* of that miracle! Stay away from all personal sense of self, body and world. Be aware that consciousness is who you are, what your body is, and what everything everywhere is. *Consciousness is the I that I am and the body that I have.*

THE BODY OF CONSCIOUSNESS

Consciousness is body, body is consciousness. I hope with all my heart that this truth has come through clearly. I hope that you understand that the entirety, the all-inclusive experience of consciousness—absolutely everything everywhere that you are conscious of—is consciousness itself, *your* consciousness. You experience oneness, not separateness and difference. You are consciousness being and experiencing itself individually and uniquely as you.

I also hope it is clear that the key to so-called "healing" of the body is the filling oneself with *living God awareness.* Belief in a being and body separate and different from God itself is the only ailment, illness and disease of experience. Your true here-and-now mind "and" body were never born, will never die, and cannot ever be injured, ill, diseased or disharmonious in any way, unhappy in any way; can never experience too much or too little of any category of life in any way; can never be too slow or sluggish in any way. Your mind "and" body are the one mind-body which is full of eternal life itself and is everywhere-present at every point of experience at the same time because life, you, your mind, body "and" world are *consciousness,* not matter.

You are filled with the fullness of God and none else (because there is none else). Think about that. The whole of you, the whole of your one mind and body, the whole of your consciousness, is overflowing, bursting forth with the fullness of God, of good without bad, God without opposite, life itself without illness, disease, old age or death—eternal life itself! You are that because you are consciousness, and your body is that because your body is consciousness, not the physical body you believe your body to be. Get all belief out of your sense. Stop being a believer. Consciousness is your body. There is no physicality. Physicality is simply a physical sense of spirit or consciousness, a corporeal sense we are having of consciousness, a local, finite, personal sense of that which is the only: God.

Forget these beliefs. All belief is false. The only truth is the infinity, omnipresence, oneness and eternity which is God, consciousness. Consciousness is your truth of being, mind, body and world. As you stay lifted in this truth, you are freeing yourself very beautifully, quickly and effectively from the false sense—from belief. Do not be too surprised about the deep peace you begin to feel, the deep rest, the relief you begin to experience as you relax and abide right in the midst of the consciousness you are, the consciousness that is your body.

Consciousness is the living truth of you, the God-filled and fully alive mind and body of you—life itself, truth itself, eternal health, vitality, harmony, and fulfillment of being itself. Awaken to your truth! Awaken to the *consciousness* you are, your mind, body "and" world are! Then your whole experience of life is awakened, and you are free.

Six

The True Body

Let us more deeply understand what the true body is and tangibly experience it here and now. Let us reach the point of awareness which enables what has been called "healing" to be perfectly evident and real throughout the multitude of ailments, diseases, injuries and dysfunctions that the physically-sensed body experiences.

All injury, sickness, disease, dysfunction and decrepitude are quickly healed and then forever avoided as we lift our conscious awareness of being and body from physical to spiritual. The "physical" is simply a physical *sense* of that which is one hundred percent spirit. As sense is illumined with truth, the body is experienced truthfully. It heals. Sense and body are one, not two—just as water and wet are one, not two. We have heard this throughout the *Miracle Self* as "consciousness is experience." The spiritual body and universe—the only true body and universe—is matter-less, therefore untouchable and forever unaffected by anything of "matter." Matter is simply *belief,* and because whatever is believed *is the form* of the believer's experience, matter seems to be real. But only God is, therefore only God or spirit is real. As sense becomes illumined with truth and lives as and by truth, the truth of the body and universe is tangibly evidenced. False sense is "healed," and the true and eternal life, health, vitality and purpose of being spring forth and live here and now.

Spiritual devotees the world over are ready to lift out of belief and into the living, real and practical experience of their spiritual mind, body and world. They—you—are ready to lose the false sense of being and body (that of belief) and be healed, whole and free.

The freedom in spirit, or better stated *of* spirit, allows us to live the freedom of the spiritual, truthful *I* we each are, and in that way escape the parenthesis of belief that keeps us imprisoned in the mind, body and world of belief. As long as we are imprisoned in and by belief, we cannot receive truth. Truth (infinity and omnipresence) cannot enter belief (finiteness and local presence). Equally, belief cannot receive truth. While we still exist in a cloud of belief, all our hearing and reading of truth, and even our feeling of truth within leaves our tangible experience devoid of truth. All the truth study we do, all the meditating we do, and all the silence we sit in still leaves us unable to lift the body out of its imprisonment of belief (which includes the good *and* bad of physical existence, the health *and* illness, disease, injury, decrepitude or pain it may be suffering) into truth and freedom. These pairs of opposites have nothing to do with God but are entirely the experience (the body) of belief—the belief in self, body and world being something in and of their own selves, separate and different from God.

LIVING YOUR TRUE PURPOSE

Only when you awaken to the one truth (that only God is) and stop believing that which seems to be, can you start living your true purpose. Your true purpose includes a healthy and vital body. The body is not only yours to run around the earth with and to enjoy and make use of personally. It *includes* individual use and enjoyment, of course—the freedom of individual health, function and practicality, love and joy, even adventure and thrill. But the true purpose of spiritual being is to give, serve and share of its spirit, its infinity and omnipresence of substance, love, kindness, happiness, wisdom; its spiritual capacity in all its ways and forms. Only as we are consciously free as spiritual being, body and world are we able to begin to truly give, serve and share. So it is important for you who are hearing this message to now lift into the truthful (spiritual) experience of being, body and world. Only then can each individual begin living and serving the truth of his or her inherent nature, that of spirit, infinity and omnipresence of all; only then does each individual discover his or her inherent fulfillment of being, mind, body and world.

And so let us realize that *only God is*. God is spirit, incorporeality, infinity, omnipresence. This being so, there is none else but God. God is the only being in existence. Existence itself *is* the one being, mind, body, world and universe. There is no "other" type of being or mind or body or universe. Only God is. However, there indeed is a *false sense* or *belief* about the truth of being, and this is the root of all duality, of all problems, of a mind and body and world full of the pairs of opposites instead of full of the freedom of that which it truly and one hundred percent is: God.

Believed being, or falsely-sensed being, has been named "human" with its mental mind and physical body living in a vast physical universe, all of which is subject to conditions of both good and bad. Belief or false sense *is itself* the pairs of opposites, the belief in difference and separateness from God. The Master explained this in the parable of the "prodigal son," the individual who believes he is different from and separate from the one being, the one all-in-all being, inclusive of his entire embodiment of experience (his consciousness) and, therefore, suffers birth and death, limit and lack, hardship and pain. Yet the truth of being is God eternal, spirit, incorporeality, infinity, omnipresence. As we each lift away from belief or false sense into a living awareness of our truth of being, we begin to experience that truth as reality. The pairs-of-opposites belief "and" experience (belief and experience being one and the same form) fade into nothingness, as dark fades into nothingness as soon as light enters the world, and the truth of oneness becomes tangible.

Lift your awareness *up* into truth. This is the secret. *Lift* up and away from material belief into spiritual reality. Remember forever, we cannot "bring truth down" to a lesser level of awareness. We cannot bring the infinite to the finite, omnipresence to local, personal presence, spirit to belief, or God to matter. All we can do is rise in awareness from belief to truth, from personal sense to omnipresence, from matter to spirit. *There,* in and as risen awareness, all the freedom of spirit, all the freedom of truth, all the oneness, all the infinity and omnipresence of God as individual and collective being is as free as the air as tangible, real, practical experience.

WHY TRUTH DOES NOT "WORK"

Any time we think in terms of a finite or local place or activity, condition, organ or function, we are living the experience of *belief* not truth. When we think of our body as being this local, personal, physical form and we experience illness, disease, injury, underweight or overweight, some kind of pain or suffering—whatever discordant condition we discover is happening to our body which we believe to be real, debilitating or threatening in some way—we are living the experience of *belief,* not truth.

As soon as we believe that there is something happening "in" or "to" this local, physical body, which we now need God or truth *for* (to heal it or save it), we are so far away from truth in belief (and so far away from being able to experience the truthful, healthy and vital body), that we are left in frustration, scratching our head or even tearing out our hair wondering why truth isn't working for us.

Why, after all these years or decades of reading, listening to, and attending spiritual classes; after meditating and sitting in silence and experiencing, very often, the most beautiful, deep peace and joy and freedom within, why does illness fail to heal? Why does disease or injury or decrepitude fail to yield and heal? Why does the body remain underweight or overweight? Why does it not adjust and become truthful and free? We even change our diet to "help spirit with the job," yet the body still refuses to adjust to its rightful, more comfortable and satisfying weight and vitality. Why?

These questions come to mind, and we cannot find the answers. We cannot understand why it is that truth isn't working for us, particularly after all our years or decades of devoted spiritual study and practice and even our weekly hours of silence.

The reason—and there is just one reason—is that we have entirely misunderstood what we, our minds and bodies are. Even as metaphysical or spiritual students we have mis-identified who and what we are, and it is this mis-identity that keeps the tangible evidence or actuality of truth from our everyday experience. Isn't it shocking that after all these years or decades of being on the spiritual path, we realize only now that we have been living a condition of mistaken identity? Now we are awakening to it.

You see, truth, once *truly known and lived,* is quickly evident as the forms of experience. In fact, truth is spontaneously evident as experience, but because we find it so difficult to release that which we have for so long believed to be true about us, our body and world, belief is often slow to dissipate. It is for this reason alone that the evident forms of harmony, health and freedom can take a few minutes, hours, days or weeks or, in some few cases, a few years to be detected by an individual who has lifted into truth, or been "given" the lift by a practitioner.

If truth is not evident, and if truth is not sustained in one's experience, there is only one reason: we have not known the truth. We cannot deny or hide from this fact. "Know the truth, and that very truth will set you free." The Master, of course, was telling us the truth—the *principle* of God or truthful being.

The very first thing we must realize, and own up to and accept, is that if we are not evidencing truth throughout our lives, we do not know the truth—just as, if we are not evidencing 2 + 2 = 4, but keep getting 3 or 5 or 17, we do not know the truth of math. At first, this is perhaps hard for us to swallow, but it also contains the kernel of our immediate healing and freedom.

Do you see how important it is to know the truth? *It is impossible to evidence or to "have" that which we do not know.* So many students I speak to or read emails or healing requests from, want only to meditate or sit in silence. They do not want to know more truth: "Enough words, all I want is healing," they say. Well, isn't it interesting that all the great mystics of the ages gave us many thousands of words, and still do today? Many words of truth are given us for one reason: we have to *know the truth* before we can be *free in truth.*

Knowing the truth does not grant or produce or give truth to an individual; knowing and living as truth *is itself the form of truth*—the "image and likeness" of itself as earth (the multiplicity of tangible experience). This is why knowing the truth is important—no, *essential.* This is why the Master, who did not waste or mince his words, made a specific point of telling us to "Know the truth, and that very truth will set you free." So let us hear the truth again and again until untruth fades from our awareness and belief dissolves:

God is the *only.*

God is infinite, never finite or local, personal or objectified. God is infinite; God is *the infinitude itself.*

God is incorporeal, never corporeal. We simply have a corporeal *sense* of that which is one hundred percent incorporeal; and sense, in and of its own self, is innocent and impotent. Sense is just sense, not power, not an actual presence or form or entity—just innocent and impotent sense. It is *belief* added to sense that gives us untruthful experience because belief *is* experience. *Belief* is the culprit, not sense. To experience the truth of being, mind, body and world we have to rise from the belief in corporeality to the reality of incorporeality.

God is omnipresence; God is omnipresent. Anywhere we care to think about or focus on throughout the whole of the infinite, there the whole of God exists and is fully evident, complete, perfect, whole and manifested as that very place we are observing. The whole of God is that very form we are observing, that very place, condition, activity or amount we are observing. Whatever it is and wherever it is we observe it, there the whole of God exists as that which we are experiencing. The whole of God, the whole of the infinite, exists fully at every point of itself simultaneously.

And what is God, the infinite, the incorporeal, the omnipresent? God is *consciousness.* Consciousness does not exist "in" the mind, nor "in" the body. To suggest that consciousness exists "in" the mind or body is like suggesting the ocean exists in wetness, or wetness exists in the ocean. This is untrue. The ocean *is,* and is all-inclusive of its character, qualities and properties. The whole of the ocean has the experience of itself which is inclusive of wetness, saltiness, waviness and so on. We can just as aptly compare the statement "I am ever with you, and all that I have is yours" to the ocean as we can to God, mind and formation. There is no part or place or form of the ocean that does not have all that the ocean is and has in just the same way as there is no being, mind, body or experience that does not have all that God is and has. The *all* of God is inseparable and indivisible from each and every point, aspect and expression of itself, just as the ocean is inseparable and indivisible from each and every point, aspect or expression of *itself.* The ocean cannot separate itself from wetness, saltiness and waviness anymore than wet, salt and waves can separate themselves from the ocean. The ocean simply *is,* and is all-inclusive of its nature, aspects and elements, qualities and conditions, character and activities. The ocean is one with and as itself—indivisible, inseparable, all-inclusive and self-inclusive one body, one self, one*ness.*

In this way, we understand that God is one with no "and" or "other," no variant or offspring, no different or lesser or separate aspect, body, form, activity or amount anywhere throughout the infinitude. God simply and all-inclusively *is,* and that *is* is consciousness.

God (consciousness) is infinite and omnipresent, the self-inclusive all-in-all and all-of-all life, substance, presence, body and universal formation. There is nothing existent but God, consciousness. "The Lord he is God in heaven above, and upon the earth beneath: there is none else." All is consciousness; all being, all body, all of the world and universe and everything everywhere in it and of it (and infinitely beyond) is consciousness. Nothing but consciousness is, and consciousness is *one* and *omnipresent.*

God (all being) therefore my being (my "I"), is consciousness. All body, therefore my body is consciousness. All formation, therefore my entire world and everything in it and of it, is consciousness.

There is none else.

Forget what belief has told you, and dismiss appearance. "Judge not by the appearance." Belief throws us into falsely sensing who we are and what presents itself to us. We are tricked into believing that each and every objective form in our world is a being or entity in and of its own right—a real and separate he, she, it, activity, amount, place or condition in and of its own self. We have been conditioned to accept the corporeal experience as being real. Yet only God, the *incorporeal,* is real. "I am the Lord, and besides me there is none else."

All is God, and because God is consciousness, all is consciousness. All is infinity, omnipresence and eternity; therefore you, your body and your universe (and all being, body and universe) are consciousness: infinity, omnipresence and eternity. "I am that I am."

There is no personal being, body or belonging in consciousness; there is no object or locality or amount or activity or place or condition in consciousness. Consciousness, which is omnipresence, cannot be objectified, localized or personalized. No one can claim consciousness as his or her own, not even Gautama or Jesus! "I of my own self am nothing. . . . Besides God [infinity and omnipresence] there is none else. . . . The rain falls equally on the just and the unjust." Omnipresence is forever impersonal, non-local, undetectable and unnameable. *Sense* is certainly *individual,* objective, local, detected and named. All experience is momentary awareness, and it is this that seems to be objective, local, detected and named. But sense in and of its own self is innocent and impotent, never being what it seems to be. *When sense is empty of belief the truth of all is evident, but when sense is full of belief, all acts as it is believed to be.*

Consciousness is infinite and omnipresent and is incapable of producing finiteness or being finite, incapable of producing locality or being local, incapable of objectifying itself or being an object, an amount, a thing; a separate, personal being or body. The whole of God is what consciousness is; the whole of consciousness is what God is. The whole of God is embodied in, and as, individual consciousness—your consciousness.

The whole of God *is the entirety of itself* as individual being, body and world—as you, your body and world; me, my body and world; all being, all body and all of the world. The whole of infinity and omnipresence exists as itself as the entirety of you, your body, your world and universe. Each and every point of you, each and every breath and moment, each and every form of your experience is the whole of God, consciousness, fully complete and self-inclusive, finished and perfect, indestructible and invariable, and eternally so.

The whole of omnipresence exists as the whole of itself at every point of infinity at the same time. There is nothing local, personal or nameable about omnipresence other than omnipresence itself. The all-inclusive *whole* is that which you are and that which you observe; but this does not make being or experience personal, local or objective. Experience is forever *individual,* yes; momentary and conceptual, yes; detectable and describable, yes. But experience never is *in and of its own self* real. Only God is real or reality. We are simply having a conceptual, individual sense of the one being and experience which is real: God, consciousness, infinity, omnipresence.

Experience inclusive of all it contains is simply moment-by-moment conceptual awareness of oneness which, at "our" degree of mind is three-dimensional and of five senses. Experience is multiple moments of now, or multiple embodiments of now, one after the other after the other throughout each twenty-four hours. And because awareness is experience, and because our degree of awareness is three-dimensional and sensed with five senses, our experience is filled with three dimensions and five senses but is never local, never objectified, never finite, never an entity in and of its own self. We are simply having a corporeal sense of the incorporeal.

Knowing this and living it is the secret of individual and collective freedom from all mistaken identity, all personal belief, all limit and lack, all illness and disease, poverty, injustice and inequality. "Know the truth, and that very truth will set you free."

Seven

One and No Other

Only God is, and God is one. Oneness has no other, no variant, no different or lesser embodiment or experience of itself. Oneness is spirit not matter, not physicality, not flesh and blood. Oneness *is*, and has nothing but spirit in and of and throughout it. And because of this, oneness cannot be influenced or changed. Nothing has power or even influence over oneness because there is nothing but oneness. The only power and influence "over" oneness is the power and influence of oneness itself.

Only oneness is; therefore, only one power is, one presence is, one being is, one body is, one world-universe is.

Oneness is infinity, omnipresence and eternity itself. Oneness cannot be made into two; infinity cannot be finitized; omnipresence cannot be made partial or local. The whole is the only and exists not as a "contained" you but as everything everywhere of your experience. "I am that I am," and that "I" I am is consciousness, inseparable and indivisible oneness. Being "and" experience are one, not two, not different, not "inner" versus "outer." Being forever experiences the oneness of itself. The only question, therefore, is what are *we being*—the oneness of truth or the multiplicity of belief?

Always remember, that which experience seems to be, isn't. Appearance in and of its own self is infallibly deceiving. Only God is; only oneness, wholeness, infinity and omnipresence is. When we know and live this truth, appearance is free to be what it truly is:

the "image and likeness" of God—whole and perfect form. When we do not know this truth, appearance cannot be free of the belief we hold about it.

The only thing that ever presents itself to you is God. The whole of God is right here where you are, as you, your mind, body and everything everywhere of your entire universe—all one with and as you. Consciousness is infinity; the consciousness of you is the infinitude itself, your boundless, unconditional all in all.

No being, no body, no thing, no amount, no activity, no place or condition anywhere under any circumstance whatsoever is different from God, separate from God, or less than God. Nothing is finite, nothing is local, nothing is personal. Only God is, and because God is omnipresent, the whole of infinity and omnipresence is right here as you and as everything everywhere of your entire experience. Never is anything of you or your experience not full of God because "something other than or different from God" does not exist.

The whole of consciousness, despite what belief would have us believe, contains no finiteness, no locality, nothing objectified. Consciousness is the infinitude itself and its only capability is infinity; consciousness is omnipresence itself and its only capability is omnipresence, not local presence, not finite presence, not personal presence or objectified presence. The one and only capability of consciousness is that which it is. That is logical, is it not?

That which *is* cannot be "different" from that which it is. Nothing has capability or power or character or nature "outside" of, different from or less than that which it or he or she *is.* This is true of anyone or anything, and of course it is even more true of God or spirit—oneness. All *one* can be, and consist of, and do is that which it is—one or oneness.

God is and can only be the fullness of God and none else; spirit is and can only be the fullness of spirit and none else; oneness is and can only be the fullness of oneness and none else; infinity is and can only be the fullness of infinity and none else; omnipresence is and can only be the fullness of omnipresence and none else; incorporeality is and can only be the fullness of incorporeality and none else.

All God can be is God. This means that all God can be is infinity, omnipresence, incorporeality—consciousness.

God is consciousness, and because there is "none else," you are that, I am that, all is that. You are consciousness. Your mind, body, world and universe is consciousness, and none else. Therefore, *all you can be* and indeed all you *are* is consciousness and everything consciousness is. You cannot be something other than or different from or less than all that consciousness is, and you cannot *have* something other than, different from or less than all that consciousness has—which is the fullness, the infinity, the omnipresence of itself.

This very presence you are is omnipresence as this (your) presence—not personal, not finite, not limited or lacking, not local, not objective, not of matter, not of physicality or materiality. There is no such being or substance or thing in God. God is *consciousness.* And because there is nothing whatsoever throughout the entirety of existence but God—"I am the Lord, and besides me there is none else. . . . The Lord he is God in heaven above, and upon the earth beneath: there is none else"—there is no power or influence upon anyone or anything whatsoever but God itself.

God, the *only,* cannot be changed into a different substance, different presence, different form or a different "type" of substance, presence or form. Infinity cannot become finite, objectified or personal. Omnipresence, which is spirit and incorporeal, cannot become the presence of matter and corporeality—the presence of flesh and blood, wood and stone, cotton and metal, cells and atoms, stars and planets. No, *only God is;* therefore, only God-mind is, only God-being is, only God-body is, only God-presence is, only God-substance is, and that is *consciousness.*

Life has only been challenging because we have grown to believe that we, our minds, bodies and world are entities in and of their own selves—different and separate from God. We have become lost in the forest of belief, all of it false; the prodigal son and daughter lost, hungry and often hopeless. And because belief is experience, our minds and our worlds are filled with the forms of belief, both good and bad. But realize here and now, no matter how deeply you may be facing ill health, lack, limitation, injustice or insecurity at this moment, that belief has no actual reality, no law or principle to sustain itself in experience. Why? It is not God.

Only God is, and God is full of only itself. God does not contain or include belief. God only contains and includes God. It is for this reason that you never need battle that which seems to be. Ignore that which seems to be, and bring your awareness straight to God itself—pure God, pure being, pure spirit, pure truth.

God is consciousness, the infinite is consciousness, and "besides consciousness there is none else."

Consciousness is incorporeal, consciousness is omnipresent, and besides consciousness there is none else. Because there is "none else," there is no power or influence that can "change" consciousness into something "else."

Only consciousness is. I am that and all is that.

God is one. There is only one—one consciousness, one spirit, one being, one body, one substance, one condition, one activity, one place, one infinity, one omnipresence, one incorporeality. And because the whole of God is equally present at every point of itself at the same time, all is the whole of oneness.

Nothing, nothing of the whole of the infinitude, the whole of eternity, is different from or separate from this very being, body and place that you are, this very second.

This very being that you and all are, this minute and forever, is all that God is. Everything you have and all beings have is everything that God has. "Son, I am ever with you, and all that I have is yours."

GOD DOES NOT "GIVE" NOR "WITHHOLD"

Because of this truth—because infinity and omnipresence are the only—God (truth) does not and cannot "give" or "withhold." *All already is,* and cannot be added to or taken from. Nothing of God can be added to you or taken from you.

Oneness is full of itself alone, throughout itself alone. Nothing of oneness can be added to oneness because it already is the whole of itself throughout. Equally, nothing of oneness can be taken from oneness because it itself is the only power, presence, substance and body. What power or idea or influence (or thief!) exists where *only oneness is?* It does not and cannot.

God is incapable of being anything "other" than itself, or acting contrary to its nature for the reasons we have just read: the fullness of God, omnipresence, infinity and eternity are already here where you are, where I am, where all is—*being* the very mind, body and world of all. The whole of God, the whole of omnipresence, the whole of infinity and eternity is already here, *being all.* There is nothing to give, nothing to withhold. God is incapable of giving and incapable of withholding because God is omnipresent. Omnipresence cannot give and cannot withhold because it is already here—eternal, unconditional and infinite.

If we ever seek some good thing, amount or condition from God, if we seek any kind of "result" from God, we are lost immediately. That which we believe we lack and need is already what we *are* and *have* and, not only that, but is *already manifested* and *demonstrated* as what we are and have. Our "lack" is a lack of *awareness of that which we actually are and have,* never a real lack. Can you hear that? If so, you will be quickly free of all lacking and limited, discordant and disharmonious, suffering and painful, ill and diseased experience.

Despite our low degree of awareness, we each are and have the entire presence, mind, body and world of God. There is none but

God, and the fullness of God. *Rise in conscious awareness of God as being everything everywhere;* this is all that is necessary. Lift your awareness from the belief that you are less than or different from or separate from that which is the only and the entirety of all, into the conscious awareness of infinity, of omnipresence, of incorporeality, of eternity, of *God as all.* Consciousness is what you are and what all is—pure consciousness with no matter in it whatsoever, no human in it, no physicality in it whatsoever. Realize this! Lift into *this* truthful awareness! Recognize nothing about you, your mind, body and world but consciousness. *Then* you will quickly witness the "image and likeness" of God (unconditional good) become perfectly real and evident as the tangible forms of your experience.

Eight

One Body

Only God is, only oneness is—inseparable, indivisible oneness, incapable of being anything but one, anything "different" from or less than itself.

Because only God—oneness—is, there is *one body alone.* Oneness does not, and cannot, produce 7.3 billion (at the time of writing) different bodies. Belief believes billions of different bodies exist, but belief has nothing to do with truth. To experience truth we must be filled with truth. If we continue to fill ourselves with belief, all we will have is more belief-form. Let us fill ourselves with truth.

Only God is, only oneness is. Nothing exists but oneness. *All* is one, and that one is God or spirit or consciousness. Only one body is—the *body of consciousness* (or God or spirit). Experience, despite the way it seems to be, is *one*—the one body of consciousness—and is itself each and every form or aspect of experience, *the one* itself. There is only one being, one body, one amount, one place, one condition, one character, one nature, and that one is God, spirit, consciousness, omnipresent as all. God is that one, spirit is that one, consciousness is that one, infinity is that one, omnipresence is that one, eternity is that one, and besides that one there is no other. Oneness is incapable of being anything different from or less than or separate from its omnipresent self. God—the one, the only—cannot and does not have an "and," "another," a "different" or a "lesser." God is God alone; one is one alone—just as white is white alone—and because God is all, God and body are one. The seeming "two"—God and body—are univocally one.[1]

[1] See Paul F. Gorman's *The 7 Spiritual Steps To Solving Any Problem* for further understanding of univocal oneness.

All of the infinitude is, and is fully occupied by, and as, the fullness of oneness. There is no space left out or left over for an "and," a difference, a lesser being or body or formation of any type, and there is no cause that could cause it because oneness itself is the only "cause." Not even one grain, not even one atom, one subatomic particle or one trillionth of a subatomic particle of you, your mind, body or universe is different from or less than the omnipresence of God, oneness. All is utterly one, fully occupied by itself, with nothing "else" because one cannot have anything "else," nothing different, no "plus" or "minus." Indeed, one cannot have less than all of itself throughout itself.

The whole of the infinitude, the whole of omnipresence and the whole of eternity, all being one as the whole of one, is eternally full of itself alone, without border, without end, without beginning or end, without change. It for this reason that there is only oneness, one body, and that oneness, that body is consciousness.

Absolutely nothing whatsoever exists but consciousness. Do you see where we have been lost in believing that the "personal, physical, local" sense of body is "our" body, whereas in actuality the real body is the body of consciousness? There isn't any "other" body because consciousness is the only existence, being and form. The body of consciousness is the only body.

Your consciousness—your all-inclusive experience, formation and activity of everything everywhere happening in and as your consciousness—is your body and everything of your body. "I am that I am." You can observe anything, at any place within your body—within your consciousness—and realize, "I am that." That which you observe, even though it appears to be a person, object, place, activity or condition "out there" different and separate from you, is not different and separate. It is the one I of you, the one consciousness being experienced as form. It is nothing different from I, consciousness. It is not "over there" but right here *as a form of consciousness* in this moment of experience. It is an aspect of your one body. The infinite variety of body, form, activity, amount, color, fragrance, quality, character, nature, place and condition we each observe is the one consciousness we are, simply experienced individually. Because all is the one consciousness, consciousness is the one body-of-being. This body-of-being is our one true body. There is no other.

ONE BODY OF CONSCIOUSNESS

Our one body of consciousness is our truthful body. Consciousness is body. As we rise into ever greater understanding of consciousness being body, we no longer "separate" or "differentiate" that which is observed and experienced from that which is consciousness, oneness, omnipresence, infinity and eternity.

All is consciousness; all is one, and that one—as individual consciousness—is individual body. Your individual consciousness is your individual body; my individual consciousness is my individual body; his and her individual consciousness is his and her individual body, yet all one, all God, the infinity of oneness, omnipresence, individually experiencing life as the being named "you," "me" and all.

Begin to understand that the organs and functions of the body, the activity of the body, the presence and purpose of the body are all consciousness. Begin also to understand that because the body is consciousness, your and my *individual experience* of the body—its individual type, character and nature, why it is healthy and why it can be ill or diseased, injured or disabled, underweight or overweight, why it ages—is all to do with individual *belief*. When you understand this, you will awaken to what it is, and how it is that the body heals.

We must lift belief, attention, interest, concern and effort away from that which is believed to be the body, the "physical, corporeal" body, to the spiritual truth of the body. We must withdraw our interest, concern and effort from the believed-body's state, its organs and functions, its flesh, bones and blood—from everything going on in and as the describable body, that which is termed the "physical."

A DISCLAIMER

We should give a disclaimer at this point, as we always need to do: please—I mean this with all sincerity and seriousness—only act and rely on spiritual awareness when you are ready and comfortable to do so. Do not make a decision about what type of attention or aid your body needs based on what I or any other practitioners or teachers say. Make spiritual decisions regarding the body only when you yourself *feel* the spiritual strength and readiness to do so. Never attempt to withdraw from maintaining or sustaining the physical sense by physical means until you have conviction about the spiritual body. Only when you feel strong in spirit, and feel the dissolving of the belief that the "physical" body has reality, are you ready to make the transition from physical aid to spiritual healing.

If you are not yet feeling ready, it does not matter. Continue to use any aid—from a simple band-aid or lotion, to medicine, or even to surgery, if you need it or feel more comfortable and safe having it. Please understand this and hear it deeply and seriously. It is simply not necessary, nor wise, to step out of your comfort zone and risk your current experience of life and health, until you feel truly ready to do so. Until that time of realization, there is no harm done to your spiritual awakening. Continue to rely on materia medica. You are not holding yourself back by using medical aid until you are spiritually stronger, anymore than a child is held back by having her parent steady and protect her from falling as she learns to ride her bicycle.

The way into spiritual readiness is to realize that no matter what any needed aid or procedure appears to be, it is *actually spirit* because there is nothing but spirit.

All is spirit no matter how it appears to be. All form, activity and procedure are spirit because spirit is the only. Therefore, a Band-Aid is actually spirit, a pill is actually spirit, a vitamin is actually spirit; even surgery is the activity of spirit because only spirit is.

In this realization you are, even as you have a physical experience, lifting your awareness and belief away from the physical into a higher awareness of spirit being the only and the all. In this way you are beautifully serving your spiritual awakening.

There is the disclaimer. I hope you take it seriously. It is very important that you do.

WHEN YOU ARE SPIRITUALLY READY

When you are ready, you take that leap and decide, "I will no longer pay that much attention to, be interested in or concerned about what is or is not going on in the physical sense of the body. I will no longer attempt to heal the physical experience by physical means.

I will now, this day, lift into pure spiritual consciousness, in the realization that consciousness is my body.

My whole experience is the one body of experience, the one body of being, my individual and unique body of experience.

Consciousness is my body . . . consciousness alone. . . .

The secret of health and healing is to lift awareness and interest into that of seeking God *as God is,* not as we believe God is or need or want God to be as human, physical, material good. "Seek not ye what ye shall eat, or what ye shall drink, neither be ye of doubtful mind . . . but rather seek ye the kingdom of God, and all these things shall be added unto you [shall become evident and tangible for you]." Hear that: the *kingdom* of God. The kingdom is the infinitude, omnipresent as all. There is no existence but the kingdom of *God itself being all.* The kingdom of God is the kingdom of consciousness, the kingdom of the incorporeal, the kingdom of the infinite, the kingdom of the omnipresent, and nothing less or different from that one and only kingdom.

Do you see why the Master told us to seek *not* the things of experience—the way in which the kingdom objectively appears to be in experience—but to seek the kingdom itself, and nothing but the kingdom itself. The moment we begin to seek *that which truly is for itself alone* and not for any "result" that "we" may desire or believe we need, *then* we discover our life filling with as much health, harmony and plenty as we could ever wish for, plus "twelve baskets full left over."

I am consciousness, and because consciousness is one and oneness, my body is consciousness.

My body, this physical sense of body, a local sense of body, is not "within" consciousness. No, "I" am consciousness. That means that my body is actually a body of awareness not physicality, and that body of awareness, being consciousness, is infinite and can be nothing less or different.

My body is incorporeal and can be nothing less or different. My body is omnipresence and can be nothing less or different.

This very second, I actually am consciousness, infinity, omnipresence, incorporeality, eternity. Even though belief may still be fighting this truth, it does not make any difference. Belief is and has no power and is proven to be and have no power the very moment we lift into consciousness as I, consciousness as body, and stick with it.

I am consciousness; therefore, I am infinite, and because all is one, my body is consciousness.

My body is the body of consciousness or awareness, which is infinite, omnipresent, incorporeal and eternal.

Everything of my tangible experience is my tangible body because my body is consciousness. And consciousness is always tangible. There is no intangible consciousness, no unmanifested or undemonstrated consciousness, no invisible consciousness, no invisible omnipresence.

But you see, belief says, "Yes, there are power and reality in experience—power and reality that are different from God." Belief makes the believer believe that God is invisible to experience, intangible to experience and, in fact, nowhere to be found in experience. Belief convinces the believer that God is ethereal not practical, that God is unmanifested and undemonstrated, requiring a formula or a code or the right spiritual thinking or attitude to make visible, tangible, manifested, demonstrated, real and practical that which isn't at this moment.

Belief believes that God which is spirit has to change itself into physicality, matter, corporeality to become a healed, healthy and harmonious body—not only that, but has to become healthy and harmonious *here* and *there* in the various local places and for the various conditions where healing is most needed. Entangled in this belief, we make attempt after attempt to convert God into corporeal good or spirit into matter, and we forever fail because God does not have any matter in it. The incorporeal does not contain an ounce of corporeality, and so you see that such belief has been folly from the moment someone decided to try it.

God is forever manifest, demonstrated, visible, tangible and real in the most practical "here and now" way. Oneness does not have different departments or states or experiences. Oneness is oneness, and because oneness is omnipresent, every place of oneness is fully one, whole and complete, finished and perfect formation. Oneness is fully manifested, fully demonstrated. Oneness does not and cannot have one part unmanifested and another manifested, one part undemonstrated and another demonstrated, one part invisible and intangible and another visible and tangible. That is nonsense and always has been. It is the product of belief and misunderstanding alone. We must "Know the *truth,*" and then "that very truth will set [us] free."

Oneness is forever the whole of itself, and because oneness *is* existence, there being none other, God *itself* is the only existence, the only manifestation, the only demonstration, the only visibility and tangibility. There is no other type of manifestation, demonstration, visibility or tangibility; there is no other state or experience. God *is,* period; oneness *is* and is the only *is,* and because God, oneness, is finished, whole and complete, all of existence is finished, whole and complete. The only requirement is a living *awareness* of this great truth.

God—because God is one, the only—is the only presence, the only being, mind and body, the only manifestation and the only demonstrated experience.

And because God is omnipresence and eternity, all presence, being, mind and body is eternally manifested and demonstrated. Eternal God, good, is fully manifested and already demonstrated here and now.

The whole of God is fully manifested and already demonstrated right here where you are, as you—being everything you are and everything you have.

The whole of God is fully manifested right here where you are, fully visible right here where you are, fully tangible right here where you are—being everything you are and everything you have.

It is time to lose the belief in an unmanifested God, an undemonstrated God, an invisible or intangible God—a God that has still to "become" our good. The whole of consciousness is wholly finished and complete, manifested and demonstrated, visible and tangible as and throughout the entirety of existence. This is why the Master tells us, "As in heaven so on earth." As God is, earth is also because God and earth (experience) are one, not two.

So there remains just one question. How is God—the *truth* of being, mind, body and earth—evidenced? How is it evidenced by you and me, here and now, today? *By rising into the living awareness of all as God, consciousness, and nothing different.* The you you are, and the I I am, and the all all is, is God because God is the one, the only.

You are *the* incorporeal, *the* infinite, *the* omnipresent itself. There is none else; therefore, your truth *has* to be that, and indeed it is. "I am that I am." "He that sees me," the Master told us, "sees him that sent me [he who is what I am]." When you observe anyone or anything, you see God, you see the spiritual, incorporeal form, being, mind and body because there is none but God, spiritual, incorporeal form, being, mind and body. It is simply that mind is objective—of three dimensions and five senses—and so the infinite variety of God is *sensed as* three-dimensional objectivity. We experience the one being as billions of different beings, and the one form as a universe of billions of different forms, things, places, activities, amounts, animals, plants, vegetables, oceans, mountains, countries, states, cities, towns, neighborhoods, houses and gardens. We have a corporeal sense of that which is one hundred percent incorporeal. We have a personal, local, finite and temporal sense of that which is one hundred percent impersonal, omnipresent, infinite and eternal.

Lift, lift, lift into the awareness of *consciousness* being the all of you, the only of you, with nothing different, nothing less, nothing changeable, and nothing *capable* of being different or less or changeable.

You are rising into the awareness of the *one* that is consciousness being the whole of you, inclusive of body. And remember, all awareness is fully embodied, demonstrated, manifested, visible and tangible. So rising in awareness—*rising in awareness*—is the most thrilling, the most exciting adventure of self. Each grain of higher spiritual awareness *is* the form of itself as greater health and harmony, peace and freedom, abundance and happiness of being.

Never try to bring God or consciousness "down here" to fix, heal, harmonize or pacify all of the experience of "down here." Forget it, forget it, forget it! If ever you try to use God "for" some nameable, local good, you are so far out of truth you may as well go to the movies instead. Never do that. God cannot be used. God *is!*

The secret is to forget about "down here," forget about what belief believes is mental, physical or material. Your sole journey in truth is to rise in awareness. We have here such a good and strong clarity about exactly how to do that.

Rise in awareness. Rise into the awareness that you are, and your mind and body are, consciousness—only consciousness. You are nothing "else." You are not what you seem to be, and your problem is not what it seems to be; nor is your solution what it seems to be. All is consciousness, period. There is nothing "else."

I am consciousness; I am the one body of consciousness; consciousness is my body. Nowhere in the entirety of my experience is "outside" of my body because consciousness is my body and consciousness is infinite and omnipresent.

I am having an infinite number of experiences of the one body I am, and in a material sense those experiences have been given an infinite number of names. In that material sense every one and every condition act in an infinite variety of ways—some good, some bad. But all of materiality is simply a believed sense of that which actually is.

When I now rise into truthful awareness of that which is, I witness the whole of my body, degree by degree by degree, becoming that of life, health, harmony, love, freedom, joy and purpose.

I am consciousness, and besides consciousness there is nothing else at all, therefore nothing else about me. For this reason, if I am ever thinking or pondering or reading about or listening to anything other than consciousness; if I am exploring or seeking anything other than pure consciousness; if ever I am wishing to understand more of truth, and it is anything other than understanding more about consciousness, I am off in the woods somewhere, and not rising in spiritual awareness.

On the other hand, every time I seek to know more about God or consciousness, every time I seek the spiritual being, the spiritual body, the spiritual experience, the spiritual thing, place, condition, amount, activity, organ, function, then I am rising in awareness.

Every minute of seeking truth for the sake of truth itself (never for a reason we can name) is a tangible raising of awareness. That is how to make the utmost use of every minute and every hour of your truth study—your soaking yourself in truth messages. Every time you read spiritual instruction, or listen to a class, make sure that what you are reading or hearing is that of God as mind as universe, or consciousness as mind as universe, not of anything to do with a lower level of awareness which accepts the "mental, physical and material" existing in "time" and "space," conditioned by "cause" and "effect."

If ever you read about, listen to, or attend a class that teaches how material experience can be healed, prospered or harmonized by God, or spirit—by "knowing the truth," by meditation or silence—then know that you're not taking in truth. You have to be aware of this; otherwise you will spend more and more time lost in a forest of belief.

I am consciousness, I am spirit, I am the infinite, and I am incapable of being anything "other" than one hundred percent what I am—consciousness, anything "other" than spirit, anything "other" than the infinite.

There is nothing about me or within me or throughout me that can cause difference. I am I, and besides I there is none else.

One can only be one; infinity can only be infinity; God can only be God. There is none else; there is no other being or state or body or world or universe oneness can be. There is no power or influencing factor in oneness that could make it into a different form or activity. Oneness is full of oneness alone. There is no "other" being or body; there is no choice but to be the fullness of the one which is the infinity, omnipresence and eternity of being, mind, body and universe. There is no "other" way of being but the one. Any "other" idea of life or body is founded on substanceless belief alone. There is no principle behind "another" idea because the only true and eternal principle is God, which is oneness. That principle is the infinite, the infinitude itself, which is omnipresent at and as every place and point of itself at the same time. Oneness is incorporeal, spiritual without name, form, shape, outline; uncontainable—pure consciousness. *I am that. I am consciousness, and besides consciousness I am none other.*

THE LIGHT OF TRUTH FILLING AWARENESS

Think now, of the entirety of your experience filled with and as, and being the one form of pure consciousness. Begin to gently ignore and let go of the belief in a material world as being an entity in and of its own self—its bodies, forms, things, activities, amounts, names, places and conditions. Gently and lovingly withdraw your fixation from belief and appearance. Begin to think about the entirety of form being one substance, one presence, that being consciousness. Fill your awareness with, and set your affection upon pure consciousness, pure presence:

I am consciousness. The whole of me is consciousness. There is nothing about me, nothing I can possibly experience, other than consciousness.

Even when belief is trying hard to convince me that matter is real—that my body is a physical entity and that it is in some way or another ill, diseased or injured, that it is suffering and painful, or that I am experiencing some form of lack or limitation, sadness or loneliness—I realize the untruth of it. I "loose it [this belief, this suggestion] and let it go." Even while the experience is happening, I realize the truth of oneness, of God, of spirit as being all I am and all I have.

I realize that what I am actually experiencing, even though I may be having a false sense of it at this moment, is pure consciousness because there is none else.

The only experience is that of God (or spirit or consciousness) because there is none else, and God is incapable of being anything other than itself.

Only God is, only spirit is, only consciousness is, only omnipresence is; therefore, I am that, and all is that.

I cannot be, and indeed am not, anything "else" or "different" or "less" because there is nothing else, different or less. How could there be when God is the fullness of itself alone—omnipresent—in and as all?

Indeed, only God is; therefore, all being-mind-body-world-universe, and everything everywhere in it and of it are the omnipresence of God.

There is no available space or place left over that could be anything else, different from or less than God itself—oneness itself, consciousness itself. Omnipresence, by definition, is full of itself, and is fully being itself alone because there cannot be omnipresence "and" something additional. And because omnipresence is God, oneness, all is full of, and being the fullness of God alone, onness alone. Therefore, all *experience* is that of omnipresence, God, oneness. There cannot be a different type of experience because there isn't a different type of omnipresence or God or oneness.

No matter what you are experiencing—whether to belief it is good or bad, or very good or bad—realize that it is actually and literally God, spirit and truth. It is absolutely—utterly—one hundred percent impossible to experience anything different from or less than God, spirit and truth because God-spirit-truth is the one and the only.

There is no space for "another type" of experience, a "different" experience or a "lesser" experience. Infinity and omnipresence are all there is and therefore, occupy the whole. Where would there be space for even one, minute grain of something "else" or "different" or "less" when infinity and omnipresence occupy all space? There is not. It is impossible. The infinite omnipresence that is God can only be, and indeed only is, its own experience, incapable of experiencing anything else, different or less.

As you experience a person, object or amount, he, she or it appears to exist in a particular location and appears to be an entity in and of its own right. Belief would have you believe it is so. But "judge not by appearance." What you are actually experiencing is the whole of God-infinity-omnipresence simply appearing to be, or objectively appearing to sense as, the person, object or amount. The way in which experience appears and the way in which it is sensed do not change God, or make God different or less as the form of experience. God is God, period, and so all formation is God and cannot be, and is not, anything different. Again, nothing of the entire infinitude consists of anything but the omnipresence of infinity itself.

Everything of experience, second by second, is the whole of God, the whole of the incorporeal, the whole of omnipresence right here where you are, as you. Nothing of God is missing, nothing is incomplete, nothing is separate from you or your experience. All of God, good, is here and omnipresent this very minute. You cannot possibly go to God and receive anything more of God than the amount you already have, because the whole, the infinity of God is right here, being you and your entire experience. The way of experiencing it is to lift into a living awareness of what God *is,* that being pure consciousness—incorporeality itself, infinity itself, omnipresence itself, oneness itself—and none else.

ONENESS ALONE

If we believe anything other than oneness (consciousness), if we believe or are bothered by or are fearful of any objective form, any finite sense of oneness—either good or bad—then we are not in oneness, but in twoness. Believing twoness (God *and*) is why we suffer and why we *continue* to suffer. As soon as we understand oneness, we fill our interest and our contemplation full of only oneness—consciousness.

There's the miracle. As soon as we do this, it's often surprising how quickly the miracles of oneness are evident—just by being consciously aware of oneness; just by seeking nothing but oneness itself, which is consciousness.

I seek to have my awareness opened and filled full with the truth that consciousness is God, consciousness is what I am, consciousness is my body.

The whole of consciousness is my body. My body does not exist "in" or "within" consciousness as a finite, local "part" of consciousness. No, my body is the body of consciousness, which means the body of infinity and omnipresence and eternity. My body, therefore, exists as and throughout infinity because my body is consciousness—indivisible, inseparable, omnipresent consciousness.

Whether I am looking out at a human being, an animal being, an insect being, a plant being, an object, amount, activity, place or condition, what I now realize is that the whole of consciousness is that which is being observed or experienced. Everything everywhere I observe or experience is the omnipresence and infinity of consciousness being the form of it in my experience. I have lost the false idea that "I"—my physically-sensed body—is separate and different from the bodies of all the other human beings in the world, or from all the trillions of other forms, beings, things, amounts and conditions in the world.

No, the whole of my experience is my body, is my consciousness. Consciousness is my body. My body is a body of awareness not a body of phys-

icality. Awareness is consciousness, and is infinite, incorporeal and omnipresent.

SEVEN DAYS OF ILLUMINED AWARENESS

For the next seven days, think continually about the infinity and omnipresence of *consciousness* as I, *consciousness* as body. Lift, minute by minute, into a greater living awareness of oneness, not multiplicity. Become aware of the entirety of your consciousness (your conscious awareness) as being the oneness of you, the oneness of your body.

Let us withdraw or begin to lose—really, truthfully begin to lose or dispel—the idea that the body is physical as it has been believed it to be.

My body, the only body, is God because God is the only, and God is consciousness; therefore, my body is consciousness.

Devote, with determination and discipline, just seven days and nights to lifting your awareness into this one truth and watch what happens. You'll feel a release from old belief and conditioned sense, and with it the release from illness or disease because release and released experience are one.

BECOMING NEWLY AWARE

Lift right up into a new paradigm, a new understanding, a new reality that completely drops and leaves behind the old belief that self is a mental being and the body is physical, local and temporal, with arms and legs, organs and functions, a head and a brain. Drop it and let it go, and realize that only God is; therefore, I am that and all is that. And because God is one, infinite and omnipresent—indivisible and inseparable—what I am is that one infinity and omnipresence, not many parts or elements or aspects, not finiteness nor local presence.

"I am the life, the water, the wine," the Master tells us. Well, what is "I"? Consciousness, God. Therefore, by definition, the body is consciousness, which is infinite, omnipresent and eternal oneness. "I" am the life, "I" am the body, which means consciousness is the life, consciousness is the body. No one in truth ever told us that self is mental, the body is physical and the world is material. Where has such belief come from? It is only because we have grown to believe appearance at its face value instead of as its truth (its reality) that we live a sense of difference and separation from God.

The collectively-believed notion that we are different and separate from God is simply untrue. It is unfounded, without principle or law to uphold it. Difference and separation simply do not exist in God and are incapable of existing in truthful experience. As you rise out of this old and unfounded belief about self and body, into *truthful* self and body—which are one, consciousness, infinity, omnipresence, eternity—you quickly begin to *experience* the truthful self and body. The "physical" body emerges through the fog of old belief as whole and healthy, vital and strong.

It is quite a miracle to observe what happens to the physical sense of body when we leave it of its own self alone, lift up into the truthful body of infinity and omnipresence, rest there, and simply behold it "happening" as and throughout our consciousness.

The physical sense of body is just one element of our infinite and omnipresent body. Our body is the entirety, the all-inclusive and self-inclusive body of consciousness—infinite, omnipresent, eternal, fully manifested and demonstrated God, good.

A living awareness of this truth is the only requirement; a lack of this living awareness is the only disease.

Nine

Go to Where God Is, Part One

There is one way only to experience actual truth—the harmony, joy, health, abundance, love, freedom and fulfillment of spiritual being. There is one way only because there is one God only—*one* itself, spirit and truth itself. There are multiple paths that *lead to* the one way, but unless the one way is eventually found and adhered to, all "other" ways are guaranteed to fail. "Strait is the gate, and narrow is the way, which leadeth unto life, and few there be that find it . . . a narrow place, where there is no way to turn either to the right or to the left."

Unfortunately, even after years or decades of reading, listening to, and attending truth classes, until the point of awareness is reached where we can *truly hear the one truth,* we have not found the single way. We, therefore, practice that which we believe is the way of truth but actually is still a way of failure. Failure indeed is what we evidence (failure to witness truthful life, God's life, "heaven as it is on earth") until the beautiful moment of awakening to the one way. Only God is, and God is *one* without variation, without difference, without choice. Therefore, only the one way, the "strait and narrow" way of God itself is the actual and fruitful way.

The guaranteed way to fail is to attempt to bring God or spirit "down here" to us, to matter, to heal it, harmonize it, pacify it; to make it loving and kind, moral, just and compassionate; to bring safety and security to it.

Attempting to "bring God down here," or "to this place" to influence or heal a human or material condition is impossible. That is why, for as long as we continue to attempt it, we are guaranteed to fail. Let me just say, I was the best at failing until that moment when, like the bursting through of springtime, the way of truth sparked within me just enough so that I could stop the nonsense of attempting to "bring God down to my level" of mentality, materiality, physicality to heal "me," to fix "me," and lift "me." Impossible!

That single spark of truth within saying, "This way, my love, my son, my daughter; come this way; come to me alone for I myself am all" is the moment our healing starts emerging. Only God is, and the moment we first truly feel that truth, we realize that we must go to where God is, rather than trying to get God to come to where we are.

As soon as we understand this, and start doing it, the miracles of truth are quickly evident in experience, and if not so quickly, then within a very short time. You see, principle, once attuned to and adhered to, is instantaneously evident throughout you and your experience. "Where the presence of the Lord is, there is liberty." Principle already exists in all its fullness, all its glory, all its freedom, all its certainty and all its formation (body). Principle is law. As soon as we recognize this and attune "our" awareness and "our" ways to *it,* as soon as we go to *it,* as soon as we go to the principle *for the principle* rather than trying to get the principle to come down to us, or come "over here" to us to rescue and fix us, to heal and pacify us despite ourselves, then it is that we quickly find ourselves on the path of truth—the beautiful "strait and narrow" path the Master showed us. "Strait is the gate, and narrow is the way, which leads to life [truth], and few there be that find it."

Indeed, as we arrive at the straight and narrow path, and as we walk it, we discover that *it itself* is the healing experience. How is it walked? How do we begin to witness our bodies healing? The way is to rise up into the consciousness of incorporeality, the consciousness of God, the consciousness of spirit, the consciousness of omnipresence, the consciousness of oneness, not "twoness." Lift and illumine your awareness—*spiritualize* your awareness. Empty yourself of material belief and fill yourself with a living awareness of *spirit as all.*

In spiritual consciousness there is no matter, no mentality, no physicality. Spirit has no locality in it whatsoever, no object, amount, place or condition. Belief does not exist; only God exists, only spirit exists—just God, spirit, the *incorporeal* everywhere present, equally and simultaneously. There is no name, no God "and," no multiplicity, no time or space, cause or effect. There is nothing but God, spirit, the infinite, the omnipresent, the incorporeal presence—pure and unconditional God presence *being all,* whole and complete, boundless and free.

When we have a grain—just a true grain—of this awareness, which means when we have lifted our awareness from everything describable, everything of matter or humanity, up into *God consciousness*—spirit, omnipresence, infinity, eternity, oneness, pure consciousness, besides which there is nothing else—once we've done this, *there is* the harmony of individual and collective being. There is the harmony of being, mind, body and world; there is the union, the love of mankind, the love of all beings, the love of all in the world, the love of God, all fully existent, fully manifested, fully demonstrated as all. Everywhere we look, everywhere we turn, everything we think and do is filled with, and is itself, God-spirit-truth.

God consciousness "and" God experience are one, not two. God consciousness does not *produce* God experience; God presence (God consciousness) does not *produce* or *make manifest* healthy, harmonious, peaceful and plentiful formation. God *is* the "image and likeness" of itself as form.

WHERE GOD IS

We have heard that the only way to experience God—our truth, our harmony, our freedom in all of life's experience—is to rise up into God consciousness. We understand that we cannot bring God "down" to materiality; we cannot bring the infinite "down" or "into" the finite, the incorporeal "down" or "into" the corporeal, spirit "down" or "into" matter. Belief that the corporeal, mental, physical, material experience is real in and of its own self is just *belief,* not reality. It is *belief about* that which is actually one hundred percent God-spirit-truth, and belief can never evidence truth. We have to lift our senses away from belief into *God itself.* This is the great key. When we have it, we have found the straight and narrow way, and we are walking right into the experience of our healed and renewed body.

Always remember, truth cannot "come to us." Is it logical to you that we cannot bring infinity and omnipresence "down" or "into" finiteness and local presence—especially as all finite and local experience is only of *belief*? How can that which is real be evident as that which is false? To expect God, which is true, to heal belief-forms which are untrue is like expecting math to heal 2 x 2 = 3. Math cannot do that; math can only *be* 2 x 2 = 4. Never again hope or expect spirit to become evident as matter—healed and healthy matter. Matter is nothing but *belief about* spirit. God consciousness *dispels* material belief leaving just God experience—God being, God mind and God formation (body or embodiment).

The entire secret of spiritual living—harmony throughout mind, body, relationship, place, amount, condition and activity—is to rise to where *it tangibly exists.* We must go to where God is; we cannot get God to come to where "we" are. All the health, harmony, peace and plenty of God (truth) already exists as perfectly tangible, visible and real formation this minute, but we cannot see it if we believe the forms of experience to be entities in and of their own selves. We must rise into *oneness* instead of dwelling in belief and multiplicity.

When we understand that all is consciousness, we quickly realize what it means to *rise to where God is* rather than getting God to come down to where we are—and we quickly stop attempting to. We must lift away from material belief to an awareness of consciousness as reality.

I am consciousness, and consciousness is the infinitude. God is the infinitude of consciousness. That is why I am, and all is, consciousness.

Existence itself is the infinitude and omnipresence of consciousness. All life, all being, all presence and all formation is consciousness. Consciousness is infinity and omnipresence; infinity and omnipresence is consciousness.

I am consciousness, and besides me there is none else. My body is consciousness, and besides consciousness it is none else.

THE CONE OF AWARENESS

What we call *experience*—inclusive of the infinite variety of being, form and activity involved—is simply a degree of God awareness. Awareness *is* experience; experience *is* awareness. There are infinite degrees of awareness (just as God itself is infinite—*the* infinitude itself). "There are many mansions in my Father's house." Any and every degree of awareness *in and of its own self* is good without opposite because all is God, which includes every degree of awareness. Never lose sight of this: awareness in and of its own self is God, good without opposite, innocent and impotent.

To illustrate the degrees of awareness, imagine a cone ten feet tall. From the apex, the cone becomes increasingly wider towards its base which is, let's say, five feet in diameter. Imagine this to be the *cone of awareness*—from pure spiritual (God) experience at the peak, to a multiplicity of objective (matter-filled or material) experience at the base.

The peak is pure consciousness aware of itself as the infinity, omnipresence and eternity of individual being and formation—pure consciousness forever being the "image and likeness" of itself alone as all being, mind, body and universe. Here, all of existence, all being and body—you, me and everything everywhere—is the being and body of pure consciousness, individual yet eternally *one* as and with all "else."

As the cone descends towards the base, imagine each "lower" degree containing more objectivity. At the peak there is no objectivity, no thing, no place, no condition, no amount, no activity. All is one and omnipresent, pure I as or being all. As we slide down the degrees of awareness, each successive degree contains more *objective* experience—from infinitesimal objectivity in the first degree, to a multiplicity of objectivity at the base.

However, each and every degree of awareness is nothing but the fullness of God and nothing else. Whether we live at the apex or the very base degree of objective awareness, we are, our mind and body are, and our world and universe and everything everywhere in it and of it are one—God and nothing but God. This is the great key to understanding experience, to understanding "this" or any "world," the "healing consciousness" that Gautama the Buddha, Jesus the Christ and every spiritual master discovers. "The earth [awareness, experience] is full of the goodness of God. . . . The earth is the Lord's, and the fullness thereof. . . . Holy is the Lord of hosts: the whole earth is full of his glory."

So far so good. But this leaves a burning question. Why, if every degree of experience (earth) is itself God, and is full of the goodness of God, do we have the experience of both good and bad? Why do we experience an infinite variety and degree of pairs of opposites? The answer is *belief.*

The moment we inject *belief* into experience (the world) we have God *and.* Belief is the *and.* We add an *opinion* about him, her or it; we add *judgment;* we hold an *idea* about our world or a person, thing, activity, amount or place in it. The moment we do this, we change our *experience* from that of purely and fully God to no God at all. We've made a "false idol." We've begun to worship a false god. We've made a prodigal of ourselves and our world. We've set up a personal, selfish self whose primary impulse is self-survival and secondary impulse is self-satisfaction. In this way we have created a *belief* of difference and separation from God, truth.

Belief *is* the pairs of opposites. With belief infusing awareness, our experience is discolored, mistaken, misperceived, confused and misunderstood. We live as a being of mistaken identity in a universe of mistakenly identified experiences. We believe we are simply "who we are"—human, of a certain gender, race, character and nature constituting some measure of good, and some of bad. Equally, we believe every person to be "who they are," a person in and of his or her own self, and every object, place, activity and amount to be "what it is," an entity in and of its own self.

Yet all is God, not different and separate "hes, shes or its." All is one, not multiplicity, difference and separateness. Unless we realize this, all the spiritual instruction we read and attempt to demonstrate is inspiring but frustrating because we cannot, no matter how hard we attempt to do it, bring God to humanity, physicality or matter. Humanity, physicality and matter are all believed reality, not reality itself. Only God-spirit is reality. But the moment we realize the mistaken identity we've lived with, then drop it and go to where God is, we quickly have our release from belief and our freedom in spirit.

ELEVATE CONSCIOUS AWARENESS

"Going to where God is" can be likened to rising in an elevator from the first to the top floor of a building. The experience available on the top floor is entirely different from that on the first. While it is true that no metaphor is adequate in explaining truth or God, an occasional metaphor is (with a little spiritual discernment) a wonderful gateway to the straight and narrow "ah hah" of realizing and evidencing God.

Let's say we have been living on the first floor of a twenty-floor building, and we now wish to experience the greater luxury, the people, the spaciousness, the harmony and the view which exist on the twentieth floor. How do we achieve it? We cannot bring the twentieth floor and everything it has down to us on the first. That is impossible. The only way we can reach and experience the twentieth floor is to *rise to where it is.* We get into the elevator and rise to the top floor. When we have arrived, the greater luxury, the people, the extra space, the harmony and the view are as free as the air to us. It *is* what the twentieth floor *is* and *has.* When we're there, we *have* it, and we can fully experience it.

If we now wish to enjoy the roof garden with its elevated vista, the sunshine and fresh air, the greenery and beautiful colors and fragrance of the flowers that exist up there on the roof garden, we again have to rise to where it is. We cannot bring the roof garden down to where we are on the twentieth floor, or any other. The only way—the one way—we can experience the roof garden is to *go to where it exists.* Once we have arrived, the entire experience is as free as the air for us to enjoy. Do you see? Then you are on the verge of witnessing miracles throughout your mind, body and world this day, this week and forevermore.

When you understand, really hear and "get," that God is *consciousness,* pure consciousness with no matter in it whatsoever; and that God is *all,* there being none but God; and then when you get on with rising to where God is instead of attempting to get God to "come down to where you are," you quickly begin to witness the truth and freedom of God throughout your life.

Rise in awareness from humanity to God, from matter to spirit, from the corporeal to the incorporeal. Empty yourself of the belief in humanity, physicality and materiality, and fill every thought and sense of you with spirit.

I am, and besides me *there is none else. Therefore, the "I" that I am—the "I" and the "I am" spoken of in all the scriptures of the world—is consciousness. I am pure consciousness, pure spirit. I am incorporeality not corporeality, infinity not finiteness, omnipresence not local, personal or temporal presence.*

Do not be concerned if belief still lingers in your mind. You will understand the truth of mind as we continue, and how to take control of the mind.

For now, be assured that when we understand God to be the *only;* and when we begin to drop concern and effort for physicality and materiality in and of its own self, and instead fill our awareness—our every thought—with spirit and truth; and as we begin to *rest, relax and be more peaceful* in or because of the truth we now know, God is able to "shine through" and reveal its image and likeness as the forms of our experience, including the healthy form and function of the body.

In and as and "through" the stillness and transparency of being, *there God is* as the tangible image and likeness of itself as experience. The fog of belief is dispelled, and the truth of mind, body and world is perfectly clear and visible. We have "risen" to where God is, to where God *as* mind *as* formation is tangible and real and as free as the air for all to experience.

Ten

Go to Where God Is, Part Two

God is consciousness, and because God is all, consciousness is all. All there is is consciousness, and "besides me [besides consciousness] there is none other."

We have to take this truth literally. If we allow belief to rule and do not sufficiently rise into an atmosphere of spiritual awareness, we will observe our world through the lens of belief, and say, "No, the world and universe are not consciousness but matter; the mind is mental and the body is physical with internal organs and functions on which life depends. Mind, body and world are exposed to both good and bad powers, conditions, characters and governments. A sleuth of the world's bad powers can hurt the mind, contaminate or injure the body, or cause it to become ill or diseased. The whole world exists separate from and outside of me, in which I have to survive and hopefully live happily, safely and securely. I can understand that consciousness exists 'in' or is the 'essence' of the universe, but my world is filled with *matter*—flesh and blood, wood, stone, metal, concrete, brick, paper and plastic. It is filled with many different varieties of life and life-form—plant life and form, flower life and form, fruit life and form, animal and insect life and form, and many others. I live in the computer and internet age which certainly affects and often governs my experience, my business, my home and family. I largely depend on the many utilities, products and services of modern day living and the dollars I need to pay for them. The fact that consciousness is all is wonderful to know, but what *practical* use is it to my every day life, happiness, security and fulfillment and to the healing of that which is lacking or limited, painful or diseased?"

You see, if we allow belief to govern our senses we cannot see through its fog to reality. Belief about what "is" and what "is not" is too strong. An internal argument begins to rage as soon as we open up spiritually. "If all is spirit, therefore harmonious and good, and if spirit heals false experience, why does my disease or lack or pain not yield? Where is the harmony and wholeness of spirit if spirit is all I am?"

The answer is that, for a short time, we still believe there is God *and;* we still believe in spirit *and* matter, or God *and* "this world." The healing of experience in all its ways and all its forms comes the moment we have *only God* as all—God *as* mind *as* form.[1] Lay belief down; put belief's ideas and convictions to bed. Now, free of belief, fill your awareness with God and spirit. Spiritualize your awareness. Use your thought as it is supposed to be used, to gently ponder and concentrate on pure spirit and truth. Then, very soon, you will see the wonder of truthful form emerse through the dissolving fog of belief.

RISE IN SPIRITUAL AWARENESS

God is consciousness, pure consciousness, and because God is all, consciousness is all. And because God, consciousness is *one*—the omnipresence of *one alone*—the whole of God exists right here as you, and as what you are, what you are made of, what your organs and functions are, what your mind, body and universe are.

One is not made of two or more. *One* does not have a sub-division or a variation of itself or different departments forming different forms from different materials. *One is.* That's it, there is nothing else about or in existence, and nothing else that *can exist. One* is all

[1] See *The 7 Spiritual Steps To Solving Any Problem* by Paul F. Gorman

there is; *one* is the only existence, the only presence, the only mind and form (or body); *one* is existence itself with "none other."

You are that one—the *whole* of that one. The whole of oneness is fully manifest, fully demonstrated, fully visible and tangible, fully existent and real as everything about you—as each and every place of your consciousness at the same time. You live and move and have your entire being as, and in the infinite ocean of, consciousness. And because consciousness is infinity, omnipresence and eternity, you live and move and have your entire being as, and in, infinity, omnipresence and eternity. Every cell of you, breath of you, step of you and place or form of your experience is the whole of God, the whole of infinity, the whole of omnipresence and eternity.

This is who you are, what you are, what you are made of, what your experience is and is made of, and what you have. Besides this one reality, there is no other reality about you.

Only oneness is. Wherever you look, there I am. *Whatever form or condition you think about or observe, it is* I *because none but I exist. And because* I *am omnipresent—never partially present, and utterly unable to be so—you and everything of your experience, every form and detail, is always the entire omnipresence of* me.

The whole of spirit and truth exists, and is the very substance and form of every breath of you, every cell, atom and subatomic particle of you, every frequency of you, every thought of you, every moment, every millisecond, every microsecond of the presence of you *happening*. That milli- or microsecond is the whole of God, fully existent, happening as you, happening as me, as all—the whole of infinity, the whole of omnipresence, the whole of eternity, the whole of one.

All there is is one, infinity, omnipresence, incorporeality, eternity—fully existent and formed at and as every place of itself at the same time. *Oneness . . . oneness . . . oneness.* And oneness is consciousness not matter, not physicality or materiality, not time and space or cause and effect, but pure and omnipresent, eternal, unchanging consciousness.

I AM THE BODY

I am the body, I am the life. I is consciousness; therefore consciousness is the body, consciousness is the life.

If you are still thinking, by any degree, in terms of locality, if you're thinking in terms of "you" as being personal, finite and local, or as your body being an isolated organism made up of complex, vital organs and functions, and consisting of a certain degree of size, weight and beauty, and having lived a certain number of years, lift out of such belief now.

Rise in awareness; spiritualize awareness. Get into that elevator and rise to the top floor. Rise to a higher level of awareness where only consciousness exists—pure consciousness with no matter in it whatsoever; spirit without form; pure existence without shape, name, activity, amount, condition or place; without cause and effect, time and space.

Rise, rise. Realize that you are consciousness. Your body is the body of consciousness. You are this very minute one hundred percent infinite, free and omnipresent at and as every place throughout infinity at the same time, the "you" of you being spirit, God. "I am that I am."

Isn't that astonishing, wondrous and beautiful? Isn't that freeing? This truth is literal. Truth is not *to become* your experience one day, year or lifetime in the future. Truth is the truth of you here and now, this minute because truth is the only reality just as the truth of math is math's only reality. Omnipresence *is* right here and now; God *is* right here and now; infinity and eternity *are* right here and now, and are the *only* here and now—not one second in the past or one second in the future. Omnipresence is forever right here and now. The whole of God, fully present and formed, fully existent, manifested, demonstrated, visible, real and tangible is what you are, and all is here, now and eternally.

Nothing more can be added to you, nothing. Nothing more of infinity can be added to you—you *are* infinity. Nothing more of life can be added to you—you *are* life. Nothing more of eternity can be added to you—you *are* eternity. The very life you are is eternity itself existing as you and your life. The very life you are is your body—life itself existing as the full embodiment, the full "image and likeness" of itself alone as your life and body. There is no other life or body, there is just *the one life* fully embodied with, and as, and being itself alone. The one life is the only life—life eternal, never born and never dead; never aging, never becoming tired or weak, worn out, decrepit and then one day dead.

Eternal life is the very life you are, and have, this minute and forever. And because life is the one embodiment, life is your body. What is that life? What is that body? What is that eternity? What is that omnipresence? What is that here and now? *Consciousness.*

You can experience your life eternal, your pure life, your free, vital, whole, limitless and perfect life this minute by realizing that it is *consciousness,* not mental, not physical. Consciousness is body, the only body. No life—consciousness—is unembodied. There is no such thing as "unembodied" God or consciousness. God is forever embodied; God is forever the body of itself, and because God is the only, you are that body, I am that body, and all is that body.

Experiencing the truth and freedom of the body is a matter of higher awareness—*spiritual* instead of material awareness. Higher awareness reveals the higher sense of body, the spiritual sense of body with no matter in it whatsoever, therefore no material or physical good *or* bad in it whatsoever. The one requirement is to *rise* into spiritual awareness. Get "into the elevator" and rise in awareness.

Consciousness is life. Consciousness does not "contain" life; consciousness is *life. Consciousness does not "become" a body; consciousness* is *the body.*

The moment you grasp this you are free! Consciousness is life. There is no other life, there is no other "place" life exists, there is no other "state" of life or form of life. Consciousness itself is the life, the "place" where life exists, and the body of life. *Rise* to where life exists. *There* your fully healthy, vital and strong body *is*—fully real and tangible. Rise to the "top floor" or "roof garden" of awareness—the spiritual kingdom where the body is forever healthy and vital—rather than dwelling on the "ground floor" of existence, the "physical" sense, which is subject to both good and bad states of health. *Rise to it,* do not expect it to come down to you. Once you have risen *to it, there it is,* the fully embodied experience of that level of awareness. Each degree of "lifted to" spiritual awareness *is itself* the healthier, more harmonious and freer forms of experience. The healthy, harmonious and free body exists this minute and forever, but it must be risen to in awareness—that's all. Healing is not what it seems to be, nor does it happen where it seems to be needed, but is the *rising in awareness* to where health and wholeness forever exist—to where there is no matter, therefore no good or bad, but spirit alone. "Where health and wholeness exist" is the state of spiritual awareness—the awareness of spirit as all, God as all, consciousness as all.

Where the belief in matter exists within us, the pairs of opposites exist in experience, but where spirit alone exists in awareness only spiritual experience exists.

"I am the Lord, and there is none else—there is no God [life, body, truth] besides me." Consciousness is the life, and besides consciousness there is none else. Life exists nowhere else, or as nothing else. Life does not exist in a form in and of its own self. Life is in, and is itself, *consciousness.*

Life *is* consciousness; consciousness *is* life. If you are seeking the truth of life or the healing of the false sense of life, seek consciousness and then you *have* all the life consciousness is and has—all the life God is and has; vital, eternal life. You are consciously eternal, and continually opening in awareness to more of your eternity—infinite, divine eternity.

Consciousness is the secret of the healthy, vital and eternal body because consciousness is life and body—life forever embodied. *Rise, rise.* Let all physical or material belief drop away. Turn to consciousness itself, and realize—

I am pure consciousness. There is nothing else about me but consciousness. The I *I am is the one, universal consciousness, the mind I have is the one, universal consciousness, and the body I have is the one, universal consciousness.*

I live and move and have my being in the infinite, omnipresent ocean of consciousness. I am consciousness; consciousness is what I am.

If you were to gather up in front of you everything you are and have, everything—your mind and body, your loved ones, your friends, neighbors and colleagues, your belongings, your home, your vehicle, your work, your neighborhood, country and world and everything everywhere of it all—all of those beings and belongings, no matter what name, character, quality, quantity or condition they appear to be in and of their own selves, are not that. None of what appears to be is what you are or have—what your "lot" in life is.

What you are and have is *consciousness.* Consciousness *is,* and is the intelligence, substance, presence, form and activity of everything of existence. Your being is consciousness, your mind is consciousness, your body including its organs and functions is consciousness; your family is consciousness; your friends, your belongings, your home, your work are all consciousness. Everything everywhere in the entirety of your existence is consciousness, not the physical or material, not the object, activity, amount, place or condition it seems to be at face value.

As you rise in spiritual awareness you rise also in spiritual experience. The rising in awareness and the rising in experience are one, not two, not separate. Higher awareness does not *produce* higher harmony; higher awareness *is* its form of higher harmony. You begin to experience the spiritual body, spiritual love and relationship, spiritual work, spiritual things, spiritual home and neighborhood, city and country, world and universe. You begin to experience the harmony, freedom, union, peace, joy, happiness and truth of the spiritual kingdom—the true kingdom.

Consciousness is your truth. Consciousness is your life. Consciousness is your body. Consciousness is the entirety of you, the wholeness and oneness of you—the one life of you, the one body of you, the one experience of you. *Oneness and wholeness, not multiplicity and separateness*—not "you" versus "me" and "all others" as personal, separate, isolated beings with minds and bodies existing in a large world filled with good and bad. This is all *belief alone,* much of it drummed into collective being by orthodoxy.

Drop all belief now and rise into *oneness*—the elevated awareness where only God exists, only consciousness exists, only spirit exists. Once you have "arrived" at an awareness of consciousness-being-all, you are and have all that consciousness is and has. Consciousness is infinity, omnipresence, eternity. The whole of good is what you are and have throughout your experience when you have consciousness-as-all filling your awareness. Good exists in all its ways and forms right at your feet, all around you, at every place you are, and as the content of every observation because as you stay in a living awareness of consciousness-being-all—as you realize that the *whole of your consciousness* is your body, and is God, is good, is harmony, is peace—then wherever you go, whatever you do, and whatever you observe are that of pure consciousness, pure God, pure spirit, pure good, pure harmony, pure peace.

You've given up judging humanly, physically, materially and you've begun to judge spiritually. The tangible experience of health, harmony and wholeness is automatic as you become ever more spiritually aware instead of materially aware, just as the tangible experience of the top floor or roof garden is automatic *when you have arrived there.* As soon as you are "up there" everything the top floor or roof garden contains is as free as the air to your experience. *But you must get there;* you must rise to where *it exists.* "Where it exists" is in spiritual awareness, the awareness of *one* not many, of omnipresent spirit without form (as far as belief would describe form), without body, without amount, without place, without activity, without name, without condition.

Leave matter behind and rise into spiritual awareness, to the incorporeal, to pure consciousness. When you are there, you will discover that everything of God is freely you, freely available to you, and freely flowing in and as and throughout everything you do. Rise into pure consciousness. Never again seek some "thing" from God. Never again go to God for some nameable good. You will fail. "Ye ask, and receive not, because ye ask amiss." You are attempting to get God to "come to where you are," to fix you, heal you, pacify you, prosper you, bring you love and happiness; yet attempting this, or expecting that it can happen, is as impossible as attempting to evidence the top floor in the basement. You cannot do it. God is not available at the "human" or "physical" or "material" level of awareness. Spirit is not available as matter, omnipresence is not available as local presence, and infinity is not available as finiteness—anymore than the top floor is available on the first.

You would think it ludicrous if flight students expected the vista of earth from 40,000 feet to be available on the ground. It simply isn't! The only way we can experience the vista of 40,000 feet is to rise to 40,000 feet! At that altitude the vista is as free as the air. Yet spiritual students expect God to heal *them* at *their* level of awareness—*their* health, finances, relationships, businesses, and world.

God *is*; God *already is*. And because "God saw everything that was made, and behold, it was very good," there is no bad in God whatsoever. *That's* where we find our health, wealth and harmony throughout life. We mustn't attempt to have God-harmony here, where "we are." We must rise to where *only* health, wealth, harmony, joy, love and freedom forever exist—and that is "up" in God consciousness. Rise to *where* God is; rise to *what* God is, to pure consciousness.

I am pure consciousness. I is consciousness, consciousness is I, and because consciousness is one, I am one. The entirety of my consciousness is not the personal sense of it I may be having, but God, the one and the only.

Because God is forever embodied, or with-body, God is my body; therefore my body is consciousness—the incorporeality, infinity and omnipresence of consciousness, which is the incorporeality, infinity and omnipresence of body.

Because my body is consciousness and not matter, it is and has nothing finite or local about it. It is and has omnipresence and infinity. It is not an object; it is never objectified—it is incorporeal, spirit and truth.

I am, and my body is infinity, not finiteness; I am, and my body is omnipresence, not local presence; I am, and my body is incorporeality, not corporeality. I am, and my body is consciousness, not mind and matter. I am, and my body is consciousness itself.

I am that I am.

Your only work is to rise in spiritual awareness. Then all "else" automatically heals, becomes healthy, harmonious, plentiful and purposeful because at the "level of spiritual awareness" all good and harmony already *is*. This is the miracle of truth.

Do not seek the forms of life as if they were an entity in and of their own selves. They are not entities. Only God is, therefore God is the only entity. Seek life itself—God itself—and all the good and abundant forms quickly emerge through the dissolving fog of belief. Do not seek to gain the good things of earth or to be rid of the bad things. Both good and bad material (earthly) things exist only at the "lower level" of human, mental, material, physical awareness. At the "higher level" of spiritual awareness good and bad do not exist; just spirit exists. This is why we seek just spirit, never matter. We cannot seek any kind of material experience spiritually. It will not work, and cannot—just as we cannot seek light by using darkness.

Jesus gave it to the world in this way: "Therefore I say unto you, Take no thought for your life, what ye shall eat, or what ye shall drink; nor yet for your body, what ye shall put on. . . . But seek ye first the kingdom of God, and his righteousness; and all these things shall be added unto you [added unto or emerge as your experience]." But never seek these good "things" *themselves* because, if you do, you are seeking thin air; you are seeking an imagined entity rather than the one real entity which is God itself. When you know this you hold in your hands the greatest secret ever given the world, and that is that *only God is*. Therefore, when you seek God alone—not for anything *else* (because there is nothing else), but seek God *as* God *for* God *to* God—then formation is revealed to be the "image and likeness" of God rather than of good and bad. The *truth* of form becomes evident—"heaven as it is on earth." This is the automatic and infallible experience of the "higher level" of awareness, *spiritual* rather than material awareness.

Rise in awareness. Seek spirit itself—pure consciousness—as and for the experience of pure spirit, pure consciousness alone.

I am consciousness—not human, not physical, not material.

I lift my entire awareness, my entire belief, my entire understanding, my entire sense up and away from that of human, physical, local and temporal, and that of internal versus external vital organs and functions in my body, to that of spirit or consciousness being what I am, what my mind is, and what my body is.

I lift away from the belief that "my mind" is "me"—the character and nature of me, the intelligence, wisdom and ability I "have." None of this is *true because only God is; therefore the only "me" I am is the me God is. "I and the Father are one.... I of my own self am nothing.... There is no God [life, mind, body, world, universe] besides me." It is not true that "my mind" is my consciousness, my intelligence, my awareness faculty. The consciousness I have, the mind I have, is the one consciousness and mind that is God—incorporeal, infinite, omnipresent and eternal.*

My consciousness, my mind and my body are just as much evident fifty feet away, one hundred feet away, 1,000, 10,000, 25,000 feet, a quarter of a million miles away, and infinitely away as they are right here because I am one and omnipresent, not separate and locally present.

I am life itself; I am omnipresence itself; I am infinity itself; I am eternity itself. "I am that I am" because the only "I" that is is the I that God is, besides which "there is none else."

The infinite is the only, and exists fully at every place of itself at the same time. Therefore, I am that; I exist at every place of my consciousness at the same time. The fullness of me exists at every place of my consciousness simultaneously. The fullness of me, the whole of God, the whole of the infinite, the whole of awareness exists at and as every place of my consciousness at the same time.

I am omnipresent; I am never local. I am infinite; I am never finite, never restricted, never bound by anything including place. Consciousness cannot *be contained or bound. There is no limit in consciousness. There is no place in consciousness.* Consciousness *is infinity, omnipresence, eternity and because consciousness is the only, I am consciousness—infinite, omnipresent and eternal.*

The health and freedom of the body is experienced as consciousness. As I rise into spiritual consciousness, I discover more and more of the truth of me, the freedom of me, the eternal life of me, the ever-present love of me and my experience.

I can never be without love as I rise into the consciousness that is love. Love is as free as the air, and witnessed everywhere about—including the one form of love that is my individual true and eternal love—as I rise in awareness. I discover that love holding hands with me, here everywhere I am, the very moment I have risen into the consciousness that is love, omnipresent.

I find that my entire consciousness is full of love, full of loving gesture, loving impulse, loving activity, as everyone and everything about, throughout the entirety of my experience, as I rise in awareness to where love is. As I walk through my consciousness in the risen degree of love-awareness, I observe and experience love everywhere about.

I observe the beauty and generosity of being. I have the constant opportunity to give love because I am and have an infinity of love. I give and serve of my substance, my truth, my spirit everywhere about. My world invites me to share with it, to serve it. My entire world invites me to give my love, my spirit, my substance to it, to him or to her, and I witness him, her and it giving to and serving me as I am living the risen degree or level of awareness where love is, where the purity and oneness of substance and truth exist.

All of this is my one being and body of consciousness without division, separation or difference. I live and move and have my being in my one body of consciousness, as my bodily function, my bodily activity and service. My consciousness is my body; therefore my entire universe is my body. I love it and I serve it, and it loves and serves me—all being one, all perfect, all the omnipresent synchronicity of love, wisdom and union happening in experience.

Every cell of my universe, every atom—my consciousness, remember, consciousness—is love, is one, therefore in oneness and love with "every other" place and form of itself. The oneness and wholeness of love exists at every point of infinity at the same time. Therefore, every place and form of my body of consciousness is the whole harmonious one. Discord, disease, lack and limitation do not exist; only oneness and wholeness exist everywhere throughout consciousness because consciousness is what I am and what I have as experience. There is none else.

Gently, ever more, let go of the sense of locality, the physical, local sense of body. Leave local sense behind and rise into spiritual awareness, into the truth of body, which is consciousness alone.

"Up here" in spiritual awareness, we can begin to understand that every cell of the body, every "cell" and "atom" of the infinity of consciousness, the body of consciousness, is love itself, life itself, God itself—fully present, fully existent, fully manifested and demonstrated, fully visible, fully tangible as the whole of itself at every point of the universe at the same time. There is no space left over throughout the entirety of you—the entirety of consciousness—for anything "else" to exist. Your whole body of consciousness is love itself, life itself, wholeness and completeness itself, in union with and as the whole of itself; your whole body is one, is love, is life, is harmony and fulfillment *being* every point and form of *itself alone* at the same time.

Nothing but love and life are evident as I realize that my body is consciousness—pure consciousness. I then have, and can rest in, and can begin to use as my divine purpose, my body, which is my consciousness, because my body, as I realize it to be pure consciousness, is now free. It is free in and as infinity. It has the resources of the infinite. It is forever vital, alive, vibrant, purposeful. I can now serve my world, my body, my kingdom with divine purpose. I can fulfill my purpose of being as I realize my body, my purpose, my service are all consciousness.

Pure consciousness is what I am. Pure consciousness is what my body is. I and my body are one, and that one is God, and God is consciousness. So I am, and my body is, and all is consciousness—pure consciousness.

When you stay at the center of your being—when you do your best to seek or "keep your mind on" God for the experience of God itself rather than for the experience of "material" health and harmony—you are safe and protected. It doesn't matter how urgent, threatening or overwhelming the problem seems to be, nor its category—health, wealth, harmony, peace or justice; neither does it matter how close to death or destruction the problem seems to leave you. When you seek God for God itself, the kingdom of consciousness for itself, then you are safe. You are protected from actual harm of any category even though the problem may often seem very real and very threatening.

Staying at the center of being not only keeps you safe but is also the beginning of your ability to witness healing and harmony of not only "the body" but of all lack, limitation, disharmony or injustice. Let's go through the healing experience now.

Let's say you are experiencing an illness, disease or injury, or any other form of discord, disharmony, pain or suffering. The first truth to realize about it is that all illness, disease, lack and limitation, no matter what its category, is not what it seems to be but is *a lack of living God awareness*. Every person is the being, presence, substance and body of God and nothing "else" or "other" or "different" because only God is. You are fully existent, alive and embodied truth this minute, and eternally. You are fully existent, pure and unblemished consciousness; you are, and all are divine being which has been mistakenly identified and labelled as "human" being. Suffering of any sort is simply an *unawareness* of this truth.

The way of witnessing the healthy, vital (healed and whole, truthful) body is to take your attention completely away from "the problem" (and, in fact, away from the whole "physical body" itself), turn to God, and then seek God's kingdom purely for the experience of *it itself*—not for the experience of "physical healing." God or spirit has no matter in it whatsoever, nothing physical or material whatsoever, and so seeking the healing of matter or physicality is a waste of time. "Ye ask, and receive not, because ye ask amiss."

Even if you are experiencing pain or fear at this moment, start lifting your awareness. Try to, as best you can, rise into spiritual awareness. Leave matter behind and fill yourself full of spiritual truth, spiritual fact, spiritual reality.

Seek pure consciousness. Realize that the sense of body or disease that is suffering and painful, is not the truth of the body. The root of all illness, disease or injury is never what it seems to be but is a *lack of God awareness*—just as the root of all incorrect math is a lack of math awareness. Four x 4 equals 12 is not an actual problem, not an actual entity or body, even though as long as we are stuck with "it" (a lack of math awareness), we experience the "illness, disease or injury" of it. The quick and infallible solution is to recognize what the problem in fact is, and then lift into the truth of math. *There* we discover the harmonious "16" of 4 x 4. The only actual problem was a lack of math awareness, and the only true and everlasting solution was heightened math awareness.

In this way, all illness, disease and injury *in and of their own selves* are illusory sense caused by a lack of awareness that all formation (all body) is God. The body is *spirit* not matter, spiritual not physical. Illness, disease, injury and dysfunction are *belief* that form is something other than or different from God. That belief—the lack of God awareness—*is itself the form* of believed experience, the pairs of opposites, the good and bad of experience. This is why health *and* ill health exist in human experience—why happiness *and* unhappiness, riches *and* poverty, love *and* hate, peace *and* war exist throughout the world *believed to be different from or separate from God.*

All discord, fear and suffering—*all,* no matter what its name or nature—is a lack of living God awareness, a lack of the light of truth. Realize this, and you are on your way directly and quickly to the freedom of spiritual being, mind, body and world which has in *it* no belief, no matter, no pairs of opposites—just God as all. The way of healing is to first know the truth, and then be still. "Be still, and know that I am God." Never attempt to "do" anything with the illness, disease, injury or dysfunction *in and of its own self.* Leave it alone. Take no thought for it whatsoever. Instead, rise in awareness.

I am pure spirit, pure consciousness, not mind and matter.

God is consciousness, and God is All, and God is omnipresence; therefore the presence that I am is God—consciousness.

The one reason I am experiencing this pain or suffering, illness, disease or injury is that I haven't fully known that I am not mind and matter but God, spirit, consciousness.

I am the body of consciousness because there is no other body, there is no other presence, there is no other being, there is no other mind and there is no other form.

I am spirit; I am consciousness.

Consciousness is the body. There is no such thing as "unembodied" consciousness; all of consciousness is embodied. The entire spiritual kingdom (the only kingdom) is with body. None of God, spirit, consciousness, life, existence is without body, unformed, intangible, invisible, unreal or impractical. Therefore, the "I" that I am is the embodiment of God, oneness embodied, the one embodied presence of existence itself, the one embodiment of consciousness. My body and all bodies are that. The body I am, the body I have discovered myself with at this period of my awareness, is the *one body* of consciousness, individually experienced as the "I" that I am. Do not localize your sense of body but magnify it into and throughout the vastness of consciousness.

I am and have the one, all-inclusive body of consciousness—infinite, omnipresent and eternal.

Consciousness is all there is; consciousness is what the infinitude is, and besides consciousness there is none else.

Rest belief. Withdraw your interest and fixation from the way belief has convinced you that the infinite variety of beings and forms in the world are real in and of their own selves. Lift into and stay in God awareness, the awareness of spirit being all, consciousness being all, God being all. It is this lifted state of awareness that reveals all form as its truthful good and wholeness with no opposite. Do not be concerned about form, about the body or any part or experience of it. Concern yourself just with God, spirit, consciousness, and then the form takes care of itself. Lift . . . lift . . . lift.

I am and my body is spirit, consciousness.

God is, period. God is consciousness; therefore all being is consciousness. I am that. I am consciousness, and because consciousness is oneness and omnipresence, my body is consciousness.

I am and my body is spirit, consciousness—pure consciousness with no shape, no form, no weight, no objectified, physical, material body or organ or function whatsoever.

All I am is all consciousness is. And because consciousness is the only, therefore can only be itself, I am the being, mind, body and function of consciousness and nothing other.

Consciousness is incapable of being anything other than or different from itself. Consciousness is the infinitude itself, and the infinitude is incapable of being anything other than infinity. And because the infinitude is omnipresence, it is fully present at every point of itself at the same time. Absolutely nothing exists but the omnipresence of infinity. The whole of the infinitude (the whole of omnipresence, the whole of consciousness and everything infinity, omnipresence and consciousness are, and have) is fully existent at every point of itself simultaneously, and because there is "none else" I am that, and all is that.

I am, my body is, and my entire world and universe are pure consciousness, pure spirit, pure infinity and omnipresence. This is life inclusive of all forms of life (life and form being one and inseparable, indivisible).

Consciousess is infinity, omnipresence, and eternity fully formed, visible, tangible and present at every point of itself simultaneously. I am, and all is consciousness; therefore I am, and all is the infinity, omnipresence and eternity of life, and besides this life I am, there is none else. I am that, I am, I—that is all.

Life can never be ill, diseased or injured, can never suffer, can never be in pain because all such experience is corporeal, yet life and body are *incorporeal*. What "other" power or formation exists that could be antagonistic towards life, make life ill, diseased or injured? There is no "other" power and there is no "other" formation. There is only one, and that one is incorporeal—consciousness, God—pure and eternal life, fully existent at every point of itself at the same time. Where is there, in that case, anything but the one, incorporeal life and formation? There is not. Therefore you are that one life, I am that one life, all is that one life.

Now that I realize that I am the life and the body of consciousness, my senses are filled full of the living awareness of life, and nothing but life.

I am and have the infinity, omnipresence and eternity of life—inclusive of all of life's forms. I am aware of life and nothing but life at every point of myself at the same time. I am and have life, and life alone. I am life—I am life infinite, omnipresent and eternal.

I am life eternal. All of life is forever fully, totally, infinitely present as formation. I am that, and there is none but this one life. As I become aware of this truth, my senses are filled with the living awareness of life and none but life; therefore all formation in my experience is the formation of the one life, the one truth.

Every being and thing I sense is that one life; every being and thing I experience is that one life and none else. As I realize this one truth, my experience becomes that of the one truth. I am the infinity, omnipresence and eternity of life itself, there being none else.

As you rise in awareness in this way—as you seek the kingdom of God, the kingdom of consciousness in this very way—you are safe. You are always safe the moment you begin to live, as best you can, at the center of your being. "The best you can" is always enough. As soon as you even "touch fingertips" with God, God has you, and you are safe and sound. Every minute you devote to seeking *I*—the kingdom of consciousness, the being, mind and body of pure consciousness—you are home, protected and safe.

Seek I for itself, not for what belief believes you need I for. Seek the infinite, the incorporeal, the omnipresent and eternal that is the true you in all its ways—the you and body of consciousness, the only you and body there is, the only I, the only presence of you there is (which is never local, never physical, never of a particular shape or size or weight, but your consciousness, infinite, omnipresent, eternal, incorporeal). In doing so you are filling your awareness with the light of truth, healing your experience, healing your senses. Every minute you devote to this is another minute of healed experience. Make sure you hear that—every minute you devote. Therefore devote as many minutes of each hour as you possibly can. This is the way.

On the other hand, every minute we attempt to "bring spirit down to our level" of material existence or experience—to heal *it,* harmonize *it,* or pacify *it*—we are failing. Let's make sure this is truly understood. Every time we think in terms of a physical or material condition, a describable and nameable condition, and then believe and hope that God will harmonize or heal *it,* we fail. "Ye ask, and receive not, because ye ask amiss."

However, every minute devoted to *rising in awareness,* to seeking the kingdom of God itself for itself alone, the kingdom of consciousness itself for itself alone, *is* the evidenced forms of mind, body and universe which exist as and at that level of higher spiritual awareness. Each degree of higher spiritual awareness *is* the universal form of itself. This is why each minute—literally each minute—devoted to seeking truth, to rising in awareness, is the healing of experience, the healing of the senses, the healing of mind and body.

Eleven

What Is Consciousness?

A student recently asked, "What is consciousness?" This is an important and fundamental question that we are never "too advanced" to explore or re-explore. In such exploration we dispel the false, personal, local, human sense of being, mind and universe and awaken to truthful, *spiritual* being living the spiritual experience. As soon as truthful awareness is attained, truthful experience stands all around us as the one formation of reality because truthful awareness *is* truthful experience. This we know, but the question is *how*? Exactly how is truthful awareness attained?

We must always start with the one premise, the one truth and principle, that *only God is*. Nothing whatsoever but *God-is* exists. Everything, everywhere present, infinitely and eternally present, is God. Nothing exists but God, and God is spirit and truth, the incorporeal. Therefore nothing exists but spirit and truth—incorporeality, infinity, omnipresence and eternity (and any other synonym we may use for God). God is spirit, truth, incorporeality, infinity, omnipresence, eternity. Therefore, what God is *not* is matter, untruth, corporeality, finiteness, locality or local presence, temporality or temporal presence.

God is spirit; God is incorporeal; God is the infinite, omnipresent, eternal one, and "besides me [that which God is] there is none else."

God is life. That which we call *life* is *God*. Being *is* life *is* God. God *is* life, life *is* God. God or life does not exist *within* being; being and everything of being, inside and out *is* God *is* life.

God is life. God is *the* life, and because God is one (there being none else) God is *the one life.* The life you are, the life I am, and the life all is is the one life that God is. There is no other type of life, no different type of life, no variation of life, no lesser life. God is life, the one life; therefore all life is that *one God-life.* The Master gave it to us: "I am the life."

I (God) am the life. I *is* the life, and there is none else. I *is* life, *the* life, there being no other or different or lesser life in all of the infinitude. God is one; therefore God is *the one life,* the one existence. There is not God "and" life, or a God who "issues" or "gives" life, or God the father-mother who creates or gives birth to God the son and daughter. With reverent spiritual discernment the ancient language of scripture must be understood and then brought up to date. Because only God is, and because God is one and omnipresent with no other, we understand that God is the one and omnipresent life, the one life of all, there being none other, none different, none less. God is *the I* of being, and besides that *I* there is none other; God is the *one life,* and besides that one life there is none other.

Life, the one life, the one existence, is the only. Life is *the* infinite itself, *the* incorporeal itself, *the* omnipresence itself, *the* spirit itself, *the* eternity itself. Life—because God is the only, the infinite, the incorporeal, the omnipresent, the eternal—*is itself* infinite, incorporeal, omnipresent and eternal.

Life is infinity; life is incorporeality; life is omnipresence; life is eternity, and life inclusive of life's experience never varies, lessens or dies.

God does not vary or change. That which is the only cannot vary or change, nor does it have a need or reason to vary or change. Why would wholeness and perfection have a reason to vary or change to become less whole and less perfect? Why would that which is infinity, omnipresence and eternity vary or change to become finite, locally-present and temporal? Why would God, which is the only, the utter and unconditional good of all, vary or change to become multiple, consisting of both good and bad? Why would it and how could it? The answer is that it would not and cannot. The only has nothing "else" or "lesser" or "different" it could change into, and no reason to do so even if it could (which it cannot).

God is incapable of becoming not-God, something other than or different from or less than God. Infinity is incapable of becoming finite; omnipresence is incapable of becoming local presence. If it were possible for infinity to become finite and omnipresence to become local presence, infinity and omnipresence never would have been infinity and omnipresence in the first place. Only finiteness can be finite, and only locality can be local—both of which are false sense alone, not reality.

God is the only, and God is incorporeal not corporeal. God is *the* infinitude itself, *the* eternal itself, *the* spirit itself—*the* life itself. Therefore, life *is* incorporeality itself, *is* infinity itself, *is* eternity itself, *is* omnipresence itself, besides which there is none else.

We must, in order to awaken to what's been said so far, completely disregard what "we" believe we are and have—"our" sense of being, mind, body, world and universe and everything everywhere of it; of thing, friend, love, relationship, amount, condition, place and activity. Forget everything we, as human beings, have been taught is real. Forget common education and sense. We do not want *common* education or sense but *spiritual* intelligence, wisdom and sense. Disregard the world view and fill your awareness with God alone. Fill your every sense with the light and magnitude of spirit, infinity and omnipresence not the dark, finiteness and limited presence of belief.

Read and re-read truth one hundred times, one thousand times, ten thousand times! Fill your every cell, every moment and every sense with spirit and truth, and nothing "else" or "less." That's what it takes for us to "shake" ourselves free of the common belief therefore the common experience. It is what every illumined being has done, including Jesus, Gautama, Mohammed, Shankara, Lao Tzu, St. John, St. Francis of Assisi and every other. "Love the Lord your God, and serve Him with all your heart and with all your soul, that I will give you the rain of your land in its due season, the first rain and the latter rain, that thou mayest gather in thy corn, and thy wine, and thine oil." Fill your every moment of awareness and every sense with the truth that *God alone is*. Flood your senses with truth until truth awareness overflows, spills out, and fills your universe.

It is the flooding of the senses or awareness that illumines and awakens being to that harmony of *is*. This is the way of it. Listen to, read, and ponder truth morning, noon and night until you feel its presence within and throughout your being. Permeate every grain and moment of you with truth. The only way to do it is to disregard the human sense—belief and appearance—and to devote the entirety of you, or at least majority of you, to truth.

Do not attempt to compare truth to human experience or condition. Do not attempt to apply truth to human experience or condition. It will not and cannot ever work because the "human" experience and condition are nothing more than *believed* experience and condition, a false *sense* of that which is true; a false sense of being, mind, body, world and universe. Completely disregard the human sense and, in an emptied, open, receptive, willing and welcoming state of being, read the pages of this book. Soak yourself in the message morning, noon and night, and you will be surprised at how quickly truth begins to take hold of you and become alive as your thinking and experience.

The truth you are to soak yourself in is the truth we are hearing throughout these pages and throughout every Miracle Self book: the truth of oneness, the truth that God is the only, and that God is consciousness, therefore that you are consciousness, your mind is consciousness, and your body is consciousness. When you are doing this, and when you begin to feel the truth of the truth, then comes the next stage. Listen to the Master: "I am the life." *I* am. *I* . . . *I* . . .

Listen to Moses: "I am that I am." Again we hear *I*.

The Master again: "Fear not, it is I. . . .You are ever with me, and all that I have is yours. . . . I am the food of the world. . . . I am the light of the world." Again and again, we are given the word *I*—the reference to *I*.

So the logical question is, what is *I*? Surely, if we can understand what *I* is, we can understand our truth of being, mind, body and world, our freedom and how to attain it. We can understand our wholeness, our purpose, our harmony, our abundance, the truth that is the truth of God, the only truth, the only being, presence and condition.

What is *I*? *I* is *consciousness, existence, life, the only*. I is your, and my, and every being's and every thing's aliveness. I is life itself, *the* life itself, *consciousness itself*. I is consciousness, aliveness, awareness, beingness, existence itself.

I am consciousness. I am the consciousness I am conscious with. Consciousness is my conscious awareness. I am conscious with consciousness, and the consciousness with which and as which I am and I live, is the consciousness with which and as which my body is and with which my body lives.

Whatever you are observing at this or any moment, you are observing with consciousness. That which you are observing is also consciousness because there is none but consciousness. All is one, and that one is *consciousness*. There is none but consciousness, God, spirit. Every being and thing that is, is consciousness being it. Consciousness is conscious of consciousness; consciousness is conscious of itself alone because there is nothing but consciousness, therefore nothing "else" to be conscious of.

That makes perfect sense, does it not? Consciousness cannot possibly be "unconscious"! There is no such thing as "unconsciousness" in the omnipresence of consciousness, which is the one and the only existence, substance and form.

Because consciousness is one, the "observer" and the "observed" are one. Oneness observes or experiences itself. Consciousness is forever conscious of itself as individual you, me and all. What "you are observing" is "observing you" too—oneness aware of the whole of itself. All is the one consciousness happening. There is no "here" or "there," "inner" or "outer," "me here" versus "him, her or it out there." All is one, omnipresence, fully aware and formed at every point of itself *of* every point of itself.

The objectivity (world and universe) of experience does not matter. It is nothing in and of its own self; just mind-formation, mind-imagery. All is consciousness no matter what mind-form is experienced. Never be too interested in form itself; never be concerned or tempted to make effort towards or for form—either to be rid of the bad or to gain more of the good. Consciousness is the real, the one, the spirit and the truth; therefore all interest and "effort" is centered in seeking the truth and living experience of consciousness, God. "Seek the kingdom of God and his righteousness [the truth of the spiritual kingdom]." Become aware that consciousness is all that exists. Consciousness is everything everywhere—omnipresent, infinite, eternal and without any "other."

Consciousness *is*. Consciousness is not conscious *of* objects of experience—the world, the universe and the infinite variety of objects and activities happening within it. Consciousness *is* the infinitude fully alive and conscious of itself. Consciousness is one omnipresent whole. Humanity believes each individual is conscious of its body, its immediate surroundings and conditions, its world. It believes it is conscious of things and conditions outside of and different from itself, and that the world of different things, powers and conditions affects it either positively or negatively.

Belief says, "I am conscious *of* the room I am sitting in. I am conscious *of* the forms in my room—the couch, chairs, a table, books and the shelves they rest on, decorations, pictures, flowers. I am conscious *of* the window and the view through the window—the trees and flowers, the birds and bird song, the colors and fragrances. I am conscious *of* all I see, hear, taste, touch and smell. I am conscious *of* the thoughts I am having moment by moment." But consciousness does not exist within or even *as* "us," a substance or faculty "we" *use* to be conscious *with*. There is no "us" or "them" or "it"; there is only God, consciousness, the one omnipresent whole.

Without consciousness I am and have nothing because consciousness *is* existence, *is* everything everywhere, *is* infinity, *is* omnipresence, *is* all form. Without consciousness there would be no existence. Consciousness *is* existence itself inclusive of the infinite forms of existence. Consciousness *is* what I am and have. Consciousness *is* my entire universal experience and its every formation. Consciousness is what *all* is. Consciousness *is* what my being, mind, body and universe *are,* what all being, mind, body and universe *are,* what all form, thing, condition, place and activity *are.* And consciousness is fully aware of its omnipresent self, not *from* a "local" position named you or me *to* a "different" position named another person, thing, place or activity but *as one, omnipresent, equally-present all-inclusive and self-inclusive, fully aware being experiencing its universal formation.* If I am not conscious, I do not exist because the I that I am is consciousness itself. I is life and that I is consciousness.

I does not exist within my mind or body or universe; I *is* being, mind, body and universe. This is the great secret—I is consciousness, I is all. "I am that I am. . . . I am the life, the water, the wine. . . . I am the Lord, and besides me there is none else. . . . The earth [all of experience, all formation] is the Lord's [I's], and the fullness thereof. . . . Fear not, it is I"—it is consciousness, pure and unconditioned consciousness, unblemished by belief and false sense.

God *is* consciousness and because God is all, all is consciousness. Everything everywhere, despite the way it appears to be, is God, consciousness—*fully* God, *fully* consciousness. God or consciousness is, to belief, invisible and intangible, unmanifested and undemonstrated versus materiality or objectivity which is visible, tangible, manifested and demonstrated. It is believed that God is the "infinite invisible" whereas the world is the "finite visible." Yet what is this belief but another pair of opposites? God is not the pairs of opposites but is one, that one being fully visible, tangible, manifested and demonstrated. There is no such thing as invisible, intangible, unmanifested and undemonstrated God. Can belief truly believe that God is invisible to itself, intangible to itself, unmanifested and undemonstrated in its own experience? Or maybe belief believes there is a self "other than" God, a "human" self which is different from God, and which has to somehow make the "infinite invisible" visible, the "intangible" tangible; that has to master manifesting and demonstrating skills in order to "bring forth" that which is real yet "unmanifested and undemonstrated" to become manifested and demonstrated. *What is such belief but utter, illogical duality!*

God *is,* and is the only *is.* God is all—the all-of-all and all-in-all. One cannot be two, the only cannot be many, the infinity of spirit cannot "also" contain matter, mentality, physicality, corporeality. All cannot contain something "else" or "additional" which is different from itself alone. Omnipresence cannot contain different states of presence, some being invisible, intangible, unmanifested and undemonstrated while "others" are the opposite: visible, tangible, manifested and demonstrated. Omnipresence is what it says, omnipresence, *the fullness of one presence being all.* We must use basic logic in truth. If God is infinite and omnipresent there cannot be anything other than or additional to that *one* which is God. God is fully itself alone as omnipresent existence. How could something "else" exist if God is all-in-all and all-as-all? An illogical mind would say there is all "and." No! How can there be all "and" something additional, something else, something different? If there was all "and," all would not be all, but partial. Of course, such belief is not only illogical but utterly untrue.

Webster defines "all" as:

1a : the whole amount, quantity, or extent of
1b: as much as possible
2: every member or individual component of
3: the whole number or sum of
4: every
5: any whatever
6: nothing but: only:
6a : completely taken up with, given to, or absorbed by
6b : having or seeming to have in conspicuous excess or prominence
6c : paying full attention with
7: used up : entirely consumed

Certainly, there is no possibility of "all" containing or including anything "else" outside of itself or additional to itself. All is literally all, leaving no "other."

In truth awareness, the word *all* or the state of *allness* is very important to understand. All is one or oneness. God is, God is all, oneness is all. All, the only, the one, is literal. Therefore, because God is consciousness, consciousness is the only, the all, the one.

What we observe as everything of "me" and "this world" is not the corporeal self and world that it seems to be at first glance. It is God, oneness, entirely incorporeal. We simply have a corporeal, objective *sense* of the incorporeal. That which is one hundred percent incorporeal and omnipresent (God, spirit, consciousness) is *sensed as* finite and local objectivity—form of infinite variety and category; bodies, activities, organs, functions, trees, flowers, birds, colors, fragrances, dollars, weights, measures, relationships, neighbors, homes—everything everywhere.

The corporeal sense is what we have named as being "real, visible, tangible, practical" because we have believed it *of its own self* to be reality. Students regularly ask about the "real world." They hear about God, about spirit and truth and the life, love, harmony and abundance that God is. "But what about the 'real world'?" they ask. Their "real world" is in fact the unreal world! We have been raised to believe the corporeal as being real when in fact the corporeal, in and of its own self, is unreal. Only God is, therefore only God is real. And because God is all, the real and in fact only world is God—the *spiritual* world (universe). This is true in the most actual and practical way, but it has to be understood before it becomes real *in experience*. "Know the truth, and that very truth will set you free."

Each level or degree of mind (one of the "many mansions in my Father's house") is its own universe of formation. What we call the "human" mind is itself the world we experience. In and of its own self our mind and its universe are pure God, entirely devoid of belief, innocent and impotent, the one existence of God as this level of mind, "earth as it is in heaven." Only belief about experience fills experience with the good and bad. Belief is itself good and bad because every belief has an opposite. Without belief only God is, only heaven is; only life, love, harmony, peace, abundance and fulfillment are.

In truth and actuality there is nothing but God in, and as, and being the multiple forms of experience. But belief fills experience (not reality) full of good and bad. With belief infused in experience, experience in its infinite variety of form appears to consist of both good and bad. It never is good and bad but it appears to be. Remove belief and all good and bad are also removed, and we are left with God alone. Our universe is experienced *as it is*—the God universe, innocent and impotent, divine and purposeful, "full of the goodness of God" alone. God is mind is universal formation. The seeming "three" (God, mind, form) are not three but one. In oneness you can see that because God is mind, mind is nothing but, and full of God—pure, unconditioned God. And because mind is formation, formation is equally nothing but, and full of pure, unconditioned God. Mind has not changed and cannot change God because God is the only presence, the only power, the only faculty. And because mind is form, form is not changed God, a substance different from God. Form is God because mind, which is form, is God. Nothing can change God! Our universe of experience—of being, mind, body, world and universe of formation—is simply *corporeally sensed* incorporeality.

Right here, in this understanding, is complete and spontaneous freedom of being if you can hear truth, and feel it, and live it, and begin to let it live you. Everything of our "humanity" and "physical" world and universe is simply corporeal sense of that which is one hundred percent incorporeal, spirit. As soon as we know this truth—really know it and begin to feel and live it—it becomes tangibly evident as the formation of our being, mind, body and world. It becomes our reality in the most palpable and practical way. We experience God as form rather than belief as form. God, spirit and truth become perfectly visible and tangible as experience because we now know that all of mind formation *is God* and nothing else or less or different.

Everything everywhere is God, therefore pure and perfect, whole and complete no matter what we may believe about it. All *is* life, *is* love, *is* whole and harmonious, complete and fulfilled. Nothing we do or fail to do, know or fail to know affects God in the slightest. God *is,* and God is all there is, and that *is* is in perfect and harmonious order now and eternally. Therefore, everything everywhere of experience, no matter what we may believe, is God, pure and perfect. It is when we *know this truth* and begin to ignore and drop belief about experience that we begin to witness God as all.

God or consciousness is the substance and formation—the very substance and body—of all. The substance that is God—the presence, the alive "stuff" of experience—is consciousness. Consciousness is awareness, beingness—your very beingness, your very presence, your very substance and form, your very aliveness and that of all. Feel the presence of you. Become aware of and *feel* the very presence, the aliveness, the beingness of your presence happening. This is God itself happening—the presence of God, of truth, *your truth* being tangibly experienced. In your stillness and quietness, the presence you feel happening, your life felt happening, your aliveness felt happening, is the very presence of God itself happening as the whole of itself, as you.

Feel the presence, the peace, the spaciousness, the sense of release, the infinity, the freedom that you are, and have this minute! This is your truth, your only truth. God *is,* and that *is* is your truthful being and body, world and universe in eternal harmony and wholeness. You are that—the whole of *I,* the whole of *is* this minute and forever. Oh, be free in truth! Know that the *I* of you is God, never any degree less than or different from God. "I and the Father are one. . . . Be still, and know that I am God." *I am,* and there is only one *I am,* that being God, spirit, truth. The "I" referred to in scripture is your I—your entirety, your *consciousness*—for there is only one. Because there is only one, the *I* of every Master's "I am that" is the *I* you are and the *I* I am—just as the "I" the sun is is the same "I" the sunbeam is.

BEING AND BODY ARE PURE CONSCIOUSNESS

Your being and body are pure consciousness, pure spirit, omnipresence, God, life-and-body eternal. When we observe or experience our body, we are having a corporeal or physical sense of that which is one hundred percent spirit or incorporeal—the divine body of pure spirit, pure consciousness without any matter in it whatsoever.

Here and now, your body is that—pure spirit, pure consciousness. Spirit is the only, therefore the only body. God has not changed, nor ever can change, into a physical body with physical organs and functions. God is God, and besides God there is none else. Therefore, here and now, your body is the body of spirit, the body of consciousness: pure spirit, pure consciousness without physical structure, form, shape, weight, organ, function or locality. Your body is free in and as spirit this very minute. It is the body of consciousness, infinity and omnipresence; not matter, finiteness and local presence.

Your body—this very body—is eternal. It is never born and it never dies; it never ages, never becomes ill, diseased, injured; it never degenerates or becomes dysfunctional because it is spirit not matter. Only matter (which is nothing but believed sense) can be born, grow, mature, and then become ill, diseased, injured, degenerated, dysfunctional and eventually dead.

You are the being of *spirit* with the body of *spirit*—eternal, almighty and omnipresent. You are infinity individually experiencing itself as "you," the individual presence of life and body itself, about individual, divine purpose. Your being, body, world and universe are infinity and omnipresence—the one power and all-knowing formation of being.

Keep your mind forever filled with the truth that God, being infinite, being the only, being omnipresent, being everything everywhere, is *consciousness*. God is not matter or objectivity; God is not a "he, she, it, thing, activity, amount, condition or place." God is everything infinitely everywhere. Sense experiences the one as multiple, as an infinite variety of beings, things, activities, amounts, places and conditions. All of this is good (God) and true as long as sensed experience in and of its own self is not *believed*. Belief misperceives and then believes its own misperception. Foolish belief! What we do to dissipate belief is realize that everything everywhere, infinitely and eternally, is the one presence that is God, that is consciousness. In this realization, we are home. We are safe and protected. We are on the straight and narrow way, walking into the awareness, therefore the tangible body of our freedom.

My very consciousness is God consciousness because consciousness,

God, is one, the only, indivisible, inseparable.

God is the only being, mind, body and universe; therefore I am that. God is the only presence; therefore the presence I am is the presence God is, all one, omnipresent and the same.

God is the only; therefore I am that one, that only because I cannot be different from the one and the only.

Truth is the infinite ocean of oneness—the one and only life, the one and only presence, the one and only being and body. You are that—individual yet inseparable as the one; I am that—individual yet inseparable as the one; all is that—individual yet inseparable as the one.

I am the infinite ocean of consciousness, forever experiencing the one I am. I observe an infinite variety of aspects of the one infinite ocean of consciousness that I is as I, that God is as all.

The more I believe belief—that which seems to be—the more I am limited by, and as, the experience (forms) of that belief. No belief is unembodied, so the belief I believe *is* my experience. I experience all the belief I entertain as my embodied mind, body, world and condition. No belief is true. No belief is reality. No belief is an entity in and of its own self. But I have to live with the forms of belief until, in the discovery that God is all, I drop belief and live in, and as, and by God as all.

As I observe what I believe to be "my" (mental and physical) self and the "real" (material) world—"my" thoughts, "my" body, "my" relationship and family, "my" neighbors and neighborhood, "my" business, "my" world and everything going on in "my" world—I am imprisoned by the limitation of whatever I believe because I believe the forms, activities, conditions and places of experience to be *real* in and of their own selves.

In material belief, I consider my mind to be a personal, private domain, and my thoughts to be personal to me. I consider my body as my personal, physical body separate from all other bodies. I consider my home, yard and the grass, trees, flowers, fruits, berries, colors and fragrances in it to be mine, different and separate from my neighbor's. And I believe that all that is mine is my responsibility to maintain, supply, nourish and protect—with much of that responsibility being dependent on my education, knowledge, skill and sometimes luck. We could carry on discussing the endless belief we as "humanity" collectively and personally have, but why would we? To do so would be to continue entertaining that which is *not*. To continue entertaining that which is *not* is as senseless as continuing to entertain 2 + 2 = 3.

Belief infuses mind, therefore formation (because mind is formation) with false or foggy imagery. Belief *is* false experience. As long as we live with belief we live with false experience—experience filled with the good and bad of the pairs of opposites. You can quickly see that this is true by examining any belief and discovering that every belief has an opposite. It doesn't matter what subject or condition the belief is about, it has an opposite, and because belief is experience, experience is filled with an infinite variety of good and bad opposites. Every step, every hour, every amount and every activity is filled with opposites, forever tugging at each other, each attempting to win the moment. Our experience is filled with conditions, concepts, opinions and convictions and until we drop them and fill ourselves with God awareness, we are imprisoned, limited to just the scope of belief.

Let us—this day!—stop the insanity of belief. Let us rise into the truth that *only God is*. Let us realize that the infinite variety of form and activity we experience is nothing in and of its own self but is actually God—therefore incorporeal, infinite, omnipresent and eternal good without opposite. Let us ignore that which seems to be—both the good and the bad—and live in and as God alone.

The only thing, the only body, the only organ and function, the only world and everything everywhere of it, therefore everything everywhere of individual experience, without exception, are actually, literally pure God, pure consciousness, without physical structure or form, without locality, without height or weight, name or gender, past or future, without age, without parent, child or grandchild.

As we observe what belief describes as a person or object or place or condition, realize that what we are actually observing is a form of God and nothing but God. The form is simply a formed experience of this level of mind, and it is good alone, God alone. The form is entirely innocent and impotent—the image and likeness of the one presence and power of God alone; the one life, love, beauty and purpose alone. As we observe moment-by-moment formation (person, place, thing or condition) we are observing the very presence of God—the whole of omnipresence, infinity and eternity as that formation. "If you see me you see the Father who sent [is] me." Yet belief will believe the form is just, and no more or less than, whatever he, she or it may appear to be in and of its own self—human, animal, vegetable, mineral, animate or inanimate. If we accept what belief reports as being reality in and of its own self, then everything we observe certainly appears to be real. And the "me" observing it all—"my" mind, "my" thoughts, "my" five senses—also seems to be real. Belief—the tricked ego—is blind to that which is.

The only presence, the only life, the only being, the only mind, the only body, the only world and everything everywhere in it, and of it, is God, spirit, oneness—*consciousness.*

I am, and all is consciousness. I am, and I live, and I move, and I have my being in, and as, the infinite ocean of consciousness. The infinite ocean of consciousness is, and lives, and moves, and has its being as me. I am consciousness. I am infinite and omnipresent. I am eternal here and now.

I am that here, now, this minute, not in some other or future lifetime.

There isn't a future or another lifetime. Where would a "future" exist in the now and oneness of omnipresence? When and where would another or different lifetime exist in the now and oneness of omnipresence? This is it! Here and now I am the life—the one, eternal and omnipresent life.

I, God, am life—life eternal, there being none other. Therefore all life, all being, all mind, all body, all experience is the one life eternal that God is. No other or different or lesser life exists.

I am that I am.

You might say, this is all well and good but how do we arrive at the place of being able to tangibly witness the good of God as all? How do we rise in spiritual awareness to the point of tangible experience? How do we achieve the promises of truth? The answer (and the way) is that we fully fill our awareness, our senses, our thinking, our contemplation, our musing minute-by-minute with exactly what we are hearing throughout these pages until the sense of *God* or *spirit* as the only reality becomes real for us; until the material sense of mind, body and world becomes unreal, and truth, spirit, omnipresence becomes our reality—our one reality.

We still see, hear, taste, touch and smell, but these senses begin to awaken spiritually rather than remain materially imprisoned. We are still aware of our being, our body, our loved ones, home, neighbors, world and universe, but we know it all to be forms of spirit not matter. "I am in this world but not of it." I am spiritual being with the spiritual body living in the spiritual universe. I live and move and have my being in and as spirit, and spirit lives and moves and has its being in and as me. In this way I am free in truth, and so is my world because I and world (experience) are one. Wherever I am, there is freedom, truth, liberty. "Where the spirit (consciousness) of the Lord is, there is liberty." Where the substance, the presence of truth is there is the image and likeness of truth as formation.

This is our work—the work of rising in awareness from material to spiritual. Jesus tells us, "The harvest is rich but the laborers are few." Yes, very few are sufficiently willing and devoted to make sure they are aware of truth morning, noon and night, to fill their minds with truth, to tenaciously withdraw belief from that which seems to be and to fill their senses with truth alone. Those who find themselves sufficiently motivated indeed discover the rich harvest of truth, the elevated awareness where the good of life is free to serve with, give and share, and where life is happy, purposeful and abundant—"heaven as it is on earth."

Constantly, day and night, night and day, be aware of this truth:

Consciousness is I, and besides I, besides consciousness, besides God, there is nothing else whatever. Therefore, by definition and perfectly logically, the entire objective form of "this world" is objective sense not reality. As "human" mind I have a corporeal sense of that which is one hundred percent incorporeal—spiritual, infinite and omnipresent.

My sense (and the collective corporeal sense) makes spirit appear to be matter, infinity appear to be finite, omnipresence appear to be locally present, and eternity appear to be temporal. The corporeal sense in and of its own self is not untrue but forever true. *Only God is; God is the only presence and power and so nothing changes God nor can it.* It is only when *belief* is added to or infused into sense that experience becomes untruthful. The minute belief is added, experience is plunged into pairs of opposites, cause and effect, time and space, variability, unreliability, temporality—untruth.

Belief—a lack of the light of truth—is experienced as illness, disease, injury and decrepitude, lack and limitation, hunger, unhappiness, cruelty, insecurity, injustice, racism and scorn. It is why and how a person catches a cold or contracts a cancer. These two extremes of bad experience (and any extremes of bad we wish to examine) are extremes of a lack of God awareness. They are the presence of shadow or dark, an unlit awareness. They are not real entities because only God is, therefore only God is entity. Both the cold and the cancer are beliefs which eventually become evident as false activity and formation *seeming to be real.*

Belief *is* unillumined awareness. The very belief in even the possibility of activity and form other than, or different from God—the *one,* the *only* presence, activity and form—is itself unillumined awareness. This lack of illumination—lack of God-filled awareness—is itself the good-versus-bad experience of mind, body and world whether that lack appears to be of health, wealth, love, beauty, talent, purpose, peace, harmony, happiness, abundance, safety, security or freedom. As soon as awareness is illumined—filled with the light of truth—all dark dissolves in awareness as naturally as night dissolves in the light of dawn. We must remember that dark is not an entity or reality but simply a *lack of light.* In this way, we realize that the dark of awareness experienced for instance, as a cold or a cancer is not an entity or reality in and of its own self. *Only God is real.* The form of unillumined awareness called either "cold" or "cancer" is quickly proven to have no actuality, no power and no formation in the light of spirit. Spiritual presence dispels and dissolves all unreal (un-God) formation as easily as light dispels and dissolves all dark.

What of the two extremes, a cold versus a cancer—or any other of the thousands of lacking, limited, unjust and painful experiences many billions suffer in one form or another? All sickness, disease, lack, limitation, pain and suffering are the belief in life, mind and form being something other than or different from God. Every experience of life which lacks a totality of good, equality and freedom of being is experience devoid of God awareness. It does not matter what the name or nature of the bad is, its root is unillumined awareness, a lack of God awareness. It is collective belief taken on as self belief—belief appearing to be real (as all belief does). As soon as belief is dispelled in the light of truth, all forms of belief (good and bad) dissolve to reveal God-form as mind, body and world. Mind, body and world are revealed to be the "image and likeness" of God rather than of belief. The pairs of opposites dissolve to become one which is good (God) alone. The belief in an "inner" versus an "outer" dissolves into the truth of oneness, *consciousness* being all and omnipresent. The belief in different-ness and separation from God or truth dissolves and omnipresent oneness emerges as reality.

I and God are one and the same because only God is, only one is, only omnipresence and infinity are.

God and experience are one because only God is, only one is, only omnipresence and infinity are.

"I and the Father are one. . . . I am the Lord, and besides me there is none else. . . . The earth [mind, formation] is full of the goodness of God. . . . I am that I am." In this living awareness all dark is spontaneously dispelled to reveal truthful being, mind and formation.

The dissolving of all that is untrue is spontaneous because dark is not an entity. If it were an entity it may require a process and time to dissolve, to heal. But an entity it is not. Dark is nothing but a lack of light, a lack of illumined (spiritualized) awareness. Because a lack of spiritual awareness is not an entity it offers no resistance to truth. The instant the light of truth begins to fill awareness unawareness dissolves. Dark exists no longer and the untruthful forms of dark (discordant and disharmonious experiences) dissolve just as quickly. Do you see that? Do you see that nothing of dark can exist in the presence of light?

Realize that your truth exists in all its form this minute. Truthful you, mind, body and world are the only real existence and are fully manifested and demonstrated this minute and forever. The only reason you do not tangibly see truth is because you live with a measure of unlit, unillumined awareness. The answer and the cure to all ills, lacks and limitations is to illumine awareness; spiritualize awareness. That is all you ever need to do, and it is all humanity as a whole ever needs to do. Spiritualizing awareness is the one, spontaneous and permanent solution to every ill, to all of life's discords and disharmonies, to every category of pain, suffering and inequality. The one truth, the one reality and therefore the one solution is God awareness and God living—"earth as it is in heaven."

God is visible and tangible as and to itself alone. The miracle of truth becomes perfectly visible, tangible and real as we fill our whole being full of God-awareness, the light of spirit and truth, and then live as the consciousness of truth.

I will no longer allow myself to be fooled by belief, by anything that appears to be not-God, finite, local, variable and temporal. I will no longer be fooled by anything that appears to be either good of its own self or bad of its own self, appears to be an entity different from or separate from God.

I now know that anything of experience in and of its own self is unreal. It is a lie of belief. It is suggestion. I know that belief hypnotizes the senses, causes misperception—a mesmerized, untrue sense of experience.

I know that, despite appearance, only God is; therefore only God is mind and formation. The forms of false sense are not entities, not real. They have no law or principle to support their existence in my experience. They have no power, no presence and no body of existence. They are false images alone—nothingness—and I know that as soon as the light of truth touches them, they dissolve into the nothingness they are to reveal truthful, God (good, whole and harmonious) formation.

This very second and eternally God alone is. God is life alone; God is good alone; God is plenty alone; God is love alone. Therefore, everything everywhere—despite the way it appears to be or act, its measure or amount, it nature, character or condition—is God, good, infinity, omnipresence, life, love and fulfillment of being. Everything everywhere is full of the goodness of God, full of oneness, infinity and omnipresence, full of eternity, happiness and purpose.

As I rise in the awareness of this one truth, my senses are being filled-full with the light of spirit, and I can begin to see clearly. I discover myself filling with peace and spaciousness, harmony and peace which fills my universe. I discover that wholeness and peace is my universe and its every formation—the one presence, everywhere and equally present, the one omnipresent formation of wholeness, harmony, spirit and love.

My senses behold the good that is God filling and being everything everywhere. I witness God as being, God as mind and God as form—the mind and formation of peace and harmony, joy and happiness.

I begin to witness the omnipresence of God as my world, my reality. More and more of truth bursts out of every being, every situation and every condition; more of infinity becomes real and tangible as every amount, every activity and every place. No longer is there an "inner me" or even an "inner God" versus an "outer" world of otherness and difference. As I become ever more aware of consciousness being all, all becomes the reality of the good and harmony of oneness and omnipresence palpably experienced.

The truth of truth is that despite the way anything anywhere appears to be—good or bad, healthy or unhealthy, rich or poor, large or small, friendly or unfriendly, young or old, vital or decrepit, happy or unhappy—the only presence is God; therefore the only presence is good, spirit, omnipresence, infinity, harmony, peace, purpose and eternity, the "land of milk and honey," heaven as earth (formation). Consciously knowing this, and resting in the *is* of it, is the secret of witnessing truth where there appears to be untruth, light where there appears to be dark.

This is how healing "works." We do not have to "do" anything to heal our bodies or aspects of our world other than lift into God awareness and then live as God-being experiencing its universe of God-formation. Never again must we be fooled by belief, by that which appears to be. We must constantly disregard that which appears to be and realize that God itself is the only being, mind, body, world and universe. Disregarding belief and its multitudinous pairs of opposites presents us with God alone, with that which *is* rather than that which is believed to be.

It is in the light of spiritual awareness that we witness truth throughout being and experience—the life, plenty, harmony, peace and fulfillment of not only individual being, family and neighborhood but of all our world. The truth and freedom of God emerges through the fog of belief to be the reality it is for everyone everywhere.

Rise in awareness, realizing that all is God. This is our one work and one effort morning, noon and night. Then we begin to witness ever more of God as all: of good, of omnipresence being the very presence and activity of all, of infinity being the substance and form of all we do and all we give, and of love and equality being the truth of all people who enter our consciousness. Everywhere we are in spiritual awareness *there* the presence of God, good is witnessed whether it appears to be human, animal, plant, vegetable, cells, atoms, animate or inanimate; *there* is the presence of love and life, the light of truth and the freedom of spirit.

"Where the spirit [consciousness] of the Lord is, there is liberty."

Twelve

The Visibility of God

Whenever truth stirs devotees into unrest you can be certain the light of spirit is breaking through. Belief is weakening and being dispelled. The personal sense becomes uncomfortable and irritable as its pairs-of-opposites mind, body and world begin to dissolve.

Fear often wracks us as we begin to awaken to truth. Lifetime after lifetime our sense has been embroiled in belief rather than free in truth. Now, everything we have known and relied upon is being taken away and replaced with *God-as-all.* A battle ensues and continues within[1] until the moment of release from everything human and material. From that moment freedom of being and world is experienced and a truthful life of unending health, love, purpose, happiness, abundance, freedom, giving and service begins.

The instruction to *rise in awareness* and *go to where God is* rather than expecting God to "come to where we are" is certainly a disturbing message for the "beginner" spiritual student. Yet it is the most beautifully clear and instantly freeing truth for those who can hear it. Let us explore it a little more and in that way release any remaining fear and attachment to the belief in materiality.

It is as impossible for God and all that God is to "come to us" as it is for the top floor and all that it is to come to the basement or the first floor. If we wish to experience all the top floor is and has, *we must go to it.* In the same way, if we wish to experience God and all that God is and has, we must go to where and what God is—to the *consciousness of God.* We must lift our awareness in order to ex-

[1] The "war within" and the struggle for self-mastery is classically depicted in *The Bhagavad Gita.*

perience the harmony and wholeness of God as our mind, body, world and universe.

Many teachings suggest that God or God consciousness, prayer, meditation or silence reach humanity—healing, pacifying, prospering or harmonizing *it,* making the world more just, moral, equal and loving. Metaphysical teaching is full of "our" being able to reach for and gain God's health, wealth, abundance and love for "our" benefit. It suggests we need to (and can by various metaphysical techniques) assist God; or even influence and persuade God to bestow its boundless good (which for some reason metaphysics believes God is withholding) upon us and our world condition. This belief explains the fundamental inability of individuals (particularly the many millions around the globe who are spiritually inclined today) to tangibly evidence the presence of *already-and-eternally-existent* truth as mind, body and world. Until the *principle* of truth is understood and lived, truth will forever remain a mystery and seemingly out of reach—seemingly invisible, intangible and impractical.

Some years ago I noticed a spiritual teacher announcing a series of classes titled "The Mystery of Truth." Well, if truth is a mystery to this teacher, we certainly do not want to study with him! Truth is *reality*—the one and only reality. *This* is what we need to study and awaken to. "Know the truth, and that very truth will set you free." As long as it is believed that God is a mystery—"invisible, intangible, unmanifested and undemonstrated"—we will continue to have teachings instructing us on how to "make God" visible and tangible, manifested and demonstrated. Friends, realize that there never is a need to "make" visible and tangible that which is already visible and tangible! There is never a need to "manifest and demonstrate" that which already and eternally is manifested and demonstrated. Would you buy into a teaching that instructs you on how to "manifest and demonstrate, and make visible and tangible" the number "4" for 2 + 2? No, 4 is *already* visible and tangible as 2 + 2.

There is no need to "make" it "visible" and "tangible," no need to "manifest" it or "demonstrate" it. The only need is to "know the truth" of math and then that truth "will set you free" with an infinite number of 4s from which you can benefit, and which you can freely give and share unto eternity.

In this way, realizing that God is *principle* (the finished kingdom, already and eternally one, whole and omnipresent, forever visible, tangible, manifested and demonstrated) let us stop the nonsense of such false metaphysical idea and hope, and lift here and now into pure and perfectly evident truth.

Realize that God is all, and because "all" means all, there is none else. *All* cannot have something "additional" or "other" or "else"; otherwise it would not have been all in the first place. God is all *means* that God is *all*. Nothing is left over; nothing but God exists. God is everywhere and equally present *as all,* there being none else. God is the only presence, the only being, the only mind, the only form, the only condition. God is itself the substance, presence and form of all—of that which is you, your mind, body, world and universe and everything in and of it; of that which is all being, all mind, body, world and universe and everything in and of it.

I am that. I am nothing less or else or different or other because there exists nothing less, else, different or other.

I am the one substance, presence, mind, body, world and universe for there is none else. I am that I am.

The key to the entire understanding and experience of awakening is captured in the realization that *I am consciousness.* God—all—is *consciousness,* and besides consciousness there is none else. God is consciousness and consciousness alone. God does not change or transform itself or become a different type of substance and form. God is God and cannot ever be different or less or changed. God has not changed into "human" form as "us." Spirit has not changed into matter as "this world" and everything in it. God is infinity, spirit and truth and has no matter in it whatsoever, nor can it have. How can infinity, which is all (otherwise it would not have been infinity in the first place), have something other than infinity in it? How can infinity have finiteness in it? Of course it does not and cannot. Infinity is infinity alone and has nothing but infinity in it and of it and throughout it.

God is not spirit *and* matter. God has no "and" in it whatsoever. God is God and God alone! God does not and cannot change into a mental being, a physical body and a material universe even for a second, even for a moment, even for one so-called lifetime. God cannot. God is *the one, the only, the all.* Only is itself alone and is forever being itself alone as all. Because God is the one, the only, the all, there is nothing "else" that can be. *Only God is;* God is the all-in-all and all-of-all.

BESIDES GOD (SPIRIT) THERE IS NONE ELSE

"I am the Lord, and besides me there is none else." Well, if "I am the Lord" which is *incorporeal* and *spiritual* (there being none else), yet you and I are believed to be *human* and our world *material,* somewhere a grave misunderstanding exists. "Lord" in scripture refers to *mind,* and because mind *is formation,* "the Lord" in "I am the Lord, and besides me there is none else" simply refers to the "human" level of mind experiencing its formation. Our human universe of formation is described by Jesus as "one of the many mansions in my Father's house." We are one of the many (infinite) degrees of mind experiencing God as its (mind's) universe of formation. We have unfortunately named ourselves "human" and our universe "material," but neither is true. We are and all is the infinity and omnipresence of God alone, simply experienced objectively by or as the formation of our level of mind. The objective, formed experience does not, nor can it change God into different material, substance and entity. God is forever God alone, forever unchanged and unchangeable, forever pure, perfect, whole and complete. We simply have a corporeal or formed sense of that which is entirely incorporeal. But sense never changes reality. Reality remains the only real entity, perfectly and forever visible, tangible, manifested and demonstrated, there being none else. No matter what *sense* we have of self and objective experience—*as long as we realize the unchanging truth of God as all*—we are and we have the freedom, the boundlessness and unbridled presence and purpose of spirit as our being, mind, body, world and universe.

There is no such thing as "unmanifest" or "undemonstrated" God. God is one and omnipresent, the one and the only presence, entirely and forever manifest, demonstrated, visible and tangible. One cannot and does not have two states of existence, or contain two different substances or materials. God is *one* and *the only*—the one reality, there being none else, none other, none different, none less. Material belief suggests that God is ethereal and unmanifest, invisible, intangible, unreal and impractical. It believes that "our" (human) experience is different—corporeal, mental, material, physical, finite, objectified, existing within time and space, subject to cause and effect and filled with pairs of opposites. It believes that "our" five senses of sight, hearing, taste, touch and smell are not God but human, which is different and separate from God. All of this misunderstanding is nothing but the belief in sensed experience, the belief that that which seems to be is an entity or reality in and of its own self. To paraphrase Lao Tzu, "If you can name it, it isn't it." If you believe in, and then name, anything of appearance, that appearance *in and of its own self* "isn't it"—isn't God. If you make an entity out of that which seems to be; if you make a "false idol" out of anyone or anything that presents itself to you, it "isn't it"—isn't God. But remove *belief* from appearance and now *only God is* appearance, formation, the totality of experience. "Do not judge by partiality, but judge a just [truthful, God-is-all] judgment." (John

7:24, Lamsa translation.) Realize forevermore, *the only thing that ever presents itself to you is God—infinity, omnipresence and eternity.*

GOD IS, NOT WILL BE

God exists fully now. God is oneness and nowness. God does not exist in the "past" or in the "future." Therefore, there is no time and space in God, in truth; and because God is omnipresence, there is no cause and effect in God; and because God is all, there is no time and space nor is there cause and effect in visibility and tangibility. Think about this; think deeply about this. This realization is the key to your freedom of the world and all of the world's goods because the world is simply God experienced as formation. Visibility and tangibility have nothing to do with time and space or cause and effect. God is the only visible, and God is the only tangible and none but God. And because all of God is visible and tangible to God (God consciousness), all that God is and has is visible and tangible to you and me the moment we live as God consciousness rather than as human belief. "Son [and daughter], you are ever with me, and all that I have is yours."

Yet does not the whole of humanity live with the belief in time and space and cause and effect? God is finished; God is whole and complete, omnipresent now. There is no such thing as incomplete or unfinished God. Yet all of humanity believes in incompleteness, evolving experience, gain, betterment and advantage. In the human world there is forever more to accomplish, more to fix, to heal, to pacify, to prosper and to harmonize. The whole of evolution is incompleteness on its way to completeness; yet God, truth, is finished, complete, perfect. Again, "If you can name it, it isn't it" and "Do not judge according to partiality [by what seems to be, or by what is believed to be], but judge a just judgment."

If that which presents itself to us moment by moment is believed to be actual, an entity in and of its own self, truth forever remains a mystery—ethereal and impractical. God forever remains—to belief—un-evidenceable, un-realizable, out of reach or invisible and intangible to practical experience. Belief believes it has only one option: to learn "manifestation" and "demonstration" skills which will cause that which is "ethereal and impractical" to "become" real and practical. The bookstores are full of such teachings so the choices are numerous. But God is; God already and forever is, and doesn't need to become anything else or different because all already is God and the fullness thereof. "The earth is the Lord's, and the fullness thereof. . . .The silver is mine, and the gold is mine, says the Lord." All of the earth and everything everywhere in it and of it, despite appearance, is God and God alone—perfectly visible infinity and omnipresence alone.

Once you understand *this one truth* you can go through all of the works of The Miracle Self and The Infinite Way, all of the Bible, *The Bhagavad-Gita*, *The Dhammapada*, the *Tao Te Ching*, *The Gospel of Thomas*, the works of Meister Eckhart, Saint Francis of Assisi, Jacob Boehme and others (all of the great spiritual masters) and you are able to—with new spiritual discernment—understand the truth revealed throughout these great and practical teachings.

WHAT IS TRUTH?

First realize that only God is, and God is omnipresent and omnipresence itself. God is fully and equally present everywhere at the same time. No being, thing, place or condition lacks anything of God. "The earth is full of the goodness of God." There is no higher or lower consciousness in God, no higher or lower, greater or lesser presence in or of God. There is not a higher self and a lower self. There isn't even a higher self and a lower self of you and me. No presence, no being, mind, body, thing, amount, activity, place or condition is less than the whole of, the entirety of God. No one and no thing anywhere, under any circumstance, lacks the fullness of

God, the omnipresence, the absolute and utter whole of God. "The place on which you stand is holy ground." You and each "he, she and it" in your universe are holy being, mind, body and world. Only God is, and God is *one,* forever the infinite and omnipresent whole of itself as all. It is impossible for God to be partial, divided, separated, diluted or weak—to be less than the whole of itself—anymore than it is possible for math or aerodynamics to be less than the whole of itself. All principle is whole, infinite and omnipresent and unable to be less. God is the greatest of all principles and is indeed whole, infinite and omnipresent and unable to be less. God is wholeness, infinity and omnipresence *being all,* besides which there is none else.

"The earth is the Lord's, and the fullness thereof." We can replace the word "earth" with "formation" or "experience" and the word "Lord" with "mind." The experience you are having and I am having—every moment and grain of it—is the formation and activity of mind because all form is mind. Mind forms; nothing "else" forms. Mind *is* form, form *is* mind. And because God is all, mind is the fullness of God, and form is equally the fullness of God. "The earth [formation, experience] is the Lord's [mind's] and the fullness thereof."

Wherever you are having this or any moment of experience, and whatever its subject; wherever you are glancing and whatever you are glancing at; whatever you are doing and whichever him, her or it you are doing it with (whatever you are seeing, hearing, tasting, touching, smelling or thinking) you are, and he, she or it is the Lord—the formation and experience of God itself, spirit itself, infinity and omnipresence itself in all its fullness. It doesn't matter what belief reports experience and its forms to be, or not to be. What all actually and literally *is,* is God, infinity and omnipresence, despite its being deemed by belief to be human and of humanity—mind, body, its organs and functions, the formation of your surroundings, your work or business, your love, your family, your home, your neighborhood, dollars, your favorite place, your government, your country, your world or your universe.

Whatever you experience, despite the way he, she or it appears to be or act, it is God and the fullness thereof—whole and complete, infinite and omnipresent, one and eternal. God is forever that which appears to be person, form, activity, amount, place or condition. Belief tempts you to believe that all is *not* God but rather human, physical or material. But only God is, period. *Only God is.*

However, here's the rub (and the secret): God is *consciousness.* God is not a physical or material being, form or structure that you can name, perceive with your physical senses and interact with; a being or form with which you can exchange conversation, ideas, goods, dollars, love, life, happiness and freedom. God is indiscernible with material sense; God cannot be seen, heard, tasted, touched, smelled or thought about by mental, material or physical faculties. God is God alone, and the forms of God are God-forms alone, entirely invisible, intangible and unobtainable by human, physical or material sense. God is, to material sense, the unnameable, unthinkable, undetectable, shapeless, formless *incorporeal* one. Yet in truth God is the infinitude itself, the eternal itself, fully present at every place and point of itself simultaneously (omnipresent). When you know this secret and live and sense by *all being consciousness,* not matter, then God is perfectly visible, tangible and real as the image and likeness of itself throughout experience. In this (spiritual) awareness, false sense heals and true sense emerges.

Everything everywhere is God because *only God is.* Whatever we observe—no matter whether it is believed to be human, animal, vegetable, mineral, animate, or inanimate (plant, wood, metal, stone, plastic, brick or any other type of matter, machinery or technology such as the computer, the internet, the automotive world, the electronic world); no matter what it is, absolutely anything and everything of experience—is God because only God is. It is only because we experience that which is altogether God with belief about our experience that that which is forever whole and perfect seems to be incomplete and imperfect. Always remember that corporeal sense in its pure (empty of belief) state is good and true—God and truth. It is only as we add belief into experience (corporeality) that we lose the God-ness of life and then have to survive, often with a battle or even a raging war, among the pairs of opposites, the good and bad of the world that seems so real.

All concepts have a name; all finiteness has a name; all experience has a name. Belief gives itself multitudinous names—ever more and more names for the infinitely evolving and magnifying pairs of opposites of material experience. Yet all is actually one, *the* one, and none else—that one being consciousness. Let us fully understand that what has been named "God" is *consciousness.* When we understand God as consciousness, we will understand the seeming anomaly of needing to rise in awareness or to "go to where God is," rather than expecting God to "come to where we are" (which is impossible).

There is none but God, which means there is none but consciousness. Therefore, we must lift our awareness away from the belief in matter to a state of pure *conscious awareness;* we must fill our awareness, our senses, full of the awareness of consciousness-as-all, and nothing but consciousness-as-all.

Realize that because God is consciousness, and because God is infinite and omnipresent, and because God does not and cannot change into something other than itself, there is none but God—none but consciousness. You are consciousness; everything of you is consciousness because there is nothing but consciousness. Your body—and every organ and function, every cell and atom, every moment and breath, and every sight, sound, touch, flavor and fragrance you experience—is consciousness.

I am consciousness. Everything of me and about me is consciousness. Everything I experience is consciousness. Consciousness is "both" the expe-

riencer and the experienced.

Forget forms, forget names, forget the seeming organs, functions, amounts and activities of experience. Forget what they do and how they do it. Forget them all. Realize that because God is the only, and God is consciousness, your body and everything of the body is consciousness; your experience and everything of experience is consciousness.

All is consciousness. The body is consciousness, and because consciousness cannot be contained, finitized, localized, or made personal or temporal, the body, despite belief and appearance, is not a container, not finite, local, personal or temporal.

Look beyond your physical sense of body and realize that everything in your consciousness—every thing you are conscious "of"—is all *one and the same* substance and presence, all consciousness itself (including "you" the observer). You are, and the infinite forms of your universal experience are, consciousness and nothing but consciousness. As you observe, for example, your room, the furniture in your room; lights, flowers, decorations; floor, walls, ceiling, windows and what is visible through the windows, the colors you see and the sounds you hear, the fragrance of the flowers—everything everywhere of your experience—realize that it is not matter; it is not physical or material; it does not have a structural body as it seems to have to sense; but it is *God, consciousness, spirit.* Nothing exists but consciousness; *all* is consciousness.

Consciousness does not, and cannot, change into different substances or materials; consciousness cannot change from infinite and omnipresent to finite and locally present; consciousness cannot change from incorporeal to corporeal. God, consciousness, does not, nor can it ever change. The corporeal, formed experience is simply our sense of that which is forever and only incorporeal.

To understand "this world" is to understand *sense*. Imagine an infinite ocean of consciousness (you are imagining truthfully as you do this). You, inclusive of the infinity of your experience and its every aspect, element and form—every activity, amount, sight, taste, touch, smell, sound, color, place and condition; absolutely everything of your universe—are limitless and omnipresent formation or image of the infinity of *oneness, consciousness*. All is consciousness. There is none else in all of existence—no other substance, no other presence, no other form; no other being, body, object, shape, activity, amount or condition. All is the one infinite ocean of consciousness, omnipresent *as* everything everywhere, including the *observer* of everything everywhere—you and me.

It seems as if we "look out" from within us, or as us, "at" our universe and all its detail; yet each point and form of our entire universe is equally aware of "us" because only *one is*—that one being omnipresence. One, omnipresence, is *consciousness,* forever vitally, fully and wholly aware of the entirety of itself—each and every point of itself (the infinitude) simultaneously. Consciousness can neither be *unconscious* of itself, of course, nor can it be local because consciousness is omnipresence which is forever omnipresent, incapable of being local. The *whole* is equally present everywhere throughout infinity at the same time—the whole is infinity everywhere and equally present. There is none but the *omnipresent whole.*

Consciousness does not exist solely "here" as you or me nor does it exist "out there" as every form and detail of the universe. Consciousness "here" is not observing or being conscious of someone or something "out there." Consciousness is all; consciousness is the entirety of existence everywhere and equally present (omnipresent). Consciousness is one, *omni-aware*. Wherever you look, there the whole is; wherever you are, there the whole is; whatever presents itself to you is the whole of one—omnipresence and infinity—omni-aware of its entirety and completeness. Every point and place of consciousness is in full awareness of every "other" point and place throughout itself (there being none other) and indeed, *is* the whole itself.

Wherever you look, there I (consciousness) am. Wherever you are, there I (consciousness) am as your all. Whatever presents itself to you is the whole of I—the whole of one, omnipresence, infinity, omni-aware of its entirety and completeness.

Thirteen

Mind is Form

Mind *is* formation; formation *is* mind. Mind is "one of the many mansions in my Father's house"—one of the infinite degrees of awareness in infinity. Our mind is our body-form, our universe of formation, and because God is all and God is infinite, mind and its formation (being one) are infinite; and because God is omnipresence, the entirety of God—the infinitude—exists *as* each of the infinite degrees of mind (awareness) and *as* each and every point and formation of mind. "Our" universe is one degree of mind (awareness) within the multiverse or omniverse.

This, in brief, is the entire explanation of "us, our body, this world and universe and everything everywhere in it and of it." It's all you need as long as you deeply and thoroughly understand it and can live rested, relaxed, free and purposeful within and as oneness. If so, skip right to the next chapter; if not, let's hear more about the wonder of oneness.

Because *only God is,* there is no human being, mental mind, physical or material body or structural universe. The words "human, mental, physical, material and structural" (plus the quarter of a million distinct English language words[1] we employ to describe ourselves and our experience) all mean (and all actually are) the *one* which is *God* or *I* or *is* or *consciousness. Only God, one, is.*

The word "God" and the distinct synonyms "I, spirit, one, consciousness, incorporeality, infinity, omnipresence, omniscience, omnipotence" all mean the same. All is God; all is the infinity of God

[1] According to the English Oxford Dictionary

omnipresent *as* all. We experience the whole *as one degree* of awareness—this one degree we have named "humanity" and "our universe," plus the infinite variety of people and things in it and of it, or Lao Tzu's "ten thousand things."

Mind forms the infinity and omnipresence of consciousness into an infinite variety of experiences, but formation does not, and cannot *change* God into another or different type of form. All is the one infinite and omnipresent substance—consciousness—appearing as our universe of variety. Experience is filled with an infinite and wondrous variety of individual beings, bodies, things, amounts, activities, places and conditions, *but all one*—all omnipresence being all; all the one infinite ocean of consciousness being all. Nothing is separate from, apart from or different from God, consciousness. All is the infinity and omnipresence of consciousness; therefore, all is whole and complete and cannot be any different. All is God; therefore, God is all existence inclusive of all forms of existence.

Existence is the one infinite and omnipresent ocean of consciousness, there being none else. Therefore, everything everywhere is infinite and omnipresent consciousness, simply formed by and of mind—but never changed.

Everything everywhere is one hundred percent consciousness because there is no other substance, therefore nothing "else" from which being can derive life, body can be experienced, form can be formed, color can be colorful, aroma can be fragrant, activity can be active.

All is consciousness. All form and shape, color and fragrance, sound and sight, activity and amount, condition and circumstance—everything of experience—is simply consciousness as mind formation. But no form is, or ever can be finite, human, material, physical, local or temporal because all is God and God is changeless.

All is God, all is infinity, all is omnipresence, all is eternity, all is the one pure substance and presence of consciousness; therefore, all is "made of" and is itself the one pure substance of consciousness and "none else."

I am consciousness because God is consciousness, and because God is the only, consciousness is the only. I therefore must be that, and indeed I am.

God is consciousness and God is infinite. Therefore my consciousness is the infinity of God being experienced at my (the "human") degree of awareness. My experience is of that one presence, that one substance which is consciousness. I am that, my experience is that, and everything everywhere of my experience is that and that alone.

KNOW THE TRUTH

Truth alone does not free us. Truth must be known before we have the freedom of truth. We are only free in or by or as the degree of truth we know; we are not free just because truth is a fact. The same is true of our freedom with any principle. We are free in math or aerodynamics only by the degree we know these principles and how to evidence them. Then we automatically have in the most real and practical way the infinity of their "fruits."

The fact that only God is; the fact that God is everywhere and equally present; the fact that God is the very being you are, I am and all are; the fact that God is all (therefore all form, object, amount, activity, place and condition) does not make it evident in experience (any more than math or aerodynamics can be evident in experience) until it is *known and applied.*

Think. If God is *able* to be evident in the human picture—the human mind, body, world and universe—why is God not? Why has God not been evident throughout humanity's history? Why, if God is *able* to be evident humanly, does God allow the terrible wars, destructive diseases, illnesses and injuries, devastating poverty, hunger, injustice, immorality, greed, cruelty and racism to run rampant alongside the many wondrous traits and accomplishments of humanity?

Is there a power blocking God from being evident in human experience? If so, that power would have to be greater than God (only greater power can overcome lesser). But God is omnipotence, the one, the only power. The belief in a power greater than God is nonsense.

So what is the answer? Surely if God, which is love, peace and harmony of all, were able to be evident throughout humanity, there would not be, nor could there be, a single war, disease, illness, injury; one condition of poverty, hunger, homelessness, unhappiness or depression; one case of injustice, immorality, greed, cruelty or racism. If God were able to be evident in humanity, could there be anything but love and union, life and happiness and freedom of all around the world? Could there be even one simple cold or sniffle, one question or doubt, one disagreement? Could fear exist, or anything to be fearful of? No. God is love, God is one, God is life eternal—*the one life eternal* of all that exists. There is "none else." Therefore, could birth and death exist? Why would birth exist if life is eternal and eternal life is forever embodied? How can death exist if life is eternal? Life "and" body are one, the life-body eternal. Life is never without body, and never can be. Life is not ethereal, nor is it a mystery as the teacher believed. Life is here and now, real and practical—the only here and now, and the only real and practical. The concepts of "not here" and "not now" and "not real" and "not practical" do not exist in God. If they did, God would be two, not one—two states of existence rather than *one* (which God is). Certainly, life cannot be born and then be dead. Such belief is nonsensical. So why does humanity *experience* both birth and death?

It takes just a little logical thinking to realize that no human or world pain and suffering would or could exist if God were in our experience or were able to be. Not even birth and death could exist if God were able to be in our experience.

The clue to the seeming enigma is in the word "our." If God is the only (the infinite and omnipresent one, which God is), what are "we"? Have we believed we are something else, something different from God, even though we've accepted intellectually that God is the one and the only? Have we believed we are "human beings" who are less than or different from God-being? Have we believed God is somewhere "in us," or is somehow "the truth of us," but in practice far away and unreachable except by the blessed few? Have we believed that we are not blessed and that therefore God is impractical and unreal in our lives and the lives of the billions on earth? Let's expunge the nonsense of such beliefs.

GOD IS LOVE

God is love and God is all; therefore, if God were in the human scene, the world would be full of love and none else. There would not exist even one moment of intolerance, argument, hate or war; not one person would harbor thoughts of greed, injustice, inequality or racism. And because there is no such thing as unembodied God, all of humanity would be fully embodied—fully fulfilled in all form. Not one person would be homeless, hungry, in lack or insecure in any way because in God the entire "body of life" is one *as* life. No "body-part," no fulfillment of form is missing, separate or limited; God is never body-less or homeless—without the fully fulfilled formation of experience at and as every level of awareness.

"I am the bread [formation] of life. . . . I am the bread which comes down from heaven [the forever-fulfilled form of experience]. . . . the bread which I give is my body [the formation of experience is God formation, forever whole and complete, fulfilled and perfect, unconditional and omnipresent] which I give [I am] for the sake of [the experience of, the oneness of] the life of the world."

I (consciousness) am the formation of life. I (consciousness) am the forever-fulfilled form of life, of experience. The formation which I (consciousness) am as the experience of all is God formation, forever whole and complete, fulfilled and perfect, unconditional and omnipresent.

I (consciousness) am the completeness and fulfillment of being; I am omnipresence being omnipresent as you, as all.

So if I (God) were in the human scene, discord, disease, lack and limitation would not and could not exist. There would not be, nor could there be, a single act of cruelty or injustice, greed or racism. Surely it is not believed that God, which is love, and nothing but love, is also cruel, unjust, covetous and racist! That is impossible because God is the *only* presence and the *only* power; the *one* presence and the *one* power, that being love. Is the one and only presence and power of love cruel, unjust, covetous and racist? Of course not. What "part" of the one presence and power of love is cruel, unjust, covetous and racist towards "another part," and where does this "other part" exist in the oneness and only-ness which is love? Such dim belief is nonsense, therefore nonsensical to entertain. So do you see, that if God were able to be evident in the human scene, no such negative experience could possibly exist?

God is joy, happiness and satisfaction, and God is the one and the only. Therefore, if God were able to be evident in the human scene, calamity, unhappiness or dissatisfaction could not exist anywhere in the world. Joy cannot also be calamity; happiness cannot also be unhappiness; satisfaction cannot also be dissatisfaction. Oneness *is*—without opposite.

Only God is; therefore only love is, only harmony is, only peace is, only fulfillment is. Therefore, if God could be evident in humanity, there would exist nothing but love, harmony, peace and fulfillment of mind, thought, body, world and universe and everything everywhere in it and of it.

If God were able to be evident in the world, no "natural disaster" would or could exist. The world would not know volcanoes, tornadoes, earthquakes or tsunamis. It would not even know of inclement weather, either too hot or too cold. Unsafe, insecure, frightening or even uncomfortable conditions would not and could not exist anywhere in the world if God could be in the world. Where and how would these multitudes of negative conditions exist in the oneness and omnipresence of love, life, harmony, peace, joy, abundance and fulfillment that is God if God were here among us?

WHY?

The very first question we have to ask is, "Why, if God is all and God is good alone, is God not evident, and not able to be evident, in human experience?"

There is no denying that God isn't evident in the human scene. We may argue that God is somewhat evident, that there is some good in the world, or even a lot of good. But God is *all* and can never be "somewhat" or even "a lot." Even "a lot" of good leaves a remainder that is not good. No, God is either fully evident or fully not evident. For God to be evident more "here" and less "there" means that, in fact, there is *no* God evident either here or there. Humanity has misunderstood what God is, therefore what *it itself* is. All "more" or "less" good is nothing but the pairs of opposites, but God isn't a pair of anything. God is neither good nor bad. Solomon warned us against believing that the pairs of opposites have anything to do with God. "Give me neither poverty nor riches." Give me neither the experience of bad materiality nor good materiality in and of its own self. God is alone, without opposite. God is one, not a pair, not two, not otherness. "I am the Lord, and besides me there is none else. . . . there is one God, and there is none other but he."

God is one and omnipresent, indivisible and inseparable. God cannot be partial. There cannot be a little of God versus a lot of God or even no God versus all of God. God is the only, the all, the one, there being none else in all of existence. God is all of existence, there being no "other" type or even choice of existence. God cannot be sliced and portioned like a cake, shared among many. God is never partially evident, versus more evident, versus fully evident. Only belief could accept such untruth! "My thoughts are not your thoughts, neither are your ways my ways, says the Lord." Either God is fully evident or not evident at all. Omnipresence cannot be partial presence. Omnipresence is forever the whole of itself, fully and equally present as all simultaneously. God cannot be anything less than or different from all of itself; God cannot and does not change, alter, transform, evolve. God cannot be less today, more tomorrow and complete eventually. God *is,* and that *is* is now, never in a future; and that *is* is *fully is,* now.

Be certain to realize that when we have God, we have the whole of God. It is impossible to have anything less than or different from the whole of God because God is *one,* omnipresent, indivisible and inseparable. There is no "other" choice or possibility. God is incapable of being anything other than, or different from, or less than itself. And what is "itself"? The one omnipresent, indivisible whole; the whole of the presence of God, which has in it no absence. Presence cannot also be absence, and because God is omnipresence, there is never absence of any good thing, any good formation, any fulfillment of experience. Being (life, existence) and formation are *one,* not two, not separate, not different. Therefore, when we have God, we infallibly and automatically have the whole of God *formation*—the whole of fulfilled experience, unto the farthest reaches of the universe.

I hear you say, "Surely we already have God!" Yes, we already have God or, better stated, our *truth* is God. But is God *evident* in our experience? Ah, here is where many spiritual seekers around the globe have missed the way. If God is our truth, yet is not *tangibly evident,* something is amiss. "Ye ask, and receive not, because ye ask amiss." The first question we must ask is, *what is amiss?* The answer is that we have believed ourselves, our minds and the forms of our bodies and world to be *something in and of their own selves* rather than the one and only presence and form which is God. We have created a belief in God *and.* The moment we believe in God *and,* we establish a sense of difference and separation from what we truly are—the being, mind, body, world and universe of God.

To tangibly experience God, we have to drop belief, and then rise in awareness to be *in and of and as God* rather than in, of and as humanity. We have to leave "ourselves" behind and go to "where God is" because where God is is our entire harmony and completeness already and forever in perfect formation. In God-alone awareness, we discover that mind which is form, is unconditioned God. Mind is not separate or different from or less than God; therefore mind does not nor can it *change* God into a separate or different or lesser substance or presence. Mind is fully God because God is fully all. Therefore, form is equally fully God—the whole of God as form. It is only *belief* that clouds form and makes it *appear to be* separate or different from or less than God. When we have lifted our awareness and filled our senses full of God alone and God as all, God's unconditioned, fully present and perfect form is perfectly real, visible, tangible, manifested and demonstrated all around us. "Where the spirit [presence, consciousness] of the Lord is, there is liberty."

"I am the bread of life: he that cometh to me shall never hunger; and he that believeth on me shall never thirst." Certainly, "He that cometh to me" does not suggest that God comes to us. Equally, "He that believeth on me" does not suggest that we can continue to believe in humanity, physicality and materiality. Indeed, *we* must rise in awareness—go to where and what God is—and *then* we "shall never hunger" and "shall never thirst" for any good and fulfilled experience. We must lose the sense of being human, physical and material, local and temporal. We and our experience are entirely of the one being, one substance and one presence because none but the one *is*. Nothing at all exists but God (consciousness). Only God sees God; only God awareness is aware of God form; only God being experiences God self, mind, body, world and universe.

Our work is to rise into God awareness and empty ourselves of human, physical and material awareness. All the scriptures of the world instruct us in this. You can read them if you would like to, and you will discover all the authority you wish to have. It will take you a dozen or a score of years (as it took me). Or you can hear it quickly and succinctly throughout the teachings of The Miracle Self and The Infinite Way; *The Bhagavad-Gita, The Dhammapada, The Gospel of Thomas,* and *Tao Te Ching;* throughout Isaiah, Jeremiah, John, Romans, and Revelation; and throughout the works of Meister Eckhart and St. Francis of Assisi—all of these and other spiritual treasures of the world.

Our entire truth journey changes as we begin to know the truth and, as best we can, live it. We quickly find ourselves on the straight and narrow path that leads to heavenly experience because we're immersing ourselves in true truth rather than metaphysics. We cease from taking an obscure journey of believed truth hoping to find God in either mental gymnastics or intellectual silence, and we come to truth itself. We have all experienced failure in our attempts to evidence the joy and freedom of God in our everyday lives. (I struggled and failed for twenty years.) Our struggle seems like an eternity, and then the moment of spiritual discernment breaks through. From that moment everything of life changes, and quickly.

That spiritual discernment reveals this: only God is; therefore God is mind, and because mind forms, formation is just as full of God as God itself. Only belief clouds divine and perfect form from tangible experience. Remove *belief* from experience and *there God is.*

Fourteen

Abide in Me

Let us understand how awareness is lifted and filled with the light of truth—the light which reveals the fullness and glory of God as formation.

Contained in the following illuminatingly-clear instruction by the Master is the authority confirming the need to rise in awareness, to "go to where God is" rather than expecting God to "come to where we are."

> I am the vine, you are the branches. He who abides in me, and I with him, will bear abundant fruit; for without me you can do nothing. Unless a man remains with me, he will be cast outside like a branch which is withered, which they pick up and throw into the fire to be burned. If you remain with me, and my words remain with you, whatever you ask shall be done for you. In this the Father will be glorified, that you bear abundant fruit and be my disciples.

If it were possible for God to be evident in the human scene, possible for God—the one almighty principle or law—to "come to where we are," why would the Master (and I don't think any will argue that Jesus, at least according to history, is the greatest spiritual master who has walked the earth), plus every other spiritual master in his or her own way, instruct us to *abide in truth*? Why would every master warn us that if we do *not* abide in truth we are like "a branch cut off which withers and is thrown into the fire"? We suffer pain, disease, injury, hate, injustice, cruelty, failure, poverty, loneliness, homelessness, famine and even natural disasters side by side with the many joys and fulfillments of life.

Every lack of good experienced today and throughout the history of humanity, no matter what its name or nature, is rooted in one lack alone: *a lack of God awareness.* We believe our human state and our material world. We are unaware of our and our world's spiritual reality. The Master tells us that by continuing to abide in mental, material and physical belief, we are like a branch cut off, and we will wither, become weak and frail and eventually die. This is the experience of every human being (human belief). Along with many good conditions we suffer with pain, disease, discord, lack and limitation, and eventually we are thrown into the fire and turned into ashes. The personal, human sense dies because it is starved of the substance and body of truth.

If it were possible to simply sit in a chair and experience God coming to us, healing, pacifying, prospering and bringing love, justice and union to us and our world, the great masters certainly would have instructed us to do so.

Sooner or later, we all discover that God does not "come to us"—even if we devotedly pray and meditate. God does not heal, prosper, harmonize or pacify us, others or our world despite our earnest efforts to "keep our minds on God," and to "be still, and know." Even during our or our world's greatest pain, suffering and disaster, God does not come to the rescue. We have all had the experience of a non-yielding problem despite much effort to "reach" God, pray to God, even beg and plead for God's help. No, God does not, nor can it "come to" and heal the human scene any more than math can "come to" 3 + 3 equals 5 and make it 6.

God is love. Can you imagine love being absent, especially in times of need? Even human love is present to help loved ones during both good and challenging times. Greater human love flows beyond the circle of immediate loved ones to support others too, often globally. If God—which is love itself as all, the one omnipresent law and principle itself and that of each individual self—were even remotely aware of so-called humanity and its material world, we and our experience would be heaven.

The fact is, God is not in the slightest aware of humanity or a material world and universe. All principle is unaware of non-principle, of anything unlike itself. Math, as 3 + 3, *is* and can only *be,* and can only be *aware of* "6." Any "other" total for 3 + 3 simply does not exist in math. Otherness would be a non-principled result that math is utterly unaware of and therefore cannot help us with—thankfully. If math had more than one perfect, whole and complete state of body, its universe would be chaos—unprincipled and volatile. Principle cannot be unprincipled, and because principle and its form are one, nothing can separate principle from its everywhere-present formation.

God is principle—the one, almighty principle of heaven and earth and all therein. God is and knows and is eternally being nothing but its omnipresent self. You are that, I am that, all is that, and the experience of all is that. There is none else because there is no other presence—God is the only presence. It is when we *know and live by* this one truth—the one, almighty principle and presence—that we discover the principled harmony of self, mind, body, world and universe standing as us and as all formation of our experience. You, I and all are the one principle fully embodied. Everything everywhere throughout experience, from a single thought to the totality of life's detail, is *oneness* fully embodied. But, to see oneness clearly as our reality, we have to drop belief about it and lift into the heavenly (spiritual, incorporeal) consciousness. We have to lift away from the false sense of God—the belief in the corporeal, material, physical and mental being real—into spiritual consciousness. We have to be aware of—conscious of—*spirit* being everything everywhere, *spirit* being the only, *spirit* being omnipresent.

God is everything everywhere. God *is* mind *is* form, and God is spirit, the *incorporeal.* Therefore being, mind and form are incorporeal, not corporeal as they are sensed to be. We accept a false sense if we *believe* appearance—either of good or bad. It is *belief,* nothing else, that appears to be the reality of our mental and physical existence and the material reality of our universe. Our believed reality seems to be different, separate and apart from God; yet only God, oneness is. When we rise into spiritual consciousness we see it, we experience it. Oneness becomes our perfectly real and tangible reality. But if we do not realize this great truth and remain living in belief, we and our world wither and eventually die. The remains are thrown into the fire.

The "withering and dying" experience is like a branch cut off from the vine, quickly becoming starved of life, substance and nourishment. It becomes depleted of its joy and happiness, its purpose and freedom. Its fulfilling universe of good fades and fails, and eventually dies. It withers and dies because it is cut off and separated from its source. But when the branch remains *one with the vine* it lives and flourishes. It is strong, happy, purposeful, beautiful and bountiful. It is free to live abundantly and to ceaselessly give its fruits to its world.

PSALM 91

The 91st Psalm instructs us in the same truth. It is captivating, poetic and crystal clear.

> He who dwells in the protection of the most High shall abide under the shadow of the Almighty.

If it were unnecessary to "dwell in the protection of the most High"—to lift awareness and dwell in spiritual consciousness (which is "what" and "where" God is)—why would we be instructed to do so? "He who dwells in the protection of the most High shall abide under the shadow of the Almighty"—shall abide in harmony and peace, abundance and freedom, safety and security.

> I will say of the Lord, He is my refuge and my fortress; my God; in him will I trust. Surely he shall deliver you from the snare of the fowler, and from vain gossip.

There it is. Whenever we experience any kind of discord, illness, disease, injury, unhappiness, loneliness, homelessness, hunger, lack or limitation, as long as we turn away from its appearance and rise into and dwell in God awareness, in the secret place of the most high, then we quickly witness that "discord" or "lack" dissolve to reveal wholeness and harmony. Good is infallible in God consciousness because God is all and God is good without opposite. "Surely [infallibly] he shall deliver you [false sense] from the snare of the fowler, and from vain gossip [vain belief, vain awareness]."

It is being lifted in God consciousness that the whole universe of harmony *is*—that the truthful universe of being and formation is visible and tangible. Nothing but harmony and wholeness exists in God, and it is *God consciousness* that enables God existence to be seen. When we dwell in God consciousness, when we make God consciousness our living place, we *feel* the peace of being, the love of being and the harmony of being. We are, and all is, peace, love and harmony, wholeness and completeness. We have arrived at the place of God-being-all. It is a relief, a satisfaction and a freedom we *feel* happening as us—just as, in our metaphor, we feel the relief, satisfaction and freedom of arriving and then dwelling on the top floor or in the penthouse. The view is better here, and indeed the view of the universe and every form of it *in God consciousness* are forever perfect, whole and harmonious—infinite, omnipresent and eternal. Now that we have "arrived here," we can rest, simply bathe in the beauty and truth of God, and *let* God be our experience *for us*. Then, indeed we discover that our illness and disease, our suffering and pain, our lack and limitation dissolve to reveal God form.

> He will cover you with his feathers, and under his wings you shall trust; his truth shall be your shield and buckler. You shall not be afraid for the terror by night, nor for the arrow that flies by day, nor for the conspiracy that spreads in darkness;

"Darkness" is belief in matter being real. The "darkness" mentioned in scripture is simply the un-illumined awareness which exists on the "ground floor" or "basement." It is belief in the corporeal or material appearance of life, in the corporeal or material sense as being reality.

> nor for the pestilence that wastes at noonday.

"Pestilence" is the pain, the suffering, the experience of both good and bad false sense caused by belief. The actual and only "pestilence" is belief. God is nowhere in belief (and believed experience), and God cannot "come to" it. We can pray and meditate for as long as we like, but God cannot come to belief, nor can it come to us who are praying and meditating for a material result. God is God alone, and exists only "where" God is—pure spirit, pure consciousness, pure incorporeality, not corporeality.

> Thousands shall fall at your side, and ten thousand at your right hand; but it shall not come near you.

Who shall witness thousands falling at their side, and ten thousand at their right hand? Who shall witness disease, lack and limitation not coming near them? *You and I who live and move and have our beings in God consciousness;* individuals who know that reality is spiritual and incorporeal, not material and corporeal. We ignore what is collectively believed to be reality and live as spiritual beings in the spiritual mind, body, and world (universe). Humanity and materiality are known to be sense alone, not reality. We live in and as and out from God consciousness: "I live and move and have my being in God." *We are they* who witness the thousand falling at our sides, and the ten thousand falling at our right hands, with pestilence—belief—no longer able to touch or disturb us.

> Only with your eyes shall thou behold the reward of the wicked.

We still witness "the reward of the wicked"—the discordant experience of belief and believers, of those who do not know the truth and therefore continue to dwell in a material sense of reality. But "it shall not come near you" because you have made the Lord "your refuge," the most high "your habitation."

> For thou, O Lord, art my trust; thou hast established thy habitation in the highest. There shall be no evil befall you, neither shall any plague come near your dwelling. For he shall give his angels charge over you to keep you in all your ways. They shall bear you up in their hands lest you dash your foot against a stone.

This beautiful verse is one of my favorites—poetic, supportive and filled with hope.

> You shall tread upon the viper and adder; you shall trample under foot the lion and the great serpent. Because he has loved me,

There it is again, "because he has loved me," because we have lifted our awareness to God, to truth, the incorporeal, the spiritual.

> therefore [and by that means] will I [will the light and presence of God consciousness] deliver him; I will set him on high because he has known my name.

As we have lifted our awareness to that of God consciousness, its light and presence deliver us, free us from the good and bad experience of belief to that of pure God (good without opposite). God consciousness "sets us on high" because *we* have lifted our sense *to it*. We have come to "know my name," to know and keep ourselves in truth consciousness, God consciousness. Because we have lifted to it, we now have the harmony and wholeness of it. The place of God consciousness and the God experience are one.

> He shall call upon me, and I will answer him; I will be with him in trouble; I will deliver him and honor him. With long life will I satisfy him, and show him my salvation.

Throughout scripture we find no plausible reference, no real explanation as to why humanity lives by belief. The story of Adam and Eve is a wonderful metaphor, but is in reality implausible. Yet we do find throughout all the scriptures of the world the instruction to lift our awareness "to where God is," to lift into God consciousness, to fill our minds full of God awareness; to dwell on, ponder and contemplate, to continually abide in the consciousness of God, the *one* and the *only*.

It is dwelling in God consciousness, and the activity of God consciousness in us (made possible by our lifting *to it*), that aligns or attunes our sense with truth itself and enables truth to be our experience *for us*. High up in God consciousness false sense dissolves and true sense emerges. Belief dissipates and dies, leaving truthful being, mind, body and world as our palpable and perfectly visible and demonstrated reality.

Always remember, at the "human" level of awareness we have a corporeal sense of the incorporeal, that's all—a material sense of the spiritual. It is only belief added to sense that makes experience seem discordant, unhappy, lacking or limited. Sense itself is unreal; sense is *sense alone* and is innocent and impotent. As we learn to sense *without belief*, reality is perfectly apparent. It is knowing this that enables us to release our senses from the apparent (belief), and allow them to live freely in the real. We lift in awareness and illumine our sense by knowing this truth, and by keeping ourselves filled with God and God alone. Then God quickly becomes and remains visible as the true forms of experience.

Every degree of higher God awareness we attain evidences itself as good and harmonious form because awareness and form are one. For every degree that we rise in God awareness, for every degree that we become more aware of God-presence and less convinced of material presence, *the form of that degree is evidenced as* the healthier, wealthier and more naturally harmonious experience. More life is tangibly evident; more harmony, more peace, more love and more abundance are evident as, and at, each degree of higher awareness until we find ourselves living daily in a new reality, *the one reality* of God as all, spirit as all.

PSALM 1

Psalm One also speaks clearly of this very need to rise in awareness, to abide in God consciousness (spirit, incorporeality), and of the tangible experience of having risen in awareness:

> Blessed is the man who walks not in the way of the ungodly, nor abides by the counsel of sinners, nor sits in the company of mockers.

Blessed are we who believe not in humanity and materiality as they appear to be—a reality in and of their own selves.

> But his delight is in the law of the Lord.

Our one delight is the presence and truth of God as all—all I am, my mind is, my body is, and my entire universe and everything everywhere in it and of it is; the all-in-all and all-of-all.

> And on his law does he meditate day and night.

On the one truth that God is all do we meditate day and night, do we maintain our awareness day and night. Never do we let this truth slip from our conscious awareness.

Now, again, to anybody who questions the need to rise in awareness, or to "go to where God is," let us ask: If God, if harmony, if truth were evidenceable in the human scene or human world, why would we be instructed to meditate day and night and delight in "his law," the law, the principle, the truth that is God? There would be no need to delight in the truth that God is all, or meditate upon it, or contemplate it if truth were able to come and do all this for us.

Then we're told of the result of lifting day and night to God:

> And he shall be like a tree planted by a stream of water, that brings forth its fruit in its season [the "season" is always here and now, the moment-by-moment of awareness or experience, the place-by-place and activity-by-activity of experience], whose leaves fall not off; and whatsoever he begins he accomplishes.

Then the psalmist switches to the fate of those who do not rise in awareness, those who still believe they can get God to come to where they are:

> The ungodly are not so, but are like the chaff which the wind drives away. Therefore the ungodly shall not be justified in the judgment, nor sinners in the congregation of the righteous; for the Lord knows the way of the righteous; but the way of the ungodly shall perish.

Listen to that: "The Lord knows the way of the righteous; but the way of the ungodly shall perish." The Lord, the consciousness and presence of truth *knows—is itself* the perfection and wholeness of God as formation, God as mind as form. Consciousness *knows*—*is itself* the fully embodied and eternally demonstrated, manifested, visible and tangible universe of self, of your self and my self. But the way of the ungodly—the individual who doesn't have God consciousness but has mental, material and physical belief—shall perish. What perishes? Belief perishes along with the believed sense of being (the personal sense of being and universe) because it was never real. Every belief perishes; truth is eternal. And because all experience is *awareness*, as soon as we lift our awareness from belief to truth, belief perishes and we awaken to our conscious eternity.

The constant and then final perishing of belief is the experience of every "human" lifespan. We are conceived of belief and develop in the womb of belief; we are born and exposed to a whole world of belief; we are educated in and by belief, churned out of belief's school at eighteen or college at twenty-something, and sent off to work in an industry or profession of belief. Many of us soon start our own family of belief, each member of whom we love very much (far more so than we love other individuals and families of belief). As our believed selves eventually become old and weary (as all belief does), and we (hopefully) see that our family is sustaining its lineage and has developed a good, strong foothold in its world, we die knowing that we'll at least be remembered by a few, for a short time. Our death is often one of suffering and sadness, one of pain, not only for us but for our family and friends.

Then, though we are not yet conscious of it, we are born anew into the same belief we just died from; we live, work, have family and die again—and on and on in an eternal cycle of belief *until*, during one lifespan, we finally awaken. Our spiritual existence emerges as the one reality, and belief is but a distant dream—a non-reality that never actually took place.

The very moment we awaken, we are free of this live-die-repeat cycle. We are free in spirit, no longer believers. We now live on the "top floor" or in the "penthouse"—in and as pure spirit, pure incorporeal being. We and our experience are full of heaven as earth—full of life eternal, life abundant, love abundant, the divine freedom and purpose of individual and collective being. We have risen out of and away from belief and its pairs-of-opposites experience—the "ungodly," the lack of God-which-I-am-and-all-truly-is awareness.

It is all a matter of conscious awareness. If you can just get this, then your awakening is assured. It is all a matter of the conscious awareness of truth, the truthful identity of all. That identity is, of course, the one "I," the one truthful life, being, presence and form of all which is God. And what is God? God is incorporeality, spirit, infinity, omnipresence, eternity, one—the one omnipresence of being, that which is unnameable, that which is formless, shapeless, unquantifiable, that which is pure spirit without matter in it, that which is never local, personal or temporary, that which has no "I, me or mine" about it. *This* is truth, *this* is truthful identity, and *this* is the way of awakening.

PSALM 23

All of scripture in one way or another instructs us to rise in awareness. There is significant spiritual receptivity today (much greater than when the scriptures of the world were written, mostly from 4000 to 2000 years ago). This greater receptivity allows us to hear simplified and clarified truth which was impossible to hear even one hundred years ago.

And so let us, with opened spiritual discernment, hear the powerful message of the Twenty-Third Psalm.

> The Lord is my shepherd; I shall not want.

This single verse, if truly spiritually understood, is enough to witness freedom this day and for eternity. "The Lord is my shepherd; I shall not want"—the "Lord," the unconditioned and unconditional mind, the mind full of God and nothing less, nothing different; the mind which *is* the formation of all. No wonder we "shall not want." What could we possibly want when our entire universe of experience is full of the good and abundant forms of God?

My conscious awareness of God being all is my "shepherd." I need only realize this truth and then joyously and purposefully live in utter safety, protection and abundance. God is my shepherd because God is all, yet this truth alone does not make it tangible in my experience. I have to be consciously aware of it. That is the entire key. "I live and move and have my being in God"; this is unalterable fact. But because all is consciousness, I have to be *consciously aware* of truth. As soon as I am, I tangibly *have* truthful experience. My conscious awareness of God being all is itself my true and harmonious experience (my mind and body, my protection and safety, my love and loving relationship with all people, my abundance, my knowing the truth of all form, my life eternal, my peace and purpose). My conscious awareness of God being all is itself my God experience—*is, is, is!*

Conscious awareness of God does not "produce" truthful experience it itself *is* truthful experience because God "and" experience are one, not two. My health, wealth, peace, harmony, love and purpose are all found in and as my conscious awareness of God as all. "The Lord is my shepherd, [therefore] I shall not want." It is *because* the Lord-God is my all-in-all and all-of-all that I shall not—cannot—want. Certainly, I shall not and never can want when I am continually consciously aware of God being the one being, the very being I am and all are because that very conscious awareness I am keeping alive twenty-four hours a day is itself my shepherd, my complete and harmonious experience of life in all its formation. Awareness is experience.

GOD HAS NOTHING TO DEMONSTRATE

God *is;* spirit *is;* spiritual being *is all* and is forever whole and complete. God, being one and all, does not need to demonstrate anything. Everything is already demonstrated because *God is* everything, and God already *is* its finished perfection. God or spirit is omnipresence, and omnipresence is here, now and forever one, whole and complete. There is no "other" type or form of presence, and there is no future in which God becomes something he-she isn't at this moment. Therefore, if God is all, which God is, and if God is omnipresence, which is the only presence, what needs to be demonstrated? It would have to be something that doesn't exist at this moment, but God is all; God is already all; God is fully existent eternally. Nothing "will be." "There is no new thing under the sun." The whole of omnipresence *is* already, and is its own demonstration, its own presence, its own form, its own manifestation. There is none else. The infinity of God, the eternity of God is right here, omnipresent wherever you are, fully demonstrated and manifested, visible and tangible as all. What, therefore, would you or I or anyone need to demonstrate? Nothing; all already is. But "we" must be or become consciously aware of it, that "it" being *God-spirit-omnipresence itself.*

The only thing we ever need to "demonstrate" is greater God awareness, greater awareness of God as all. When we truly know that God appears as formed being, mind, body and thing because mind forms, then we relax in our world of people, things, amounts, activities, places and conditions because we know that, despite appearance, it is all God. Because all is God, all is good, and is proved to be when we stay in God awareness. If we fall out of God awareness, all seems to be both good and bad, but in God-as-all awareness, all is witnessed as the one good that it truthfully is.

Do you see it? Because all is God and nothing but God, the only need is to demonstrate more God awareness, more God experience

(God felt happening within). The only need is to become more consciously aware of God as the only one, without opposite, without exception; to become consciously aware of the one presence, the one being, the one form—infinite, omnipresent, eternal, incorporeal, non-local and impersonal.

> He makes me to rest in green pastures; he leads me beside still waters.

We are not made to labor, to have to exert effort just to survive and find security, to have to struggle and strive through life just to maintain sufficiency, achieve some measure of success, feed our family and pay our bills. We are the full presence of God as individual being, the presence of divine being on earth. "Ye are gods; and all of you are children of the most High." Our purpose is to reveal earth as the heaven it is and all beings as the divinity they are. We are to be the light of the world, to feed and free the world of its material belief.

I am not human being but God being. Only God is; therefore only God being is—"there is none else."

I do not have a personal, mental mind; I have the one God mind individually experienced. My body is not physical and temporal but spiritual and eternal.

I am and I embody the entirety of God being, God mind, God body and God universe. My mind, body, universe and every form in it and of it is "full of the goodness of God."

I am consciousness not matter—not human, mental and physical; therefore I am infinite not finite, omnipresent not locally present, and eternal not temporal.

My body is not just what appears as my "physical" body, but is consciousness itself. The whole of my consciousness is my body.

I am and have the body of consciousness. There is nothing mental or physical about me, my body or universe; there is nothing material about any form in and of my universe. I am and all is God, consciousness, spirit, therefore infinite, omnipresent and eternal.

I now know my truthful identity: consciousness. I am one with and as all because consciousness is one and all.

The whole of God is embodied in, and is being, every aspect of the I that I am, right here, right now—this very I I am. I am the one consciousness, the one all-embodied, all-inclusive, self-inclusive God consciousness being the I that I am, the mind and the body I am and have, and the totality of experience I am and have. I am and have all that consciousness is and has—which is infinity, omnipresence and eternity.

As God being, I am free being. I am whole and complete. I am one, my body is one and my entire experience is one because I, my body and my experience are spirit, not matter. And because I and form are the same one, the entire formation of me (my universal body of experience) is forever whole and complete.

I and form are one. Only one is, and that one is God. God is self-mind-body-universe—one and omnipresent. I am (inclusive of my experience and every detail of it) fully manifested and demonstrated spiritual being. Nothing is separate or different, nothing is "unmanifested" or "undemonstrated." All is whole and complete, finished and perfect because I and form are one.

For this reason, I am made to "rest in green pastures," and am led "beside still waters." I rest in the consciousness of God-as-all, and then discover myself led beside still and harmonious conditions—peaceful, complete and fulfilled formation—because I and form are one; consciousness and experience are one. Consciousness is experience; experience is consciousness.

> He restores my soul. He leads me in the paths of righteousness
> for his name's sake.

Yes! When I rise into God consciousness, when I stop seeking mental, physical or material good, but seek only the awareness of the presence of God, the being and body of God, the things of God (the spiritual things, the incorporeal things, the heavenly things which have no name, no shape, no amount and no locality), and when I have given up attempting to get or gain something from God in the realization that in and as God consciousness I am and have all, then my experience is restored. "He restores my soul." I am now filled with the light and clear sight of God. My senses are picked up by the light and love of the God consciousness I am now living, and the light of truth reveals truthful formation all around me. My path is now full of God-good rather than material good and bad. "He leads me in the paths of righteousness for his name's sake."

God awareness is awakening in and as individual being because we have lifted our awareness to where "His name's sake" exists. We have lifted ourselves to the level of God consciousness, and *there* fulfillment of all *is*. Remember the Master telling us, "In this way God is glorified in you."

God consciousness is God alone, God for God—God experience for the sake of God experience—not God for improved humanity or satisfying material good. Why? There is nothing but God. So if we wish to seek and experience truth, we have to seek and experience God alone, God for God; truth for truth experience alone, spirit for spiritual experience alone. That's the secret—the secret so few can hear.

As I seek nothing but God for God, I feel myself filled with peace. I am lifted in spirit—in spiritual awareness. I feel myself filled with the light of heaven, the light of truth, and I am lifted. My senses are illumined and I begin to see clearly.

As I have attained some measure of God awareness, and as I become still and open (receptive), God itself is now able to fill my senses. But you see, I've had to first rise to that place where the "filling station" is. When I have arrived, my senses can be filled. I have had to first "walk to and enter the elevator" before I can rise to where God is, to where the filling of the senses is continually taking place—up in God consciousness. But if I haven't stepped into and risen in the elevator, how can I sit and complain that (or wonder why) I am not being spiritually lifted and filled, that I still cannot see clearly, and that my good is not yet evident—anymore than I could complain, or wonder why I'm not experiencing the roof garden if I've not first taken myself there?

> Yea, though I walk through the valley of the shadow of death,

Yes, though I still experience pain or illness or disease or injury; though I still experience lack or limitation of health or money or love or peace or harmony or security or freedom—yea, though I walk through any discordant or threatening experience,

> I will fear no evil; for thou art with me; thy rod and thy staff they comfort me.

I will fear no experience because the presence of truth and peace and harmony is with me. The almighty power and presence of God comfort me, keep me safe and protected in the most real and practical way. I consciously experience the presence and peace of God "happening within" as I stay in God consciousness. That presence, that peace *felt happening* is itself my comfort, the rod and staff of safety and protection, the harmonizing and pacifying presence of truth as all experience.

I know that that very truth, that very peace, *is itself* the risen level of consciousness, and at that level of consciousness, there peace *is*, there harmony *is*, there liberty *is*. I am now protected, literally and tangibly. I need not fear any appearing discord or condition. I am in the "roof garden," in God experience, and in God experience there is nothing to fear. In God experience—God felt happening within—there is nothing to fear, and there is nothing to "do" to overcome that which seems to be discordant or ill. There is only God in God consciousness, God experience; therefore there is only love and the formation of love, peace and the formation of peace, harmony and wholeness and the formation of harmony and wholeness. Therefore, everyone is and everything is not only the being and form of God itself, but is *of* God itself; all people, things, activities, places, amounts and conditions are God, and *of* God in nature and character, presence and form. "Fear not, it is I. . . . there is none but Me." This is my rod, this is my staff, and indeed, this is my comfort.

> Thou preparest a table before me in the presence of mine enemies; thou anointest my head with oil; my cup runneth over.

As soon as we have risen into God consciousness we instantaneously *have* the forms of health, wealth, peace, harmony and wholeness of experience. God consciousness experienced (felt happening as we are up in God awareness) and form are one. It is impossible to experience God without "also" experiencing the "image and likeness"—the forms of God—because God and form are one.

Form is like an image in the mirror; the instant a subject is placed in front of the mirror, the object (image) is present—perfectly visible, tangible, manifested and demonstrated. Subject and object are one, not two, not different. One is not less than the other; "both" are one. This is exactly the relationship between God and formation. God (subject) and form (object) are one and the very same experience. Once we experience (feel) God "happening" within, we instantaneously *have* all of God formation. The experience of God felt happening "and" the experience of God (good) formation are the same one experience.

Make sure you understand this. Work to eradicate the belief in two-ness. Meditate on and as oneness, sit still and receptive to the truth of oneness, and let it begin to fill your awareness and live *for you.* It is the secret of the visibility of God as all formation. It is the secret of healing, health and vitality; love, abundance and freedom. It is the greatest secret on earth (for what greater secret could there be?).

Human, material awareness is a false sense of reality. It believes that that which *appears to be* is real. But now we have risen and have a new, more spiritual awareness of reality, the one reality that is spirit alone. Our greater conscious awareness *is* our greater tangible reality. At this greater or higher level of awareness—even a grain higher, just one degree higher—the hand of God comes forth, taking ours. Now indeed, that which *is* lifts us, lifts every sense of us, filling us with the light and tangibility of spirit and truth. Once we have taken ourselves to where God is (and is *being felt*) God "takes over," and truth experiences life *for us.* We are no longer involved; truth lives us. "I live, yet not I, Christ [spirit, truth] lives my life."

> Thou preparest a table before me in the presence of mine enemies.

A "table" is prepared before us—the entire body and form of our good—in the presence of our illness, injury, disease, lack, loneliness, insecurity; or threat to our life or safety or finances or whatever the problem may be. Right there in the presence of these discords—as long as we have risen (or are rising in awareness) and the minute we begin to feel even a grain of peace happening within—we are safe. We are protected and secure. No actual harm will take hold of us. Even though it sometimes seems to get very close or even touch noses with us, the problem can never actually take hold of us and destroy us or our lot. The table of truth, the very presence of health or healing, of peace and harmony, of plentiful resources and abundant finances, of love and relationship, home and security, and right and fulfilling opportunity, is already prepared and laid out before us with wholeness and completeness everywhere about.

This is the fully manifest and demonstrated self, the perfect and finished kingdom of self. God is already and forever whole and complete, perfect and demonstrated, and now here it is, laid out before us on the table of our experience. It is the "fruit" of our having risen to where God is, and our experience of God happening within, or as our being. We are consciously in and experiencing the presence of God, living by God instead of by belief and personal sense.

> Thou anointest my head with oil; my cup runneth over.

Why is my head anointed (my being filled with spiritual awareness) and why does my cup (my experience) run over with God (good)? It is because neither my head nor my cup is mine in reality, but is God and God's. All is God, and now that I have lifted up into God awareness, I experience the infinity and omnipresence of God's good happening as my life. *God itself* is the only presence and the only cup of life and is the only substance that can be running from that cup. Now that I have risen to where God is—to God consciousness—I am able to experience God's cup running over throughout my experience, for me, as me, and as everything I touch and do.

The cup of good forever runs over at and as the level of God awareness and actual God experience. *There* the cup is always running over—running over with all the good of earthly formation: the forms of life, vitality, happiness, love, wealth and fulfillment in every department of life.

ABIDE IN ME

> Surely thy goodness and mercy shall follow me all the days of my life; and I will dwell in the house of the Lord forever.

This would be better stated, "*as I dwell* in the house of the Lord forever." It is only *as I dwell* in the house (consciousness) of God that the world of God-experience opens out and becomes my actual, discernable reality.

It is our job to dwell in the awareness of God-as-all forever. God cannot do it for us. It is only when we dwell in spiritual awareness that "thy goodness and mercy shall follow [us] all the days of [our lives]." God cannot do anything for us, just as math cannot do anything for us. We have to do it. Just as we have to "dwell in the house of math forever" if we wish to experience the fullness and freedom of math, so we have to forever dwell in God consciousness to experience the fullness and freedom of God. It is *as we dwell in* God consciousness that we tangibly experience the eternal health, love, abundance, freedom, purpose and joy of our truthful being and universe. God consciousness *is* God experience; God consciousness "and" God experience are one.

Never again be confused about why God is not apparent in the human scene, mental mind, physical body or material world. God cannot be evident anywhere but the place of God; *God cannot be evident where God is not consciously present.*

Also, remember that the one path to God experience is the straight and narrow path. Taking that path means rising out of the belief in humanity, mentality, physicality and materiality, into God itself; lifting into God consciousness; lifting awareness and abiding in the presence of God, spirit, the incorporeal as all.

Realize that all form is mind-form, and that in and of its own self it is nothing—just imagery, just concept, just passing experience. The *reality* of all form is God itself—the fullness of spirit, infinity and omnipresence; the spiritual being living in the spiritual universe, filled with and being the goodness of God.

Fifteen

Now I Can See

Without an understanding of God, which is consciousness, being all, we cannot progress in truth. Consciousness is being, mind, body and universe and everything in and of the universe. If we do not lift into at least a measure of this awareness, we are unable to experience the health, harmonies and treasures which are the truth of being; we cannot have the "demonstration" of healing and health, love and abundance, purpose and fulfillment of being.

We have to understand the truth of truth before we can tangibly experience truth as our mind, body and universe—the truth of the infinity and eternity of our consciousness. We have to know the truth before that truth sets us free. Truth *is itself* our formed health, vitality and freedom, and is forever in perfect order; but because life is consciousness, we must be consciously aware of truth in order to "have" it as tangible experience. "Know the truth, and that very truth will make you free." Let us know that truth now.

ONLY GOD IS

Only God is. We must always start with God—*only God is*. If we realized that one truth alone, throughout our experience, we would never again be confused about a seeming absence of God, or about an unyielding problem.

Only God is. Literally nothing but God exists. If we still have God "and" as a belief (if we still believe we have a mind, body or worldly condition other than *God alone*) that is why we are unable to witness the harmony and wholeness of God alone *as* our mind, body and condition.

Existence, life, self, mind, body and everything everywhere throughout the universe is God. Besides that one, there is none else; besides that one there is no variation, no difference, no lesser self or lesser formation. Only God is.

God is spirit and truth. Therefore, when we hear "I am the Lord, and there is none else; there is no God besides me," we can realize, I am spirit and truth, and besides me—besides spirit and truth—there is none else. Not even temporarily is there anything but spirit and truth. Not even the mind's seemingly real corporeal formation changes spirit and truth into matter and untruth. Mind does not, nor can it ever *change* God into something else, different or less. Nothing can change God—the only, the all. That which is sensed is sense alone, not reality in and of its own self.

Only God is; therefore I must be that, and indeed am. My mind, body and whole universe and everything everywhere in it and of it must be that, and indeed are that.

I am, and all is spirit and truth, and besides spirit and truth there is none else. I am that I am, and all is that I am.

Because God is one and none else, only oneness is. Only I is—oneness, one. Only God is, only one is, only I is. I am God; I am that I am.

Listen to that: *I* am God, and *I* am that *I* am. What is *I*? Consciousness. So we can realize that consciousness is God, and besides consciousness there is none else.

None but God exists. Existence in all its form, character and nature is God, the infinitude itself; and because God is all and God is consciousness, the infinitude of existence in all its variety is consciousness itself. "All things were made by him; and without him was not any thing made that was made." From this we understand that all things are made by consciousness; and without consciousness is not any thing made that is made; that all experience is made by consciousness; and without consciousness is not any experience made that is made.

Everything everywhere is consciousness simply observed as itself and by itself as mind forms (images). Consciousness witnesses itself as the infinity of universal mind formation. But those forms or images are *just that*—forms or images. They are not real in and of their own selves. The one reality is pure consciousness. *Nothing but consciousness is.*

When we hear that "God made everything that was made," we are hearing about the finished kingdom that is God or consciousness. God or consciousness is forever whole and complete at every point of itself, divinely and gracefully finished, omnipresent as all. Every moment, every he, she and it, every amount and activity, every place and condition are consciousness.

GOD IS CONSCIOUSNESS

God is consciousness, the I of being, the oneness of being; and besides God—consciousness, I, oneness—there is none else. Only God is, only consciousness is, only I is, and that is one or oneness. What else do we know about what God is, therefore what we and all are? God is infinity, omnipresence, omniscience, omnipotence, eternity, incorporeality.

Only one is, only infinity is, only omnipresence is. What appears to be personal being and body is none other than the infinitude itself—incorporeality, omnipresence, eternity *its self,* oneness *its self,* God *its self.* God or truth is never local or contained or formed or finite. God is incapable of locality or containment or local form or finiteness.

God is incapable of being anything but itself—everywhere and equally present at the same time, being all. Therefore, all being and form are incapable of being anything but infinite. Even a single moment of experience or a single form is incapable of being anything less than or different from infinite. Whether we are experiencing a single moment of form or an entire human or animal lifespan of form, it is infinite because God is all, and God is incapable of being finite. Humanity is only a finite and temporal *sense* of that which is actually God, therefore infinite and eternal. All life is, and all form is infinite, omnipresent, omnipotent and eternal and is incapable of being anything less or different.

INFINITY CAN ONLY BE INFINITE

Infinity can only be itself—infinity—and none else. Finiteness cannot be formed from infinity. Only infinity is—indivisible and inseparable infinity. Finiteness is not reality but *sense*. Only in sense does finiteness seem to be, but sense does not make it so.

The same is true of all synonyms we may use for God. Oneness, incorporeality, omnipresence, omniscience, omnipotence, consciousness, I—all of these synonyms can only be, and are, the whole of themselves. They are incapable of being anything less than or different from the whole of themselves as all, that "whole" being God. Therefore, because God (and any and every synonym for God) is all, experience is incapable of being anything less than or different from the whole of God. Appearance may testify differently, but that testimony is a lie. "Judge not according to the appearance, but judge righteous judgment." Despite appearance and despite any belief about appearance, you, your mind, body, world and universe and every grain of it are the whole of God.

Be absolutely sure you understand this; otherwise you cannot go any further in truth. Unless you understand that individual being is the whole of God (all that God is and all that God has because God is infinite and omnipresent, therefore forever whole and complete, indivisible and inseparable), the rest of truth, the truth that sets us free, cannot be grasped. Might we intellectually understand more truth? Yes, we can probably hear every truth which has ever been given the world or ever will be. But intellectual understanding is not spiritual understanding. "My thoughts are not your thoughts, neither are my ways your ways, says the Lord." It is only spiritually discerned truth that becomes evident as the good and harmonious forms of experience. This is why Jesus instructed, "Know the truth, and that very truth will make you free." Truth known *is itself* wholeness and freedom experienced. Truth known *is itself* the penthouse experienced in all its form. That penthouse does not *produce* its experience; it *is* its experience. And the same is true of known truth.

Be absolutely sure you understand: Only *one is*. Therefore, there is only one being, one body, one organ, one function, one activity, one presence, one amount; and that one is God, incorporeality, infinity, omnipresence—incapable of being matter, corporeal, finite or local.

You are and have infinity. You are not a being "within" infinity; you do not have infinity "available" to you. Be careful to understand this subtle truth. You *are* infinity, and it is because you are infinity that you have infinity as every form of your entire experience. Everything about you is infinity experienced because there is none but infinity. You are infinity sensing itself corporeally and objectively as what has been named a "human" being. But "humanity" is just a name (and not a particularly accurate name). The only actual being is God-being, because *only God is*. You are the infinity of being. This very second and forever you are and have infinity. You are infinity itself being itself as all the formation of your experience.

You are eternity itself being itself as your being, mind, body and world; you are incorporeality itself being itself as your being, mind, body and world; you are omnipresence itself being itself as your being, mind, body and world. You are nothing but and you have nothing but incorporeality, infinity, omnipresence and eternity (and every other synonym for God).

You do not exist "within" infinity or eternity or incorporeality or omnipresence. You *are it*. If you did not exist, infinity would not exist because "I am that I am." This very second you are and you have all, and without you there would not be a single breath of life whatsoever. This, of course, is true of all beings. What seems like many is actually one alone.

You do not have truth within you somewhere, you *are* the presence of truth. You, your mind, your body and every organ and function appearing to make up the physical body—plus the infinite variety of people, animals, objects, forms, amounts, activities, places, conditions and circumstances experienced each day—are not at all what they appear to be. They are (all of them, without exception) infinity, omnipresence, eternity simply *sensed* as what we call corporeal, material, physical, existing in time and space, subject to cause and effect. But actually—in the most literal sense—all form and activity of experience are infinity, omnipresence and eternity itself, incapable of being (or being an experience) "different" from its infinite, omnipresent and eternal self. There is no "other type" of being or formation. There is no other presence, being, body, thing, world or universe.

Perhaps the most important truth we can hear is that only God is, only the incorporeal is, only spirit is; and that which we call "human, mental, physical and material" is simply a *corporeal sense* of that which is one hundred percent incorporeal. If we could really grasp this truth, we could rest from all material concern and experience a significantly greater degree of freedom this day.

GOD IS INCORPOREAL

Only God (spirit and truth) is, and God is incorporeal, not corporeal. We are simply having a corporeal sense of the incorporeal—a material sense of spirit.

Our world and worldly experience seem to be, and seem to act as, matter only because we have believed them to be. We have lost our God awareness. We accept (believe) our selves, our mind, body and world (and everything happening in it) all at face value. We believe that which appears as our formed experience (including the form we are) to be real of its own self, instead of realizing that God is all, and that the objective experience we name "us and our world" is simply mind-formation of God. God never changes, nor can it ever—including as form. Only belief believes form to be something less than and different from God. But belief is not truth. All is one, and that one is God and God alone. "I am the Lord, and there is none else; there is no God besides me."

All is one—infinity, omnipresence and eternity itself, incapable of being anything different or other than itself even in temporary experience. Even this experience we call "human" actually isn't human at all but is the very infinity of being, mind, body, thing, place, condition and activity itself. It is the whole of God in experience; it is eternity itself, omnipresence itself simply sensed as corporeal, finite, objectified, separate, local and temporal. But sense in and of its own self is not reality. Sense alone is never what it seems to be. Without exception, everything sensed is actually the one infinity and omnipresence of God fully manifested as all. And because God is finished (forever manifested and demonstrated, visible and tangible), all of experience (each and every being, form, place, activity and condition) is equally the one infinity and omnipresence of God fully present as all—forever manifested and demonstrated, visible and tangible.

How is God witnessed as all? *Only God consciousness sees (experiences) God being and form.* It is only as we attune *our* awareness, *our* sense of self, body and world to God itself that we begin to experience that which is. The whole of God is already and fully available as every form and amount of experience, but we believe God isn't. When we realize the one truth of God as all, and then attune ourselves to the presence and activity of God alone, the kingdom of harmony becomes visible. *We* must rise in spiritual awareness to the point of conscious oneness with God. Truthfully stated, it is the point of conscious oneness *as* God because "I and the Father are one." All personal sense is dropped and dissipates, and God itself is experienced. We must spiritualize our awareness to the point of no (or very little remaining) personal self and of being able to simply *rest* in conscious oneness, receptive and open, a vacuum of being, beholding God happening as all.

God already is. It is *we* who must spiritualize or purify our awareness (make a nothing of the personal sense of self) to the point of conscious oneness: a state of silence and receptivity of being that beholds the God experience "happening." We shed the belief in corporeal, human, personal, mental, material, physical, local and temporal identity for that which is true, which is God alone as all. In this way we are empty and receptive for the God experience itself.

WHOLENESS AND PERFECTION

You and all are, this second, whole and perfect life, mind and body. You are, this second, the fullness of life itself. Your body, this second, is omnipresence, omni-body itself, not local body. You are, your body is, and your entire world is the oneness, the wholeness of God, infinity—omnipresent right here as you, and where every moment and form of your awareness is.

You are, and the entirety of your activity and experience is, omnipresence itself. Omnipresence is I, mind and body; omnipresence is form, activity, amount, and condition; omnipresence is all. You are and have the whole of omnipresence as your life, your mind, your body, your strength and vitality, and your ever-present resource of all that omnipresence is and has at every moment, every breath, every step. We can simplify it: you are and have omnipresence. You are and have the whole of God and all that God is, infinitely and eternally, this very second. All that God is and has is "closer than breathing and nearer than hands and feet." The very I that you are *is* infinity itself, *is* omnipresence itself, *is* eternity itself—everything infinity, omnipresence and eternity is and has.

"I and the father are one"—the same one presence, one being, one body, one universe, one as all. It is because you are one with and as God (the only) that your life, body, world and universe are incapable of being human, personal, mental, physical, material, local, finite, separate, different, born and then dead. "I am ever with you [I am ever you, your life, your body, your universe and all the form of it], and all that I have is yours [is you, is your being, is your body, is your world and everything everywhere in it]." I (God) am you and you are me (God) because I (God) am the only. I and you are the very same *one* being, *one* mind, *one* body, *one* universe because one cannot be two—or 7.2 billion. One is one: "I am the Lord, and there is none else; there is no God besides me."

You are God-being, one with and as the Father (God), and God-being is all you are and all you have because the only existence, the only being, the only life and the only universe is God. Therefore you have just one mind, capacity, character, nature and ability; and that is the mind, capacity, character, nature and ability that is God—infinity. Everything you are and everything you have is not discovered by looking "out" at your life or even looking "in" at your intellect or your body, but is discovered by awakening to the infinity, omnipresence, omniscience, omnipotence and eternity that is your God-being. God-being is your one and only truth, and that truth not only exists fully manifest this minute but is incapable of being different from or less than its full capacity as you, in you and through you. It is incapable of being unavailable in any way or as any form to your every moment of existence. This is your, my and all people's truthful identity, and it is real and practical at every moment. This is the truthful identity of the entirety of your conscious experience which is the entirety of your body. It is the one truth of your body, forever real and practical as actual bodily experience.

Consciousness is body, and consciousness is infinity itself, omnipresence itself, eternity itself, God itself. *Infinity, omnipresence, eternity* are synonyms for consciousness or God. Therefore, consciousness (you, I, all) is non-local, non-personal—consists of nothing else, no opposite, forever boundless, whole and harmonious. You are and I am that; you have and I have that. The whole is omnipresent as every moment and form of you and your experience (universe). Never are you without the whole because the whole is what you are and what you have. Nothing you do or fail to do can change or lessen this eternal, here-and-now truth.

You are and have omnipresence omnipresent. Do you hear that? *You are and have omnipresence omnipresent.* Every moment and everything experienced as every moment (each person, thing, activity, amount and condition of which every moment consists) is—despite appearance—infinity, omnipresence and eternity itself.

MIND DOES NOT CHANGE GOD

God is infinite and omnipresent; therefore what we call "mind" is God. Mind forms. All formation (the universe) is mind formation. Without mind there is no formation. The universe and everything in it and of it is infinite and omnipresent because its form—mind—is God, which is infinite and omnipresent.

God *is* mind *is* form. And because God is one, the seeming three aspects of being (God, mind, form) are not three separate or different aspects, but one. So we can understand that because God is mind is form, all form is of the very same substance, nature and quality of God (infinite, omnipresent and eternal), incapable of being different from or less than God. Infinity forever remains infinity, omnipresence forever remains omnipresence, eternity forever remains eternity. You cannot change that which is the only into something different. Infinity is incapable of becoming finite;

omnipresence is incapable of becoming locally present; eternity is incapable of becoming temporal—even a temporal human life of seventy, eighty, ninety or one hundred years.

Such belief is nonsensical the moment it is realized that God is the only, and God is infinity, omnipresence and eternity. If God is the only, which is true, then all is infinite, omnipresent and eternal; if God is the only, God is completely and utterly unchangeable. Think. It would take "another" power "additional" to God and acting over God to change God. Not only "another" and "additional-to-God" power, it would take a "greater" power than God to change God. Surely then, the greater power would have to be God, and the God we thought was God would not be God but something less than God. Do you see how nonsensical all this is?

GOD IS THE ONLY

God is the only, therefore the only power. God is the infinite, eternal, omnipresent one power. There is nothing "other" than God; therefore the only power is God (good) power. There is no other power, therefore no other influence or condition that can "change" God into something different from or less than itself—even for a second.

We begin to realize the utter impossibility of the infinitude of God "and" a different or lesser experience when we lift our awareness into that of God alone. All the scriptures of the world, in their own way, have given us the truth of God being the only life, presence, power and form. "I am the Lord, and there is none else; there is no God besides me." If "the Lord" is the one and only (which the Lord is), then we and all are that. Let us then get on with knowing what "the Lord" is because only in discovering what the Lord is do we discover who and what we are, what our truth is, what our world and its truth is.

I am God, and there is none else.[1]
I am God, and not man.[2]
There is one God; and there is none other but he.[3]

Only I (consciousness) am, and that I is God. This being true, you and I and all have to be, and are, that same I alone because there is no other. Because God is the only, in order to know yourself you have to get to know God. When we get to know God as being the one spiritual, incorporeal, omnipresent and eternal presence, the one life alone, then we discover that we are that. We discover the truth that "I am that I am," and in so doing, walk into our truth and freedom of being.

Certainly, as we observe truth through the mind, we experience it conceptually and objectively. We experience our God-being and -world as seemingly objectified, finite, local form, condition, place, activity and amount. But "judge not by the appearance" because all is God—unchanged God. Our objective experience of God does not change God into *actual* objectified form. All is forever God and nothing less than God. As we awaken to this truth, we arrive at a tremendous point in our lives: the fact that all form is—despite appearance—as good, infinite, omnipresent and eternal as God. *Mind, body and world, and everything everywhere in and of the world are as good, infinite, omnipresent and eternal as God because there is none else but God.*

CONSCIOUSNESS *IS* EXPERIENCE

Whatever is happening in individual consciousness *is* individual experience. If belief is happening in your or my consciousness, then belief—and its pairs of good and bad—is our experience. The degree to which God is happening in consciousness is the degree to which God is the good and harmony of our experience.

A being filled with God evidences his or her consciousness as

[1] Isaiah 45:22 [2] Hosea 11:19 [3] Mark 12:23

the forms of God. The forms that make up his and her world experience are God-like (good without opposite) instead of belief-like (good and bad). The important truth to realize is this: God consciousness *is* God form or God world; God consciousness *is* "earth as it is in heaven." Do not wish for God consciousness to heal or pacify, prosper or harmonize that which is believed, by its appearance, to be sick or diseased, lacking or limited, discordant or unfulfilled. God consciousness reveals all to be good, healthy, abundant, harmonious and peaceful. "The earth [consciousness-experience] is full of the goodness of God."

God consciousness has been called the healing consciousness. But God consciousness does not actually heal anyone or anything—even though, to material sense, it appears to. God consciousness *is* forever the wholeness and harmony of itself, simply now witnessed as good form wherever its presence is experienced. "Where the spirit [presence] of the Lord is, there is liberty."

People are healed of their diseases, fed when they are hungry, comforted when they are afraid, freely supplied when they lack any good thing or condition, made safe and secure, and presented with glorious opportunity when their world seems shut to them. Injustice and cruelty dissolve. All of these miracles of truth and countless others become evident where the presence of spirit is, but what is actually witnessed is the spiritualizing of awareness which reveals truth where untruth seemed to exist.

God, therefore mind and form, is the quality and condition of itself alone. Truth does not have illness, disease, injury, sadness, loneliness, lack, limitation or discord. These conditions simply do not exist in God, therefore not in God-being, -mind, -body and -world. There is nothing disharmonious—not even a single breath or hair—in God, in truth. As truthful consciousness is lived as the totality of experience, then all "else," all "shadows," all lower levels of awareness simply dissipate as the dark of night melts in the presence of dawn.

The dark, the discord, of our experience never is reality. It is false experience without principle or law to support it, without the substance of God (the only reality) to support and sustain it. Discord of any name or nature is not an entity but a lack of God awareness, just as dark is not an entity but a lack of light.

Only God is; therefore only God-entity is. Nothing "else" has reality; nothing "else" is a real entity; everything "else" is simply believed entity. Disease and discord are nothing but collectively believed and individually accepted difference from God, or separation from God—a believed lesser state of being than God-being. As we continue to believe we are different from, less than, and separate from God, certainly we suffer in many if not all departments of life, just as the vine quickly and continuously suffers if it is pulled and separated from the earth.

As the dawn of truth rises in the individual, lifting awareness from materiality to a degree of spirituality, the more harmonious, healthy and bountiful forms of that degree of spiritual awareness become evident. Nothing *actual* has changed or improved. It is *our higher awareness of God as all* that evidences itself as the greater visible and tangible reality of our experience. It *appears as if* wonderful healing of discordant experience takes place. That which was diseased, ill, injured, lacking, limited or discordant in any way quickly or gradually dissolves; and truthful, healthy, abundant, peaceful and harmonious form emerges.

PERSONALIZATION "IMPRISONS" TRUTH

One of the greatest secrets of healing, and being healed, is impersonalization. Even if we've taken in and digested all the truth of life and healing there is to know, if we continue to believe that we, our minds and our bodies are personal, physical, structural and local, we "imprison" truth within that belief. Locked within belief, truth cannot "escape" into our senses, and if our senses are not filled with the presence of truth, our body-sense remains absent of the abundance of life it actually is and has. The visibility of the fullness of life and health remains "locked inside" our conviction of I, me, mine. We must enable truth to "escape" and fill our senses, and this occurs the moment we impersonalize our sense of being, body and world.

The presence of life and health cannot be evident as a personal sense any more than light can be evident as dark. Personal sense is a "dark" or unillumined state of awareness. As we impersonalize our awareness, truth instantly "escapes" and floods our senses. The dam of personal belief is breached and an infinity of truth-water floods the land of our being. Our senses are filled with the light of truth, and the body is quickly experienced as the perfection it truly is and always has been—the "image and likeness" of God, healthy, whole and vital.

THE KEY

We have believed ourselves to be personal beings with a personal mind and body, living in a personally experienced world filled with possessions, qualities and conditions personal to us. The truth is entirely different, and that truth is this: Only God is, and God is one and impersonal, spirit not matter, eternal and unchanging. God is infinite and omnipresent; therefore the whole of God exists equally and simultaneously, fully manifest as each being and form throughout infinity. God is *individual* being, mind, body and world and all that the world contains—but never *personal* being. And because God is all, all is spirit not mental, physical, or material; not personal, local, finite, or temporal.

The only presence is God, the only form is God, the only activity is God. The only life, therefore, is God. The only mind is God, the only body is God. And God is one. *I am that I am. . . . and besides me there is none else.*

God is consciousness; therefore life is consciousness, I is consciousness, mind is consciousness, body is consciousness, world and everything it contains are consciousness. And consciousness is infinite—infinity itself, omnipresent—omnipresence itself, eternal—eternity itself. Consciousness is never local, never personal, never mental, never physical, never material, and cannot be.

In this way we hear and understand the truth of God being all, therefore the truth about us, our body and our world being nothing other than God. When the truth (that being, mind and body are consciousness) first breaks through, it is a revelation that instantly and forever changes one's life experience.

I is consciousness not mentality, body is consciousness not physicality, world is consciousness not materiality; every thing, amount, activity, place, condition and circumstance are consciousness not matter.

You see, even as long-time truth students, many have not yet connected the truth that consciousness, being all (infinite and omnipresent), is what mind *is,* what body *is,* what world and everything in it *is*. In this "disconnected" state of awareness we have fallen into the trap of believing that we are mental and physical beings, existing locally, temporarily "alive" for a short span of years before "death." We have believed that our human self with its physical body has a spiritual *aspect* to it, buried so deeply within that it's difficult if not impossible to find. Not a word of this is true, and it is nothing but this belief that makes it difficult to awaken.

Only God is, which means humanity, mentality, physicality and materiality are nothing but *sense*. Sense is never reality but always a sense *of* reality. We are having a material *sense* of that which is one hundred percent spirit or God. As long as we do not infuse sense with belief, we experience the true "image-and-likeness" forms of God. But the moment we believe something—anything—about the forms of sense, we immediately "imprison" God within us and leave ourselves exposed to the good and bad of belief. Realize that the only truth about self, mind, body and world is consciousness itself, and because God is infinite and omnipresent, all form (including the body) is totally (inside and out) consciousness.

The one, the only and literal truth of the body is that it is the infinity, omnipresence and eternality of consciousness. The body is God consciousness, there being no other substance, life or form. Like gravity, the body is never local but is individually experienced as each now moment. We have mistaken each moment of now to be a local moment, even a local position. But only consciousness is, which means locality and position are just sense, not reality. Such is the magnificence and freedom of the body.

THE BODY IS LIFE ETERNAL

Even though the appearance is convincingly corporeal and physical, life, the body, and everything in and of life and the body (absolutely everything happening in life and absolutely all bodily organs and functions) are infinite, omnipresent and eternal.

Nothing of life or body is *actually* mental, physical or material even though it appears to be. "Judge not by the appearance." All of life and body (and world) is incorporeal, spirit, consciousness, therefore infinite, omnipresent and eternal. Infinity cannot be made finite, omnipresence cannot be made local, and eternity cannot be made temporal. We *experience* moment by objective moment, but our experience is of the only substance, presence and form that exists: *consciousness*—infinity, omnipresence and eternity. "I am in the world but not of it." Despite belief, despite appearance, and despite every testimony to the contrary, *only God is*; therefore only consciousness is—only infinity, omnipresence and eternity is. There is no existence other than God existence because God is the only, and God *is* existence. There is no alternative or lesser or different nature or quality of true life and body, of true world and everything everywhere in it. There is no other actual life, body or world we can experience because *only God is.* "I am the Lord, and there is none else; there is no God besides me."

Everything everywhere, no matter what belief names it (self, mind, body, thing, amount, activity, place or condition), is infinity, omnipresence, eternity. And because infinity-omnipresence-eternity is the *only,* it is incapable of being anything different from or less than itself alone. Our level of awareness has moment-by-moment *experience* of life (God) which, if we believe appearance at face value, makes infinity appear to be finite, omnipresence appear to be locally present, and eternity appear to be temporal. Again and again we are reminded, "Judge not by the appearance, but judge righteous judgment."

You are, your body is, and all the organs, functions, cells, atoms, and sub-atomic particles are, this minute and forever, life eternal, infinite, omnipresent, incorporeal God itself—even in what we call "human" experience. Nothing can change the one truth that God alone is. Yes, we are having a finite and ever-local *sense* of the infinity and omnipresence and eternity that we are. But sense does not make it real. It only seems to be real if we attach our belief to sense itself.

Our body sense or that of a loved one's or student's or neighbor's may be suffering in some way or a number of ways. A local place or function of the body may be painful, injured, aging or decrepit, may be lacking vitality, youthfulness or strength. Certainly we may be struggling with our body. I know it; I had such an experience, so I have particular love and compassion for anyone who is suffering in any way.

But you see, the way we become free (as I did and as you can too) of that diseased and painful body experience and the suffering it brings with it, is exactly in the way described throughout these pages. Wellness and wholeness (healing) become evident by the spiritualizing of awareness. In this lifted state of awareness, the whole and perfect body of consciousness becomes tangible and real to our experience. It has always been right here in its whole and perfect state, but we have lived with a false *sense* of it. We have accepted a collective belief about what the body is—human, physical and temporary, subject to both good and bad. But even as we have entertained that belief (therefore experienced it) the true and perfect body has been standing right there, unaffected by our belief (as all truth is). The moment truth is realized, we can rest the false experience. We withdraw our belief and attachment to the appearance of disease and the pain and suffering we experience, and in and "through" our released and rested state begin to *feel* the true body of consciousness "happening." It is the feeling of God happening within that reveals the truthful body through the now dissipating fog of belief. Healing has no trouble becoming evident when we are released, rested, receptive, and feeling the presence of God taking place.

NOTHING RESISTS TRUTH

Because truth is the only presence, there is no resistance to truth. It would take a "second" or "obstructing" presence to resist truth, but there is no "other" presence in all of the infinitude. Nothing resists the full experience of the spiritual body appearing as our whole and healthy physical sense of body; rather belief merely *clouds* our body experience.

As soon as we know this truth, release ourselves from the cloudy sense-experience of the body, and then rest openly and receptively in God, we quickly begin to witness the true body coming into tangible experience as the clouds of belief are dissolved. We simply sit still, open and receptive in the presence of God, and *let* our true body become real and tangible to our senses. The experience happens for us—for our sense of being and body. "The father [the truth] that dwells in me, he does the works." As we feel "the works [the presence]" of truth happening within, the clouds of belief are dissolved for us by those works, not by any effort we make or can make. *Only God is;* therefore only *God can.* Truth does the work, and as it is felt happening within, our cloudy sense is cleared to reveal the truthful body which has forever stood right where we are as our one and only true body.

To human sense a healing takes place. But actually the true and eternally present and perfect spiritual body is *revealed* as the clouds of belief are dissolved.

Sixteen

Nothing "Local" Can Be Healed

Our realized spiritual identity must become the very blood of our blood and bone of our bone. We must have a living awareness of God as all, a conviction. Our state of being changes from that of personal need, desire and effort to that of impersonal relaxation, spaciousness, receptivity and beholder. It is at this point that a sufficient measure of God consciousness has been attained, and once it has, not only are the fruits plainly visible for all to see and to share in, but no one in the world can persuade us otherwise. It is at this point that we truly know the truth, that we discover the authority, conviction and strength of our spiritual identity actually living in and as and through us. Truth has become the very breath of our existence, the very substance of our being, the impulse of our activity and the fulfillment of our purpose.

This is what God realization or God consciousness means. It is never an intellectual knowledge alone, but truth itself living us, the reality and principle of *God-as-all* alive, vital and visible throughout our consciousness.

The intellect alone cannot know or behold truth; remember this. The intellect is an "outer" awareness faculty—humanly, mentally, physically and materially adept. But God, our one truth and reality and the one truth and reality of all is before the intellect—"closer than breathing, nearer than hands and feet." God is found in a place of awareness far deeper within our being, undetectable by the intellect, in "the secret place of the most high [the most deep and pure]."

"The kingdom of God is within you." Spiritual awareness is released from deep within, and must be spiritually nourished and nurtured so that it is able to take root. It grows in the silence and spiritual receptivity of being. In the garden of silence and receptivity, it soon "pushes through" into the earthly awareness, appearing "materially" like a young vine pushing through the soil. This is when material awareness describes it as being "real and tangible," but the reality of it has been realized and evidenced well before material awareness has been able to detect it.

THE HEALING EXPERIENCE

Let us now experience healing. Divine wisdom tells us that if we wish to know and evidence the truth of being (mind, body, world and universe), we must know and evidence the truth of God because God is all. Man (all being) and all that man is and experiences (man's universe and everything everywhere in it and of it) is God.

"I am the Lord, and besides me there is none else." Each and every being, thing, activity, amount, place and condition is God. We, at our current level of awareness, simply *sense* that which we are and have (God) objectively, three-dimensionally, as the multiplicity of our universal form and activity. But sense does not change God or truth. That which we sense as "ourselves" and "our" objective, three-dimensional universe of mind, body and form is God—each and every grain of it.

"I and the father are one." Only God is, only one is—only one life, one being, one mind, one body and one presence is. God is the one, the only life, being, mind, body and truth, and God is infinite, omnipresent and eternal. This is why, when students attempt to heal their or their loved one's "personal, local, temporal" body, they fail. *Nothing "local" can be healed.* Better stated, nothing local can be *revealed* as its true health, vitality, harmony, wholeness and perfection because the truth of being and body is God; and God is not personal, local or temporal but is infinite, omnipresent and eternal.

Let us understand this healing truth now. Hear this thoroughly and deeply, with vitality, with a sense of reality. If only God is (and of course only God is; therefore only infinity, omnipresence and eternity is), then "locality" does not exist. The experience of being local and personal, and existing for only a certain number of years or decades is simply a false sense of the infinity, omnipresence and eternity of being that we all truthfully are. Therefore, because nothing local actually exists, nothing sensed as personal, local or temporary can be healed (revealed as its true form).

Because only God is, only God can evidence God. Only God can reveal the truth of form—the "image and likeness" of God as the forms of experience. And because truth is not local but omnipresent, truthful form cannot be evidenced in or through the belief in locality. God or truth is incapable of being personal, local or temporary. This is why it is utterly impossible to evidence God in, or for what is believed to be a personal, local, temporal being and body. God, therefore form, is infinite, omnipresent and eternal, all one. God *is* the infinitude; the infinitude *is* what God is, omnipresent as the infinity and eternity of perfect form, fully existent at every point of the infinitude at the same time.

Many metaphysics students tell me they have experienced healing. But their healing does not last; these students have to keep working at their health, their relationships, their prosperity and their harmony. And so realize this: if you have ever experienced what you believed was the healing of a *local* being, body, thing, amount, place, activity or condition, it had nothing to do with true healing (God realization or illumined consciousness). This may be shocking, but it is very important to realize if you are now to lift into and experience true healing and transformation of being.

Any unsustained healing is not true healing. True healing sustains because God is invariable. Once God has truly been experienced as the health and vitality of the body, the healing is invariable. Any variable state of life or health is so only because it is not truly evidenced God-life or God-health. It is a temporary bout of greater life or health awareness—an improved belief—but it isn't God. God is infinite, omnipresent and eternal and can only be evident *as* infinity, omnipresence and eternity. True healing lasts forever because *God itself is evident.*

OMNIPRESENCE, NOT LOCAL PRESENCE

God is omnipresent, not locally present, and can only be evident as omnipresence. Equally, God is eternal and can only be evident as eternity. To evidence God we have to "seek the kingdom of God," the kingdom of infinity, omnipresence and eternity, rather than the kingdom of that which seems to be (finiteness, local presence, and temporal life). "Seek not [the things of experience, that which seems to be], but rather seek ye the kingdom of God, and all these things shall be added unto you [will populate your senses of mind, body, and everything everywhere in your world]."

God is incorporeal, not corporeal. To seek the kingdom of God we have to seek the incorporeal, not the corporeal. The corporeal experience is just our sense of that which is entirely incorporeal with no corporeality in it whatsoever. The corporeal sense is true and good, and acts as true and good *as long as we do not believe it to be reality in and of its own self.* Only the incorporeal is God, reality, truth—the actual. Therefore, to seek God is to seek the kingdom of incorporeality (infinity, omnipresence, eternity) which has in it, by definition, no corporeality, no finiteness or locality, or personal "him, her, it or condition." It is and has nothing but the whole of God, fully present, visible and tangible, fully living and perfectly formed, therefore nothing that requires healing.

At this level of awareness, the "things" of experience are no longer real to us in and of their own selves. The thousands of things and conditions in our experience each day are finite, local and temporal mind pictures or images. They are mind forms of the one infinity, omnipresence and eternity that is spirit or God. Only God itself (incorporeality, infinity, omnipresence, eternity) is real to us, and indeed *is* the only reality. And that one reality is incapable of being, or being witnessed, in or as or for that which is unreal (human, mental, physical, material, local, finite belief).

Do you see, therefore, that any health or harmony evidenced by an individual's effort—even if they succeed—is not, and cannot be, truth evidenced because God *is,* and does not require effort to *be is. Is* already is, and is fully present, visible and tangible to its own consciousness—the God or incorporeal consciousness. That consciousness does not have a problem or any person, thing or condition that *can* be ill, discordant, poor or incomplete. It has God alone in it and as it, as all. This is the consciousness that evidences the forms of itself, which to material belief *appears to be* the healing of that which was ill, discordant, poor or incomplete.

Any "healing" that is impermanent is a form of improved belief about that which is, in appearance, a "real problem" occurring in or to or against the physical body. Illness, disease or injury is always local, objective "bad" form and activity, occurring in a personal, local, physical body. This is all the experience of *belief about* that which is actually the one body of God, the spiritual, incorporeal body which is forever whole, healthy and perfect and forever remains unaffected by belief or matter. And because all belief has an opposite, a healthy, youthful and vital body can be (and almost infallibly is sooner or later) affected by the opposite belief—ill health, senescence and languor, and finally death. It is because the substance and form of both the good and bad of this body experience are belief, that belief can also "heal" it by replacing "ill, diseased or injured" belief with "healthy, youthful and vital" belief. It is mental effort and conviction, and at its own level it is good and fine. But it is not God, nor is it the God experience of the body which is both effortless in experience and permanent in form.

All belief is temporal. Sooner or later, the effects of belief change and let us down, and we find ourselves back to square one with the same problem of illness, disease or injury hounding us again, usually worse than before. "Except the Lord build the house, they labor in vain that build it."

HEALING BY A PRACTITIONER

Spiritual healing is permanent as long as the practitioner is of true spiritual consciousness. True spiritual consciousness is that which never attempts to heal a local, personal problem or disease or disharmony, but evidences the presence of God as individual being and body. In that way, true and permanent health and wholeness are brought through.

However, if you have experienced healing from a practitioner, yet after a time you became ill again, it is because you unwittingly "sinned again," as it is coined in scripture. When we drop from the spiritually illumined experience a practitioner provides, back to physical belief and material living, back to the sense of separation and difference from God, we either quickly or eventually experience the problem returning. But when, following healing, we "ride the wave" of illumined awareness given us and begin to be aware and live more spiritually, the healing is permanent. Hence the Master told all he healed to "go and sin no more."

The experience of healing—which is spiritually lifted or illumined experience provided by the practitioner, revealing itself as health and wholeness—should always be received and honored by the recipient as a gift of illumined awareness and then maintained. When illumined awareness is kept alight (as the Olympic flame is kept alight) by studying truth, meditating, and beginning to live by periods of silence throughout the day, an individual finds him or herself released from belief and entering the doorway of heaven. All the treasures of heaven open to any individual who devotes a good measure of each day to God, to spirit and truth.

Those who have received healing, yet do not know of the wonders and miracles available to them as they maintain even a measure of God awareness and spiritual living, fail to realize what their healing experience actually was. Their healing experience was the practitioner's illumined consciousness, which imbued their senses with the light of truth, revealing the truthful body. They believe a personal, local body was healed of a physical, local illness, disease or injury, and then run back into the mental and material world, happy with their healing and their new-found vitality and strength, telling everyone they know about the miracle that occurred. Unfortunately they are headed right back into, not only the reverse of the healing, but in most cases, a worse problem than the one which was healed. "Behold, thou art made whole: sin no more, lest a worse thing come unto thee."

It's a hard thing to have to tell people and it's a harder thing to have to watch. But I think it is important that we make this clear because it is time for us who are hearing this message to lift and stay lifted in truth, thereby being the illumined consciousness that is the liberty of experience, is the life and harmony of the body and all of this world's experience.

You see, we are dealing with principle, the one supreme principle itself. It is only as we attune *ourselves*—lift and spiritualize *our* awareness—to the consciousness, the principle of oneness, infinity, omnipresence, eternity, the incorporeal that we witness it throughout our formed (earthly) experience. But if we drop in awareness again, if we ignore the principle of God-as-all, then our God experience crashes and burns just as the harmony of our math would collapse if we ignored the principle of math.

The same is true of our experience of any principle. If we do not adhere to the principle of aerodynamics, then our plane is either unable to fly or quickly drops from the sky if it does manage to lift from the ground. It is impossible to take off and keep our airplane in the sky if we do not attune ourselves and our aircraft design to the principle of aerodynamics. Aerodynamics will never, in a thousand years, come "down" to our level of non-aerodynamics and make our non-aerodynamically-designed plane fly. No non-aerodynamically-designed craft is able to fly, and no non-God consciousness is able to evidence the world's true health, harmony, love, abundance, peace and fulfillment of God.

NO "LOCAL" TRUTH

Expecting or assuming truth, God, life itself (which, remember, is infinity, omnipresence, eternity, the incorporeal) to heal or reveal itself in or as or for a "local, human" being, with a "local, physical" body, suffering from a "local" organ that is diseased, injured or malfunctioning, or some other malfunction is utterly impossible.

Such expectation is utterly out of truth or spirit. It is a metaphysical rather than spiritual degree of awareness, which has no God in it whatsoever. God is omnipresent, impartial and unconditional; God is spirit "and in him is no darkness [matter or materiality] whatsoever." The whole of God exists in and as each and every being, body, thing, amount and place. God *is* all being; God *is all,* period. No person or practice can gain favor from God to "heal" that which God is not. No person or practice can gain more of God where it is believed that less than the fullness of God currently exists.

God is forever the whole of itself as all! There is no favored locality, no favored person, place, condition or circumstance. There isn't a person in the world—even the greatest saint or master who ever lived—who has more God than the rest of us less saintly people, or who is able to receive favors from God versus the rest of us who cannot. "He maketh his sun to rise on the evil and on the good, and sendeth rain on the just and on the unjust." All is one-and-omnipresent; all is the very presence and form of oneness-and-omnipresence which is entirely impartial. Oneness and omnipresence are as incapable of partiality as is math or aerodynamics. God is the *entirety of all* and the *only;* therefore "I am that I am," and all is that I am. Then, not only is no person, place or condition able to gain the favor of God, but none needs to. God is already fully present even where God seems not to be.

Indeed, it is impossible for God to have favorites. God is principle and cannot dish out favors anymore than the principle of math can dish out the number 100 as a favor when we're in need of 10 x 10. God does not and cannot favor us as a result of our steadfast study of truth, while those who have studied less steadfastly receive less favor from God. God doesn't care how faithfully we've studied, nor does God know. God knows nothing about our efforts or non-efforts, nor does God know anything about our pain and struggling, our desires and needs. All such belief that God does know is nonsense. Nothing we do or fail to do affects God in the slightest. God *is*—period. God is principle, and as such is fully, equally and unconditionally present everywhere throughout infinity at the same time. *We* have to attune *ourselves to God,* rather than expecting God, and all the good that God is, to bend in favor of us and our needs and desires.

TRUTH CANNOT BE PERSONALIZED

No one can personalize God and the good that God is. It is impossible to personalize principle, including the principle that is God, truth. It is impossible to "bring" truth "down to" or "into" a personal being or condition and have truth heal, love, pacify, harmonize or prosper him, her or it. God knows nothing about our sense of personal being and condition. No such being or condition actually exists because God is all; therefore *God itself* is the actuality of all being, condition and existence. That which is real cannot be made to exist in or for that which is unreal. The "human" being and body are just believed (dreamed) being and body. Nothing real can be brought to exist in a belief or dream. If you attempted to place real furniture in a home of your dreams, the furniture has nowhere to exist. It cannot exist or be visible and real to you because the home exists as a dream only. In the same way, God cannot exist (in experience) as your real being and body when you're attempting to evidence God in or for your believed (dreamed) being and body.

One cannot bring truth "to," or make it evident "for," or experience it "heal" a non-existent being, body, body part, or any other "local" him, her, it or condition. One cannot bring God to a locality and reveal that locality's truth. There is no truth to a locality. There is no "local" God. God is omnipresence, incapable of becoming local presence. Therefore, because God is all, there is no local or personal state of health, love, harmony, abundance, joy, freedom or justice, or the opposites of these. These are appearances only, belief only. It is simply impossible to evidence God locally or personally, in a finite, space-based, time-based form. God is infinite and omnipresent, not finite and locally present. And because God is all, incapable of changing into something God is not, God can only be evident *as itself.*

God can only be evident as infinity and omnipresence. This is the key. "Who sends an angel here to potentize this pool for just a favored few?" There are no God-favored people, places or substances on earth, or anywhere throughout infinity. No one, not even the Master, is a special dispensation of God. No substance or place has more God to it, or in it, or available as it than any other. God is one and omnipresent. The *whole* is, and fully exists, and is fully and freely available to experience at every point and place throughout infinity, without limit. Any lesser experience is simply lesser *God awareness* and has nothing to do with fact and reality. All less-than-God experience is our limited or lowly illumined *sense* of being, not our reality.

"I know it is not God who could potentize the pool for just a favored few." There it is. God cannot dish out favors; God cannot be more present anywhere than God already is; God cannot be made evident locally, for a particular person or group of people, or a particular condition or event. *God already fully is!* And the fullness of God-is is everywhere and equally present, right where you are, as you, already manifested and demonstrated. God cannot be evidenced locally. God cannot be witnessed or "demonstrated" locally.

> I know it is not God, for he deals just the same with everyone. One has no better chance in heaven's healing fountain than another. The fount of health is in your soul, it has a door locked fast, the key is faith. And everyone can have this key and may unlock the door and plunge into the healing fount and be made whole.

The healing fountain is *God awareness,* the awareness that God is one and omnipresent, unconditionally equal, with no more or less, no bias, no favor. To receive favor or preference from any principle is impossible, including from the supreme principle that is God. To ask or pray to God to heal "me or mine" is nonsensical and impossible. *Ye ask, and receive not, because ye ask amiss.*

Your father in heaven . . . he maketh his sun to rise on the evil and on the good, and sendeth rain on the just and on the unjust. Imploring or expecting God to heal you or another is like asking God to pour rain in your yard alone or in the yard of someone you favor, rather than expecting rain to fall in all yards for everyone equally. No one in his or her right mind would ask favors of the rain or of math, and we in our right mind—in God mind—would not ask favors of God. God *already is*—this is what we must know.

Seventeen

God Is Not Personal

Can you imagine the folly of a friend praying for rain in his garden alone? Can you envisage that friend believing he has achieved sufficient rain realization, and then sitting in silence waiting for his demonstration of rain? He'd wait forever, and he would deserve the wait! Expecting rain to fall for him personally is nonsensical, and worse, expecting the principle of rain to be unprincipled is more nonsensical. Principle can only be itself, never unlike itself.

God cannot be unlike God. Therefore, the demonstration of God cannot be unlike God. If we expect it to be, we fail. Hear that. God does not fail, *we do.* We may well utter the most graceful prayer, have the most extraordinary meditation, sit in the most blissful silence. We may well experience euphoric peace flooding our being. But all of this cannot "get out" into experience if we expect it to bring us personal good or gain. Personalization blocks God from being tangible and visible to our senses. It is folly to believe in a personal God who will dish out favors, healing, prosperity, safety, security, justice or peace to some but not all. If we believe in such a God, we are attempting to personalize God, localize God, and finitize God. But God—including our experience (demonstration) of God—*cannot be unlike God.*

Do you see the folly of personalizing God, and the folly of expecting personal results? Yet millions pray to God in just this way. Even spiritual students the world over meditate for such personal good, and sit in hours of silence waiting for their "ordered good" to arrive from their God. Oh yes, they use "spiritual" terms for their attempts, such as *meditation, demonstration* and *manifestation,* but still they wait and wait forever. Why? There is no such God that can make these demonstrations or produce these manifestations!

"Ye ask, and receive not, because ye ask amiss." You study truth, you pray and meditate, and you sit in hours of silence; yet you see no evidence of your good, because you study, pray, meditate and sit in silence amiss. The root of asking and expecting amiss is attempting to personalize God, believing that God can be evident for you and your needs, or for the good of any person, thing or condition in your world.

Let us hear and understand the principle of God once and for all. God (and any synonym for God—spirit, truth, "I," consciousness, incorporeality, infinity, omnipresence, omniscience, omnipotence, life, love, prosperity, peace, harmony) cannot be witnessed "for" or "in" or "by" a personal, local "him, her or it," no matter how "spiritual" that person, desire or need may be.

WHY GOOD PEOPLE SUFFER

This is why we witness even the holiest, most selfless, loving and generous people—those who devote their whole lives to helping others—suffer with the same measure of illness, disease, injury or injustice the rest of the population does. This is why we witness spiritual students no more protected from or immune to the world's pain and suffering than is the general populace. It should not be this way. You would assume the experience of spiritual students would be different, at least that of the majority of them. It isn't so. Why? Surely as we seek truth and begin to live by truth we suffer less, we are less likely to become ill or diseased, are immune to the lacks and limitations affecting the rest of the world. But this is not the case. We all know many truth students who suffer health problems, lack and limitation problems, financial problems, relationship problems, home and business problems, stress and unhappiness problems. It's sad and hard to watch. But when we watch such struggle in our realization of the one *principle* of truth, we have light on the reason: *Ye ask amiss.*

It is up to us, my friends—each individually—to take truth so seriously, to be so devoted and dedicated to truth by such a degree that we may be and show the way. The Master tells us this very thing: *It is the father's good pleasure to give you the kingdom* . . . and *By their fruits shall you know them.* It is the "good pleasure" of the principle that is God to give us the limitless and unconditional fruits of good, and in this way—by the tangible and visible fruits filling every area of our life—does the world know and see that we have truth. Only in this way is "my father glorified": by our being God-fruitful beings, beholding and giving to the world the treasures of heaven which are abundantly evident as we live as and by the principle of God as all.

Only by your understanding and living the God (truth) principle is "my Father glorified"—is truth made tangible and real in every-day experience. Only as the impersonal self can you live in the impersonal world, filled with impersonal people, things, activities, amounts, places and conditions; only then can God be tangibly evident as all that you are and have. Only as the impersonal self can you "give" to or evidence God for others, and for all that you touch and do in the world. Only as the impersonal self do you have the "healing consciousness," the presence of being that raises the ill and diseased and even the dead into life and vitality; that beholds illness, disease and injury being dissolved and repaired right in front of your eyes; that multiplies the loaves, fishes and dollars for those who are hungry and in lack; and that pacifies disagreement, unrest or even war.

WITNESSING HARMONY THROUGHOUT THE BODY OF AWARENESS

As we expand our awareness into and throughout our true body—the infinity of our consciousness—knowing that God is all, and remain rested and relaxed, beholding God itself taking place, we watch our bodies heal, our relationships fill with love and peace and purpose, our businesses prosper, and our world harmonize.

It is as we continually impersonalize self and every form of experience and, in the silence and receptivity of the impersonal self, *behold God taking place as all,* that we are being the god of our experience. In this way alone are we "glorifying God." We are doing God's work only when we realize God has no work to do. We are "doing the works you see me do, and greater than these" only when we live the impersonal self that God is as us, and when we live the experience of the beholder of God revealing itself as all being, thing, amount, place and condition.

We are being the god (truth) of our experience only as we have no preference, no opinion, no idea, and no judgment ("Judge not according to the appearance"), but give ourselves and our world and every detail and form of it to God, and *let God get on with being God* as all we are and have. *Then* is God "glorified" (visible and tangible) by our existence; then is God fulfilled in and as and throughout our consciousness, and as every person, place and thing that touches our consciousness.

Despite belief and appearance, God is the only, and God is impersonal and impartial; therefore all is impersonal and impartial. God "makes his sun [truth] shine on the evil and the good, and his rain [truth] fall on the just and the unjust" only because God and all that God is and has is impersonal and impartial. Hear that! *All* that God is and has is impersonal and impartial. If we want the life, love, limitlessness, harmony and wholeness that God is, we must seek God impersonally and impartially, for impersonal and impartial good. When we do, we can have as much good in our experience as we wish to have—the treasures of truthful self, mind, body and world without limit.

Speaking metaphorically, the sun and the rain are experienced only when we understand that they are universal not personal. We can neither expect the sun to shine *for us,* in our garden alone, nor the rain to fall *for us,* in our neighborhood alone. The sun and the rain simply *are* and never can be personal or partial.

Ah, we say we know this of the principle of the sun and of the rain, and would never expect a personal demonstration from them, yet when it comes to the principle of God, practically every person on earth seeks a personal demonstration. Again, *ye receive not, because ye ask amiss.* To evidence the boundless treasures of God as individual being and as earth, we have to lift our awareness into the universal, impersonal and impartial from the local, personal and partial. When we catch ourselves believing that a particular area, organ or function of the body is ill or diseased or injured, or that another area of our expanded world body is suffering lack or limitation, and then seek God for its healing, we must quickly realize the folly of our effort and stop. Living from this level of awareness, and our effort to get God to heal it, result in only one thing—failure.

THE SECRET OF DEMONSTRATION

This is why even long-time spiritual students struggle to live a life of health, abundance, harmony and wholeness. They still believe they need the apparent good things of life, and still attempt to demonstrate them instead of seeking a greater awareness of what the things truly are. If they sought a greater awareness of the presence of God as all, they would have as many good things and conditions as they wish to have. Having an ever greater living awareness of the presence of God as being the one and the only is the great secret of demonstration. Once we have God as our constant, conscious awareness, we have an abundance of all good things and conditions because God and form are one.

We must relinquish our take on life and give our entire selves to that which self (including its universe of form and experience) truly is—God. As we do, we discover, "I live, yet not I, Christ lives my life." God lives my life because God is the only life I am and have; the one presence lives my life because the one presence is the only presence I am and have. That means infinity and omnipresence are living as I and the universe of I.

As God lives my life, all is infinite and omnipresent. Nothing is limited, finite or lacking because God is infinite and omnipresent, and God is all. In truth—in God awareness—all of being, form and activity is infinite and omnipresent, never finite, local, limited or lacking. But again, hear it deeply: *God* is all, *God* is infinite and omnipresent, *God* is life and health, *God* is abundance, safety and security, and *God* is truth and freedom. *God itself* is all, with none else but God itself needed for the tangible good and plentiful experience of all. It is the *God-lived self* that experiences the infinity and omnipresence of the *God-filled world.* This is the key. When mind, body and world is filled with God, the tangible experience of mind, body and world is *of* God: of infinity, omnipresence, life, harmony, peace, freedom and fulfillment of purpose.

Do you now see that any he, she or it which appears to exist locally is just a local or finite sense of reality, not reality itself. God does not exist locally, and because God is the one reality, nothing local is real in and of its own self. Locality is simply a finite sense of that which is forever non-local, universal, infinite, omnipresent, and incorporeal. If we *believe* any beings or objects to be entities in and of their own selves, their presence appears real to us. But belief is just belief, not reality. Only God is real, and it is only reality that evidences itself. Only reality *can* evidence reality.

If you can hear that, you have the entire secret of demonstration. Only God evidences itself, and only God *can.* I cannot, you cannot, and even Jesus cannot: "I of my own self am [and can do] nothing. . . . The Father that dwells in me, he does the works. . . . All things are delivered unto me of my Father." The "Father" is God, which is infinite not finite, omnipresent not locally present, spirit not matter. It is the Father consciousness—God consciousness—that "does the works," heals and pacifies, prospers and harmonizes that of experience which seems to belief to be ill, poor, hungry, incomplete and unfulfilled. God consciousness is the consciousness of spirit, infinity, omnipresence, one. God is not a finite, local being or entity; and it is for this reason that God cannot be made evident finitely or locally no matter how much we need or desire, or how much we pray, meditate and sit in silence for God to be.

GOD EVIDENT AS ITSELF

God, which is omnipresent, can only be evident *as itself.* Omnipresence is fully present at every place and point of the infinite at the same time. But listen to that: *omnipresence* is fully present. Omnipresence cannot be evident as something it is not. Omnipresence does not (nor can it) become "local" presence, "objectified" presence, "finite" presence, or "personal" presence. Omnipresence is incapable of changing, of becoming anything different from or less than itself alone.

Omnipresence, which is incapable of being anything different from or less than itself, is fully evident at and as every point throughout infinity at the same time—*as itself.* There is the key. If we search for evidence of something omnipresence *is not,* we cannot see the very omnipresence that is perfectly visible and tangible right where we're searching.

In the same way, God which is infinity, is incapable of being finite, local, personal, an object, a shape. Infinity is incapable of being reduced to a name, a finite entity that exists at a certain time and occupies a certain amount of space. Infinity is incapable of being finitized, reduced or contained. Infinity is indeed present at every point of itself at the same time; but, again, we have to realize that infinity is (and can only be) present *as itself*—infinity itself—at every point of itself at the same time.

God which is incorporeality is the only presence. Even though there is no denying that that which is one hundred percent incorporeal appears to be corporeal (solid, finite, local, objectified, separate from every "other" person, thing and place), it isn't. Appearance is not truth. We have a corporeal *sense* of that which is incorporeal. The incorporeal is *forever incorporeal,* even as we sense it corporeally as a "him, her, it, activity, amount or place." Our belief and confusion about the apparent corporeal self, body and world do not change the fact that all is incorporeal. It is for this reason that it is a waste of effort reaching up to God, the incorporeal, expecting the healing of our corporeal problems and diseases. These problems exist only in our corporeal belief. The moment we lift our awareness to that which is (the incorporeality of all), we discover our experience to be free of all problems and diseases.

God cannot heal our false sense of corporeality and make it a better false sense. No principle can heal non-principle; the principle of math cannot heal a mistake in math and make it a lesser mistake. Math can only be itself and the fullness of itself. In the same way, God can only be itself and the fullness of itself. And because God is incorporeal, infinite, omnipresent and eternal, perfectly whole and complete and invariably so, all is forever perfectly whole and complete and invariably so—*but corporeal belief cannot see it.* It is we who have to lift our awareness into God, into the incorporeal, the infinite, the omnipresent, the eternal. Then we see the wholeness, harmony and health of all formation.

It is impossible to evidence God as real and truthful form while we continue to have personal, local, material (un-God-like) belief. Only God is, and God is fully and ever present as all, including the very experience that we (in our un-God-like state) believe needs

God. In other words, what we wish for, pray for, meditate for and sit in silence for is already fully present and already perfectly visible, tangible, manifested and demonstrated as its truthful, whole and harmonious form. *But we cannot see its truthful form while we believe it is something different, something less, something corporeal.*

When we fill ourselves with spiritual sense, we are able, despite appearance, to discern omnipresence, not local presence; the incorporeal, not the corporeal; the infinite, not the finite.

When we know (deeply enough) the truth that all is omnipresence, all is incorporeal, all is infinite, all is the one eternal presence, the only presence; when we really know this truth to the point that it has become the life of our life, the blood of our blood, the bone of our bone, the breath of our breath, the sight of our sight; when no one and no condition can convince us otherwise—despite appearance—then all we have to do is rest in that conviction and behold God becoming tangible as our daily forms of experience.

In this God state of being, omnipresence illumines and fills our awareness with itself so that we become consciously aware of *it* as all, rather than the foggy sense of it we were experiencing as we were filled with belief. As omnipresence (truth) fills our senses, we often feel the presence of peace, or light, or heat, or joy, or release and freedom in spirit. It doesn't matter how it is felt; what matters is that we know truth is now filling our senses and revealing its image and likeness throughout our experience, that the truth of all is emerging as the fog of belief is dispelled.

Being and form sensed through the mind remain the same. All still appears to be human, worldly, corporeal, material, finite, objective, local. But illumined awareness knows and experiences the truth—the infinity, omnipresence, life, harmony and wholeness of all. This is what has been called the "healing consciousness." Illumined awareness is the liberty of unillumined experience. "Where the spirit of the Lord is, there is liberty." The "dark" forms of unillumined awareness are filled with the light of truth to reveal whole and harmonious being, body and world.

"Whereas I was blind, now I see."

Realize that God is, this second and eternally, fully present, fully whole and complete, and fully formed as everything everywhere throughout infinity. There is no such thing as "unformed" God, absent or invisible or intangible or incomplete God, no matter where we find ourselves or what *seems* to be. God is *the one and the only* existence—finished and omnipresent as all, and fully visibly so. There is no "inner" versus "outer" in omnipresence; there is no esoteric versus exoteric, no hidden versus revealed, no here versus there, no within versus without in omnipresence. God is *one,* existing as the whole of itself at and as each point of experience. All mind form is God-form, and as we are filled with God-sense and devoid of belief, we clearly see and *have* God form as the reality of our being, body and world.

Everything everywhere is the fullness of God, therefore the fullness of life, love and harmony, oneness, union, companionship and divine purpose. All is the one (harmonious, perfectly balanced and ordered), working in experience as the one synchronistic whole. All is omnipresent, infinite and perfect God—good without opposite. And that perfect God-good is fully present and real throughout infinity as you and all in your consciousness. In other words, every person, thing, activity, amount, place and condition throughout your universe is fully and already present and tangible as God-good and none else. *Seeing it as it truly is* is the only need.

NO LACK, LIMITATION OR DELAY

There is no lack, no limitation, no delay. God (therefore all good) *is.* This very moment and eternally the whole of God is fully present, fully manifested and already demonstrated at every point throughout infinity at the same time.

It is only by the degree that we do *not* know this truth and fail to *be* this truth that we finitize our sense consciousness. We are being a sense of finiteness instead of infinity, of corporeality instead of incorporeality, of local or personal presence instead of omnipresence, and of temporality instead of eternality. In other words, as we continue to believe we and our body and world condition are something different from God, something other than God, something less than God, the perfect harmony of our conceptual experience remains intangible to us. Being unaware of truth and failing to *be* truth are the only reasons pain and suffering continue in any department of life.

REALIZATION OF OMNIPRESENCE

As we awaken and realize the omnipresence of God, we are opening the windows of awareness through which wholeness and harmony become visible. Omnipresence is whole and equally-present God, therefore whole and equally-present God-good. At each point throughout the infinity of consciousness (any person, thing, activity or place you are conscious of) *there* the whole and equally-present God-good *is*—not only *is*, but is the *totality of the form and life* we observe. "Within" and "without"—*all* is God, one, omnipresence.

Omnipresence is the one and only presence. It does not matter what a particular presence seems to be—human, animal, vegetable, mineral; animate or inanimate. All is God, consciousness, omnipresence, one, and forever whole, without division and category. Only belief divides and categorizes. When we can truly recognize God as the presence appearing to us as Jesus or Gautama *and* the presence appearing to as of a blade of grass, a pebble, a mountain, an ocean, a dollar, a flower and the color and scent of the flower, then we have the consciousness of omnipresence. And when we have the consciousness of omnipresence, we have infinity, harmony and fulfillment as our experience in all departments of life. We have life, love, abundance, happiness, wholeness and nothing less than these because we accept nothing less than the omnipresence of God's being all.

However, by the degree we still believe that appearance is real in and of its own self, we tightly close the windows of awareness, and truth is unavailable to our experience. Lift your awareness to that which is, and in that way keep your senses open and alive to the God-filled universe. *Be* the living God awareness that sees God as everything everywhere. Keep yourself filled with oneness. Know that all is *the one* presence and form despite the multiplicity of apparently different beings, bodies, characters, qualities, things, places and conditions.

Only the one eternal presence exists. Drop the belief in multiplicity, in otherness, in difference—in anything being different from or less than God or one. Forget about decades or years, about days, hours and minutes. Forget about time altogether. God is the all and the only, and because God is eternal, all is eternal. That which seems to be is nothing real at all; therefore multiplicity and its apparent evolution in time is nothing real at all.

Forget about space altogether. There is only one space, and it is called God, and is wholly here, now. The whole of God (therefore the whole infinity and eternity of space) exists in and as the point of a pin, a grain of sand, a cell, an atom and as the totality of you, me and all.

GOD IS

God *is;* God is the *only is.* Whoever or whatever *is,* is not at all what appears to be, but is God. Every point of awareness, every form, every moment of experience *is* and *contains* the whole of God, and none else. "Inside" and "out," only God is.

The whole of God is fully embodied, fully manifested and demonstrated, fully visible and tangible, fully here and now, fully complete. God cannot give you more of itself because you already *are* and *have* and observe nothing but the whole of God as everything everywhere. Equally, God cannot withhold even one grain of itself from you because you *are* the one whole, indivisible and inseparable.

God *is*. Nothing of God can be added; nothing of God can be taken away. You are the very presence called God. All that God is and has is you and yours because God is one, indivisible and omnipresent. "Is it not written in your law [that] ye are gods. . . . You are ever with me, and all that I have is yours." God "and" you are not two, but one; God "and" every thing, place, amount, activity and condition throughout the universe are not two or multiple, but one. *All*, without exception, is God. Knowing this truth, lift into the conscious awareness of God as all—of omnipresence not local presence, of infinity not finiteness, of spirit not matter.

Work out of your consciousness (just as a washing machine works soil out of clothes), and erase entirely the belief in locality being real. Let go of the belief in a personal being named "you" versus other personal beings named John, Mary, Peter and Jane. Drop the belief in objectivity, place and condition being or having any kind of reality in and of their own selves. *Only God is.*

Lift your awareness into *omnipresence*. Lift into the *incorporeal,* into life-form eternal and invariable. Dismiss the belief in age, truly forgetting about calendars and birthdays. They do not mean anything in truth. Celebrate the eternal day, the eternal now. That is your birthday—the eternally new day, the fresh manna of every moment. Celebrate the birth of new awareness at every moment, not a particular calendar date. As you celebrate the ever new birth of awareness you discover ever greater harmony and fulfillment filling your mind, body and world.

Let us celebrate our "birthdays" every minute, every hour, every day. Let us celebrate together, as the spiritual family, because certainly each and every reader of the spiritual message is rising into a greater measure of illumined awareness and the glory and freedom of one being, one mind, one body and one harmonious and divinely purposeful world. The collective spiritualization of being taking place around the globe is a wonder to behold.

I wish to be aware of the one reality alone: God, omnipresence. I wish to understand the truth and reality of omnipresence being the one and only presence no matter how it appears to be to sense. I wish to seek the kingdom of truth alone—the kingdom of God, the kingdom of the omnipresence of spirit alone.

I wish to ever more fully know, understand and rest in the truth that God is all, and that, despite appearance, there is none else. I wish to ever more deeply know and rely on the one truth that God, being all, is the unconditional omnipresence and infinity of all in my experience, that there is none but life, love, harmony, peace and fulfillment of being, body and world.

I wish to ever more continually seek God, spirit and truth alone. I wish to stop seeking that which appears to be needed or desired—that which is personal, local, objective, finite and temporary—and to seek that which all actually is: God, spirit and truth.

By seeking God as all, rather than that which seems to be all, I seek aright and thereby witness the omnipresent life, love, abundance, harmony and freedom that all truly is.

If we wish to evidence the wholeness and harmony of form where, to personal and local sense, form seems to be discordant, diseased or lacking, we must first realize that what we are witnessing is just an image of belief, a false image or form, because we have unwittingly taken on a collective belief, and because all belief has form in our experience, here it is presenting itself to us. It appears to have reality, and to the believer it is real. But to spiritual awareness it is nothing but false imagery, without power, substance, law or principle to sustain itself in experience.

Anything appearing to be local, personal or finite is false imagery, false sense, with no actual reality to it whatsoever. It is belief that closes our awareness, therefore our experience, to that which is. As believers we cannot see God. If we believe an appearance of illness, disease or discord to be real in and of its own self, and then get busy attempting to heal it, we fail because in our state of belief, God is invisible to our senses.

The same applies to our world awareness. If we look out into our wider body of consciousness—our true one body—and believe we are witnessing someone or something incomplete or lacking or discordant (disharmonious life, love, finances, relationship or business "out there"), and then get busy attempting to heal it of its own self, we again fail. Whenever we believe an "it" of any nature, category or character, then attempt to heal that "it" of its own self (prosper "it," harmonize "it," bring life or love or freedom to "it" of its own self) we fail. The very belief in an "it" happening in or to or against us or our world *is itself* the fog that keeps truth from being visible and tangible to us.

LIFT INTO SPIRITUAL AWARENESS

Lift from local, personal, finite sense to *omnipresence*. Lift into and live in God awareness until omnipresence becomes the blood of your blood, the bone of your bone, filling your senses to overflowing.

"Set your affection on things above [God, spirit and truth; infinity and omnipresence as the only reality], not on things of the earth [things of belief]." Cease from believing that you need a personal good or personal healing, and setting your affection on these things. Cease from attempting to have rain fall in "your" yard, or "his" or "hers." Refuse to believe and accept the experience of a diseased organ or function of your or another's physical body; or of a lack of your or another's supply; or of your or another's limited business activity; or of disharmony in your or another's family or neighborhood. These are all personal-sense problems, but nothing *is* personal, either yours or another's; nothing is isolated, separate or different from the whole. All is one and impersonal.

In the realization of oneness, we lose the personal belief of self, and in losing it, we find our freedom in spirit. We awaken to the truth that the sun and the rain are universal, never personal. "God causes his sun to shine upon the good and upon the bad, and pours down his rain upon the just and upon the unjust." Rise into the consciousness of omnipresence. Forget about the way "he, she and it" (the personal sense) appears to be. Nothing of appearance in and of its own self is truth. Only God is; therefore only God itself is truth and its forms.

The only reason there appears to be lack, limitation, disease or discord is the belief that our life, body and world are different, separate and less than God. We have unwittingly adopted a personal, local, finite belief, and we suffer it. And because every belief has an opposite, and every belief has form in our experience, we are caught up in a mind, body and world experience full of opposites. Every good has its opposite. Nowhere in the universe of belief can we find good without opposite—truly reliable and invariable life, health, love, relationship, family, supply, purpose, freedom and fulfillment. We are imprisoned in an existence of belief which is itself the root of all pain and suffering.

What is belief, and how can we be permanently free of it? Belief is the sense of God "and." As soon as we accept God "and" (which we have unwittingly accepted eternally until now, as we awaken), we are filled with a false sense of self, mind, body and world—a self, mind, body and world full of opposites. We break free of the entire universe of belief by awakening to the one universal actuality of God, spirit and truth being the only existence—God (good) without opposite.

How? Ignore appearance and lift into the conscious awareness of God, spirit and truth being the *all* and the *only*. Learn to live with a conscious awareness of *omni*presence being the only presence, and all seeming personal, local or finite presence being appearance only, not reality.

Seek "universal sun and rain" rather than personal, local and finite sun and rain. Seek the experience of *God itself* rather than an experience of personal good and gain. This is the entire secret of healing. We must lift our senses away from personal, local and finite belief, need and desire into the one whole, universal presence that is God. The moment we have achieved it, our senses are filled with spirit and truth instead of humanity and matter. We are now able to see, hear, taste, touch and smell this very world as God sees, hears, tastes, touches and smells it. We experience "earth as it is in heaven." We are aware *as a god* instead of as a human, material believer. We know and experience *God* as every person, thing, place and condition. What appears to humanity to be personal, local, finite and limited is "released" to be impersonal, omnipresent, infinite and free, available fully and equally to and as all. No matter where we look and what we observe, *there God is* as *its* invariable, limitless and unconditional life, love, abundance, harmony, peace and fulfillment of being.

THE INFINITY OF SENSE

Every moment, seek to become aware of the omnipresence of infinity rather than accepting the appearance of locality and finiteness. Infinity is the truth of all, and by filling our senses with infinity, we begin to experience the tangible limitlessness of all in our experience. Do not accept the apparent reality of local or finite person, thing, place or condition. "Judge not by the appearance." Do not judge the objective or corporeal appearance of the world, but "judge by righteous judgment," by the infinity and omnipresence and incorporeality of God as all. Judge by and seek the incorporeal, not the corporeal. Judge by and seek the *one whole* that is God, therefore all. Never seek a particular thing, but seek the *one whole* that is

God itself. Never seek a personal good or healed or prospered or harmonized condition, but seek the *one whole* that is God itself. Paradoxically *this* is how to evidence the truth of any and all seemingly personal, local and finite thing, amount, place and condition.

Fill the whole of your awareness and every detail of it with God, spirit and truth as all. When you have achieved that—and keep on keeping on with this awareness, despite all suggestion to the contrary—then you will begin witnessing the infinity and omnipresence, the life and vitality, the love and freedom of not only the body, but of all experience.

We cannot witness truth through the lens of belief or heal or save a form of belief. We can only evidence truth *as truth,* God *as god,* spiritual wholeness, harmony and abundance *as spiritual* being, body and form.

We have to "meet up" with the principle, attune our awareness to and as the principle—the principle of omnipresence, infinity, incorporeality, eternity. Then we have the forms of the principle throughout our bodies and world.

FINALLY, REST

When we are filled with God as all, and can feel the sense of release and relief it gives us, it is time to rest and relax, and simply *behold* God taking place as our experience—just as we would rest and relax and behold the sunrise taking place as our experience.

Rest in "the secret place of the most high"—the secret place of God-as-all awareness—and watch the miracles that become real and visible throughout your mind, body and world. In our rested, relaxed and receptive god-state of being we "see clearly." The windows of our being are open to the forms of "earth as it is in heaven": the health, wealth, peace, harmony and fulfillment of the real, belief-less forms of God as all. We *have* and we tangibly *see* the "image and likeness" of God instead of the image and likeness of belief. We are free in spiritual being, body and world.

You could take this one paragraph, write it out in your notebook, and live with it morning, noon and night for many weeks until it becomes alive and vital within you and overflows as your awareness of all. Your whole life would change and be transformed in just a few weeks. I encourage you to do it.

Truth *is already* everything everywhere. None but God is. "I am the Lord, and besides me there is none else." But belief clouds our senses, leaving us with the forms and conditions of belief rather than the clear vision of truth. Our task, therefore, is not to change that which is untrue into truth, but to spiritualize our awareness so that we can *see clearly* that which *is*. "Whereas I was blind, now I see." In spiritual awareness, the forms and conditions of mind are witnessed as true instead of as clouded. Spiritual seeing is spiritual health, wealth, harmony and fulfillment of all.

We have lifted to that point where the corporeal is now unreal to us, the finite is now unreal to us, the limited or local or personal is now unreal to us; birth, time span, years, birthdays, decrepitude and, finally, death are now unreal to us. We are living the tangible, palpable *truth* of being.

Indeed, God, spirit and truth are the blood of our blood and the bone of our bone. It is every breath we breathe, every sight we behold, every sound we hear, every fragrance with which we're filled, and every form filling our experience. It is our lifted awareness of reality, our "penthouse" self, body and world. We no longer dwell in the lower levels of awareness—the level of belief. We dwell in truth, in God as all. We are "in this world" but not "of it" of its own self.

Keep in mind now and forevermore: nothing local can be healed. Make truth your *living truth*. Lift into and remain aware of the one living truth, the illumined awareness that sees clearly. Then give yourself (and your body and world) the gift of simply resting in silence, beholding God taking place without and without and experiencing harmony, health, love and joy springing up everywhere. "Where the spirit of the Lord is [where spiritualized mind is], there is liberty."

Let us sit with the Master as he teaches us.

> The virtues of the heavens are in God's hands. And every loyal son [and daughter] may use these virtues and these powers. Man is the delegate of God to do his will on earth. And man can heal the sick, control the spirits of the air, and raise the dead. Because I have the power to do these things is nothing strange. All men may gain the power to do these things, but they must conquer all the passions of the lower self [the personal sense of self and world] and they can conquer if they will.

To discover your infinity and freedom of being—your fulfillment of being and purpose—devote yourself to truth. The miracle of life stands within you, as you, and all around you this minute, and as you spiritualize your every moment of awareness, you will quickly see and experience clearly.

Truly seek the kingdom of God, spirit and truth *for its own self,* never for your or my own self; never for the things the personal sense of self believes it needs or desires. Never attempt to heal, harmonize, prosper or pacify anything personal, objective, local, finite—anything with a name, anything detectable and describable. Instead, realize that all already is God, whole, healthy, perfect, boundless, free and true, and that the only need is to clear the clouds of belief by filling the senses with spiritual awareness.

Then, quickly, all becomes evident as the image and likeness of God, good. The clouds of belief have dissipated, and the clear atmosphere of God is perfectly visible and tangible.

Realize that I and form are one; therefore as "I" is filled with spiritual awareness, to the point where the "outer" is as equally full of spirit as the "inner," nothing in the universe can cloud the presence of God as the only reality of all. Lift and remain in the awareness of infinity, omnipresence, eternity, incorporeality as the one universal and equally present reality. This is the god-state of awareness that evidences the miracles of life.

> Man is God on earth and he who honors God must honor Man . . .

The one truth is that "man" (humanity and its world), despite belief and appearance, isn't man, but is God, infinity itself, omnipresence itself, eternal life-body itself—the incorporeal, spiritual, divine one being itself. There is none else.

> . . . for God and Man are one. Behold, I say the hour has come [the moment of awakened awareness]; the dead [human, material belief, those who believe in God "and"] will hear the voice of Man and live because the son of Man is son of God.

We might say it this way: Because the presence of man (each individual who is apparently human, personal, separate and different from God) is actually the very presence, spirit and truth of God, the mind, body and world of the lifted, spiritually aware individual heals and becomes alive, strong, purposeful and fulfilled in truth. *Then* is the true freedom of being experienced.

Eighteen

Sensory Experience

If God is impersonal, and if nothing local can be healed, how do we experience the healing of illness, disease or injury? How do we experience the healing of our greater body of awareness, our world, suffering, disease, poverty, greed, injustice, accident, immorality, racism? Whether we sense a problem happening "to us or in our body," or "out there in the world," it is, despite appearance, the same one problem taking place in the same one place—collective *belief* unwittingly taking place and being accepted within us.

Always remember this: All is God; therefore all is actually perfect and whole despite a him, her or it appearing as either good or bad character or condition. Whatever we observe or experience, we are observing or experiencing God—*including* the perfect body or form of God (good without opposite). Only *our* cloudy sense makes the perfect appear to be imperfect.

Yet it is undeniable that when we experience some form of illness, disease or injury, it seems to be taking place personally and locally "in us" or "to us" or "to our loved one." Even people on the other side of the world experiencing disease appear, to every material sense, to have personal, local problems—problems in "their bodies" or problems of immorality or injustice or poverty in "their families or communities." So let us make sure we understand what these experiences actually are and, therefore, how to free ourselves of them, not only individually but collectively.

The answer is contained in the understanding that God is the *only* and the *all*. There is nothing at all but God itself throughout the entirety of existence. God is the only life, the only mind, the only body, the only presence, the only form. God is incorporeal, infinite and omnipresent and can never be corporeal, finite or locally present. Yes, we (with our five, three-dimensional senses) *sense* God as corporeal, finite and local. But sense is not reality. Sense is sense alone. Just as all our sense can be focused on one small area of the ocean without making the ocean local and small, so our "human" sense is typically focused on one small area of experience at a time, and that does not make God local and small.

Our sense is objective, local and finite, but sense is sense alone, and has no effect on the truth or actuality that what we are observing is nothing but our human *sense* of that which is one hundred percent God—incorporeal, infinite and omnipresent. Once we know this, we hold the secret of healing in our hands. We stop judging by the appearance of either good or bad, and judge "righteously"—truthfully. We lift away from all belief about experience into God itself, and *there,* in God consciousness, we see clearly, the true and perfect person, body and world. As we "see clearly" the healing is accomplished because God consciousness *is* true and perfect being, body and world; God consciousness *is* "earth as it is in heaven."

The only being is God-being because God is *the only.* The only body is God-body because God is *the only.* The only thing, condition, amount, activity, place, world and universe is God because God is *the only.* God is the only and the all, and God is incorporeal; therefore all is incorporeal. Nothing but the incorporeal exists. Being, mind, body, world, universe—all is incorporeal simply *sensed* by us as corporeal. Right here is the key. If you can grasp it, you are on your way to freedom and wholeness in every way—the healing of self, body and world.

God is incorporeal. And because God is all, you are incorporeal, I am incorporeal, all is incorporeal. At our current level of awareness, that which is one hundred percent incorporeal seems to be corporeal, objectified, finite, local and personal. But sense is innocent, powerless and divine, and does not and cannot change the incorporeal into corporeality.

Nothing, nothing, *nothing* can change God! The level of sense we call "human, physical and material" (and every level of the infinity of awareness) is God and full of the goodness of God, good without opposite. It does not matter how many faculties and dimensions we (or any others of the infinity of being) use to *sense* the one and only life. Regardless of the degree at which we may be experiencing our existence, what does matter is knowing and living in the freedom and purpose of God as all; knowing and relying on the reality and absolute practicality of God as the harmony and fulfillment of all.

God is entirely undetectable by humanity, which believes nothing but the objectified, structural universe of sense. Human belief is limited to five senses, three dimensions, time, space, cause and effect; and belief can detect only its *own form,* nothing beyond. Operating within the confines of belief, a doctor or a surgeon can do very good work. He can reduce a fever, set a bone, purify the blood, treat cancer and remove a tumor. But he has no idea how these same ailments can be healed by an individual in spiritual consciousness, even from half way around the world. The individual in spiritual awareness does not operate within the restrictions of time and space, cause and effect. He is not attempting to improve or heal anything of structure. He is lifting an individual's awareness which gives the patient a higher sense of his non-structural actuality (his truth); and in that higher state of awareness, the patient experiences his health, wholeness and harmony of body.

Spiritual being, mind and body are entirely invisible, intangible, incomprehensible and nonsensical to belief and the believer, yet are so real and practical that they achieve boundlessly more than doctors, surgeons and charities can achieve. Spiritual consciousness, in experience, reduces fevers, heals bones, dissolves tumors, purifies blood, renews and replaces organs; it feeds the hungry with actual loaves and fishes, actual hot or cold meals of every nourishing variety; it brings tangible safety and security to the threatened and insecure, homes for the homeless, abundance for the poor and struggling; new customers, clients and patients for the businesses; love and comfort for the afflicted; peace to the warmongers.

It is only belief that throws us into the experience of lack and limitation, disease and poverty, frustration and war. Only belief is finite, has opposites, and seems to be an existence full of good *and bad.* Only belief seems to lack God, and seems to be unable to reach God, even when it screams for his help—as we, in belief, very often find ourselves doing in the agony of pain and suffering.

What seems, to belief, to lack the good, wholeness and harmony of God is not lacking God (therefore good) at all, but is simply lacking the *living awareness of God.* God is all, and God is forever whole, complete and harmonious, but God must be *realized* for the good without opposite to be visible and real to our senses.

The incorporeal is never corporeal although it appears to be (whether we know it or not, and humanity does not know it). If we are unaware of this, then the belief in humanity, materiality—a structural being, body and universe existing within time and space, full of cause and effect—will make the wholeness and perfection of the incorporeal appear to be the good *and bad* of the corporeal. Whatever of corporeal good (healthy and abundant form) we believe we lack or need isn't what is needed. The only need is greater God awareness. The one need is greater awareness of the incorporeal being—the only and the all. When we have *that,* we have the good, healthy and abundant forms of corporeal sense right where we are and wherever we are, in unconditional and limitless quantity.

ONENESS IS

Oneness *is,* and is full of the goodness of God and none else.

Oneness is the infinite, the omnipresent, the eternal. Oneness is the abundant life the Master told us about. "I [oneness, God] am come [into individual awareness] so that ye may have life, and have it more abundantly." The greater amount of God awareness we have, the greater amount of corporeal good we experience because God is good alone, and God is all.

There is nothing "more" of God or oneness to demonstrate or manifest, or to somehow make visible and tangible. Oneness *is,* and because the entire universe of experience is that oneness (and not different or separate, not a different state of existence but the one and the same) all we have to do is become ever more aware of *oneness* to witness it as ever greater "corporeal" life, love, harmony, peace and prosperity.

The incorporeal (God) is forever whole and omnipresent, perfect and incorruptible. Any degree of absence or incompleteness is unknown to it, and impossible for it to form. Illness, disease, injury, youth, middle age and old age, birth and then death, lack and limitation, poverty and hunger, immorality and injustice are all unknown to it, and impossible for it to form.

Oneness is *one,* the *same,* and *omnipresent* throughout. The concepts of invisibility versus visibility, intangibility versus tangibility, unmanifested versus manifested, undemonstrated versus demonstrated, God versus man, spirit versus matter are entirely unknown to God, and impossible for God to form.

Oneness *is*—period. Oneness is the whole truth. In oneness, nothing remains to be "done" or formed or overcome or healed or transformed in any of experience whatsoever, because oneness has only one experience, and that is oneness itself, and the fullness thereof. Nothing "needs to happen" before we experience the fullness of life, relationship, business, affluence, harmony and peace throughout, because all is already done. All already is God (oneness, the incorporeal), and when we know this and then lift into and maintain the awareness of God (oneness, incorporeality), we see it, have it, and can absolutely rely on its presence as the harmony and completeness of everything we experience.

Nothing of God, good, remains to be demonstrated or manifested. Oneness is eternally fully demonstrated and manifested. Better stated, oneness *is* demonstration and manifestation. There is no other. If there were something remaining to be "demonstrated," oneness would not be one, but two or more. One is one alone, and cannot be two. And for one *to be one,* it has to be one throughout, which God is. Oneness cannot and does not consist of one half invisible and the other visible, one half intangible and the other tangible, one half manifested and demonstrated and the other half still needing to be—with a middle-man named you or me performing some spiritual trickery that gets the job done. The whole concept is nonsense, of course, and can only have been dreamed up by nonsensical belief. Oneness is one, and because oneness is all, you are that, I am that, and all are that.

I AM THAT

"I am that I am," and "besides me [besides oneness] there is none other." Throughout all the scriptures of the ages, we have the same message: *I am that, the one and the only, and besides me—besides one or oneness—there is none else.* Indeed, it is not possible for any other being or thing to exist in the oneness that is God.

Besides God, one, infinity, omnipresence, eternity—the incorporeal—there is none else. Do not make false idols of oneness. Know and rely on oneness as oneness, never as two or more, never as different or less or separate. Do not believe that there is something "other" than oneness, other than God itself fully visible and tangible as itself, because if you do, you'll suffer by that belief. There is never a need to suffer. All one needs, despite appearance, is to lift into greater living awareness of oneness being all, God being all, the incorporeal being the one reality and form of all.

"Ye are gods, and all of you are children of the most High." I am the child, the offspring, the very presence, being and form of God. I am that, and all is that.

I, empty of personal self, am one with God (God as me). There is no difference between God and my selfless self because all is one, and there is no lesser or greater in oneness.

As the sunbeam is one with the sun, I am one with God. As the whole universe of light is one with the sun, I and my whole universe are one with God. No difference exists anywhere throughout the infinitude; no lesser or greater amount of God, oneness, exists anywhere throughout the infinitude; nothing is separate and isolated from God, oneness. Indeed, all is the one, fully and tangibly present as all the forms of existence, including the form I am, and the form all is.

SENSE EXPERIENCE

Being, body, mind, world and universe at "our" level of three-dimensional and five-sense awareness appear to be, without spiritual discernment, personal, finite, local, objectified; of time, space, cause and effect. But appearance does not change actuality. The one actuality is God, spirit and truth. *All* is God, and besides God there is absolutely none else. No matter what the appearance may be at any moment, or what we believe about it, *all is God, good without opposite,* and nothing in the universe can change this one actuality, this one truth. Everything everywhere, despite his, her or its appearance (human, animal, plant, vegetable, mineral, animate or inanimate, good or bad) is actually God. And because all is God, all is spirit, incorporeality, infinity, omnipresence, eternality, oneness—wholeness and perfection without opposite.

Sense is a wondrous and miraculous faculty. As we awaken to the truth of all being God, we know that everything we sense is nothing but God. When we know that nothing but God exists, sense appearance can no longer fool us. Sense is simply a moment-by-moment objective experience of God ("earth as it is in heaven") and is laden with God. "The earth is full of the goodness of God."

Sense has no power, therefore has no power of change. Sense does not and cannot change God. Sense is innocent and impotent, and is, as its truth, the divine faculty of awareness. We do not create, gain, achieve, fix or heal with sense; we simply behold and serve God as sensed experience.

Sense can be likened to a filter on a camera. We can attach numerous different filters to our camera—one making the sky appear to be purple, another making the sun appear to be a starburst, another twisting people into distorted aliens, another polarizing the atmosphere. If we look at the image alone, without knowing a filter has been used, we could well believe the image. Yet the filter image and our belief about its reality do not change the object one iota. The sky, the sun, the person and the atmosphere remain as they are. Only the *image* of them appears to be different.

Equally, we know that the filter contains no power, therefore no power of change. All power is in reality, not the filter. The filter is incapable of *actually changing* the sky, sun, person or atmosphere—or anything whatsoever. It simply filters or changes the *image of* the object, but never reality.

In this way we understand sense. All power and presence is in God, not sense. Our entire sense experience—appearing, at face value, to be human, personal, objective, finite, local; of time, space, cause and effect—is not what it appears to be, but is unchanged and unchange*able* God. We are simply having a corporeal sense of the incorporeal, but the incorporeal remains unchanged, therefore forever whole and complete. God is never absent but always fully present. "When all material streams are dried, thy fullness remains the same." And because God is life, love, harmony, peace, oneness and fulfillment eternal, "thy fullness" is always fully present, never absent, never lacking and never different.

Because God is never absent, *the visibility, tangibility and here-and-*

now reality of God are equally never absent. The belief in God being invisible and intangible is just what it says—*belief.*

All belief is unfounded in truth. Whoever suggested that God is invisible did not have the whole truth, or at least was unable to clearly explain it. The whole truth is that God is invisible to belief, therefore to the person who believes belief. God is, of course, not invisible or intangible or unreal or impractical to itself. Therein lies the answer to the truth that has forever been a mystery to mankind and even to the majority of spiritual students. God is entirely invisible and unreal to belief and to the believer, but is entirely visible, tangible, real and practical to God and gods. "Ye are gods, and all of you children of the most High." To one in a God-state of being, all of God is perfectly clear and visible, but to one in a belief-state of being (a "filter-state" of being), none of God is visible. To one in a belief-state of being, God is not anywhere to be found. Belief can only see itself and nothing more than itself; belief can only experience its reality, but never the one actual reality that is God, unconditional good without opposite.

It is only as we introduce *belief* to sense, that our sensed experience becomes that *of* belief. And because every belief has an opposite, our experience is filled with the pairs of opposites—a universe (mind, body and world and every detail, form and activity of these) of both good and bad.

The belief-world is entirely unreal and untrue. The being we have believed we are is not the being we actually are. The mind, body and world we have believed to be real have no reality or truth. The hindering and limiting condition of mind, body or world we have believed to be real, and which somehow needs to be overcome, has no reality or truth.

Belief-sense does nothing but assume that imagery (apparent condition) is reality, whereas God-sense does nothing but behold God in action as all.

Knowing the truth that God is all and that sense is simply powerless imagery of God as all, we relax our effort to survive, to heal, to attain, to gain, to satisfy and parade the personal self (the ego self or selfish self). We begin worshiping, giving, serving and sharing God as the very purpose and fulfillment of our being, and this way we experience our true, full, free, boundless and purposeful self.

Nineteen

The Living Light

The chapter "Sensory Experience" has just been finished. It has existed eternally and has forever been available to our awareness, but it took a God-state of being to hear it and see it, and therefore enable the world to see it—to *have* it as the real and tangible truth message given in that chapter.

This is the secret of all discovery, all health, wealth, loving relationship, peace among men and women, and harmony throughout the world. It is the secret of fulfillment of purpose, of successful and prosperous business, charity or church, and of union among neighbors, governments and countries. It is the secret of "earth as it is in heaven," earth full of the goodness of God.

The wholeness (harmony, fulfillment) of any and every category of life that seems to be—and *is* to belief—ill, diseased, injured, weak, poor, unstable, unjust, immoral, insecure, unsafe, unhappy, unsuccessful or decrepit exists here and now, and is fully visible, tangible, manifested and already demonstrated in and as your presence this minute.

It has existed eternally but belief cannot see it, cannot have it as real and tangible. Belief cannot detect its reality and fully visible presence because belief can only see itself—the pairs of opposites. But remember, "When all material streams are dried, thy fullness remains the same." No matter what material belief suggests of good or bad, presence or absence, truth stands right there in all its fullness. It takes only a God-state of being (our natural and true state of being) to dispel the clouds of belief and bring truth forth—to see its perfectly-formed presence and visibility standing right where we are. "Whereas I was blind, now I see."

Let us assume that, at this moment, there is something disharmonious or discordant going on with the body: illness, disease, injury, weakness, old age or decrepitude. Why is this our experience? It is the unwitting acceptance of imagery (form) as reality—the experience of belief and nothing else. And because it is belief, it has no power in the presence of God; it has no ability to remain in your experience (or that of another) because belief has no law or principle to sustain it.

The more of belief we are filled with, and the less of spirit, the more belief-forms (good and bad) we unwittingly accept as being real. Belief is pervasively hypnotic. We must continuously guard our awareness by knowing the truth of oneness, and by keeping ourselves in a God-state of being.

To experience God as all, we have to be in a god-as-all state of being. A belief- or material-state of being cannot see God. Equally, God knows nothing about belief or matter and so cannot help or heal it. What appears to be belief or matter is actually the fullness of God. The one state of being (awareness) required in order to have and to tangibly see God as the forms of our worldly life is a God-state of being.

Being in a God-state of being *is to have* a god-state of mind, body and world. A God-state of being does not *produce*—but *is itself*—healthy, wealthy and harmonious form. God and god-experience are one and the same presence and form, not two, not different, not separate. God, oneness, consists of *only God, only one throughout,* not God "and," not two, not different, not less. Oneness consists of—or better stated, *is itself*—life, wholeness, abundance, love, union and none other. Oneness is full of and omnipresent as itself alone. Oneness does not contain time, space, cause or effect, good versus bad. Belief-sense is these, but reality is one and invariable, fully and perfectly existent at every place throughout the infinitude (which *is* oneness). Oneness is wholly one as and throughout itself (the only), eternally intact, unadulterated and incorruptible.

Nothing of oneness is lacking something else. There *is nothing else* in oneness; therefore there is never lack or limitation, need or desire. To be in need of or desire anything at all would require two states of existence, one who lacks something of good and another who can supply it. In twoness, one of the two could easily lack the other, or a measure of the other. In multiplicity, one state of being can (and usually does) need or desire many other "improved" states, things, amounts, qualities and conditions which it sets out to gain from other members of multiplicity. But in oneness, only one is, which eternally *has* and *experiences* the whole of itself—the whole being infinite, omnipresent, omnipotent and omniscient.

A God-state of being is God-filled awareness, with no or little belief in it. It is the conscious state of oneness without "otherness"—the fulfilled state of oneness with nothing to demonstrate. There is no such thing as "undemonstrated" oneness, "undemonstrated" God. Oneness is already and forever demonstrated and the God-state of being knows it and lives the freedom of oneness—never wanting, never desiring, never making effort to gain a form of good or to be rid of or heal a form of bad. Good and bad are nothing to the God-state of being. Only *God is* to the God-state of being. Appearance no longer fools it.

In conscious oneness, all of sense and its forms are spontaneously fulfilled at each moment. Oneness *is itself* the fulfillment of all sense and all form. Indeed, conscious oneness *is* all sense and all form (the seeming two being one), invariably whole and complete at and as every moment of experience. Need and desire no longer exist. Oneness *is*.

LIGHT OF THE WORLD

> In Him is life; and the life is the light of men. And the light shines in darkness; and the darkness comprehends it not. The true Light lights every man that comes into the world.

> God is light, and in Him is no darkness at all.

The further we are drawn from a God-state of being (our natural and true illumined state of being), the "darker" is our awareness. Just as in the dark of night we cannot see clearly, so in unillumined awareness we cannot see God-form clearly. In the dark of unawareness, we have misidentified who we are, what our bodies are, and what our world and everything in it are. We have unwittingly accepted what we've been taught by the world—to believe the little we can see as being reality.

In our state of belief, we stumble and search for our good in the dark. We make effort to gain that which we already are and have, but cannot see. We believe we are mere and temporary human beings with physical bodies existing in a world of both good and bad. We believe we "do not have" the infinite and divinely purposeful life that God is as all, so we invest our years in attempting to be of some worth, to get and to gain, to be recognized and rewarded, to find some purpose and accomplishment from our existence. When we are presented with a problem of ill health, poverty, unloving relationship, unhappiness, limitation, or restriction of expression, we seek to heal, rectify, pacify, prosper or harmonize our problem. Finally, as the "end of our life" approaches for one or other physical reason, we struggle to survive another few years, months, weeks, days or hours. This entire "human" account is mis-identity and mis-effort believed to be real, and is ours for one reason alone: we have not realized that we are the "true Light [that] lights every man that comes into the world."

All of humanity's problems, no matter what we believe they are or what name we give them are rooted in *one* problem alone: the "dark" of belief in which we cannot see our truth. The one root solution or healing of any and every problem is to awaken to the light that we are and have, to illumine individual and then collective awareness, to realize that because God is infinite and omnipresent, God is all; therefore we and all are that. In the light of truth, all is whole and complete, loving and harmonious, peaceful and true.

A LACK OF LIGHT

Dark is not an entity but just a *lack of light.* When we understand that all problems are nothing but forms of dark awareness—which we've believed are real but are actually nothing more than a lack of spiritual awareness—we can see that healing is as spontaneous as the morning light "healing" the dark of night.

As the light of truth fills the dark of human belief, any and every need or desire is spontaneously fulfilled. All fulfillment already and forever exists right where we are. It is only our dark awareness that seems to leave us "without" all and unconditional good. As soon as we are filled with the light of spirit, we *see* and *have* all good. "Whereas I was blind, now I see."

The former concepts of need and desire are obsolete in the light of truth. Good and bad are non-existent; therefore need and desire are non-existent. *Only God is,* and God alone is real and tangible when we have awakened to and are alive to the light of God as all.

In the light of the infinity and omnipresence of spirit we are free and limitless. Our minds are known as the one mind and are full of light, spirit and truth. Our bodies are known as the one body and are full of health, vitality and purpose. Our world is known as the one world and is full of milk and honey, silver and gold, love, harmony and peace—"earth as it is in heaven." Each moment of illumined mind, body and world experience is the fullness of God, spontaneously evident hour by hour, step by step. In fact, God experience is quicker than spontaneously evident experience because "Before ye call, I will answer." Before we are aware of the next hour, the next step or the next activity, *there God is* because God *already is*. Just as when we turn a corner and are presented with a new view (not *made* spontaneously evident, but *already existent* before our awareness arrives at the scene) so God exists as the perfect harmony and wholeness of all, even before we arrive on the scene. This is the meaning of the statement, "I will go before thee, and make the crooked places straight." The crooked places of belief are made straight before we get there as long as we are in a God-state of being, an illumined state of spiritual awareness (of God as all).

The kingdom of God (truth) is finished, whole and complete. Therefore the kingdom of you, me and all is finished, whole and complete. God *is*, not "will be" or "is evolving towards," perfection, but *is* already and eternally whole and in (and existent as) perfect and equal order. God *is*, and God is omnipresent; therefore omnipresence *is*. Omnipresence is the only presence—the only type, form, visibility, tangibility and experience of presence. Whether we are aware of this truth or not, there is none other. All of God (good) is already "here, there and everywhere," fully complete and perfect, fully manifested and demonstrated, before "our" awareness arrives "there"—wherever, whoever or whatever "there" is.

Omnipresence is the whole of God; therefore every "here, there and everywhere," and every person and form are and have the *whole* of God. God is one, indivisible and inseparable. This is why you can rest assured—with absolute conviction and trust—that only the *whole* exists whether he, she or it *appears to be* one solitary cell or all the cells in 7.3 billion bodies, one breath or all the breaths of humanity, one small pebble or an entire mountain range, one dollar or all the currency on earth.

And because God is all, and God is good without opposite, all of experience and all of its trillions of forms are life, love, infinity, omnipresence, omniscience, omnipotence, peace, bliss; freedom of being, purpose and expression, harmony and oneness throughout—unconditionally and eternally as the *is* of all existence.

Being full of God awareness is to be in a God-state of being. The further away from God we are in conscious awareness, the more "dark" (belief, materiality) we have in our "house," and therefore, the more of the pairs of opposites (good *and bad*) as our experience.

Even one degree away from God awareness has an "and" in it—God "and." Right there, with that "and" sitting in us, we are the "prodigal" son or daughter and open to the hypnotic belief of a mind, body and world different and separate from God, exposed to a tricky balance of good versus bad, or more accurately, good battling bad. The "God-and" in us is making "false idols" of the oneness that all is. As soon as we have a false idol (a belief in an existence or entity other than God) we fall for it. It is collective belief self-accepted, therefore self-believed. We fall for our self-accepted "he, she or it" idol. We believe he, she or it to be real, and we then get busy catering to that believed reality. We start making all the effort needed to gain and maintain health and harmony, love and prosperity, reward and recognition. Even nearing the end of our belief-lifespan, we invest the last of our money, time and effort attempting to keep alive an existence that is nothing more than concept. We've drifted away in conscious awareness from pure God, pure truth, pure spirit, pure oneness; and we suffer it.

We have God "and" a personal sense of being, body and world. We have God "within," but we also have "me" and "my body" and "my world circumstance" out here. There's the "and"—the "prodigal son," the "divided house," the "false idol." We can intellectually accept that God is all, and that God is therefore the truth of our beings and bodies, but then the personal I has a problem for which God is needed. There's the belief in separation, in life and body being different from or less than the very life and body of God itself.

THE SENSE OF NEED OR DESIRE

As soon as an "and" exists in us, it is sensed as a need or desire. The "and" *is* the sense of need or desire because everything we *have* occupying our belief has form. Belief "and" form are one just as consciousness "and" form are one. Oneness is an unavoidable principle. The belief in an "and" different and separate from God *is itself* the sensed separation and division from God, therefore the need or desire for good to be added, attained or achieved. Whatever occupies your awareness populates your experience because awareness and form are one.

When we have God alone filling our awareness, we have God alone filling our experience. But if we have God "and" as a belief, then we have God "and" (good and bad) as our experience. Either God is our experience or belief is our experience because the principle of oneness cannot be avoided. In the Master's words, "If you know yourselves, then you will be known and you will know that you are the sons of the living Father [the living truth]. But if you do not know yourselves, then you are in poverty and you are poverty."

There is no "and" in actuality or principle—in God. There is *only* actuality, *only* principle, *only* God—one. God is one, self-complete and perfect, fully demonstrated and manifested throughout. The only existence is God existence—complete, whole and perfect existence. Only life is, only love is, infinity is, only omnipresence is, only freedom is; only the bliss, only the peace of true and boundless being is, and besides that "is," there is nothing else.

Every degree "further away" from God awareness we allow ourselves to be—every degree by which our awareness is more dense, more material, less illumined, less spiritual—the seemingly "darker," more "separated," more "needy" is our experience. On the other hand, every degree of God-as-all that fills our awareness fills our experience with the light and omnipresence of truth (including all truth's form). True God awareness and true God form are one. The oneness of God-as-all becomes ever more visible and tangible as we keep our awareness filled *with it,* and live our lives *as it*—as the being, body and expression of God, oneness.

"God is light, and in Him is no darkness at all." The words "dark" and "darkness" used in scripture mean "a lack of God awareness." A God-state of being (God awareness) is illumined awareness; a human state of being (a lack of God awareness) is unillumined or dark awareness.

Our state of awareness is our *all.* Our universe of awareness *is* our universe of experience. This is why every spiritual master teaches us that we need to, and teaches us how to, illumine (spiritualize) our awareness. Illumined awareness *is* illumined (whole, harmonious, abundant and free) being, mind, body and world experience.

Whereas the human or material state of being is the "dark" (good and bad) of its world, Jesus told us, "I (God and the God-state of being, or illumined being) am the light of the world." But all of the good and bad being and world is nothing of its own self. It is a lack of God awareness, a lack of illumined awareness, rather than an actuality, a real entity. There is nothing real or sustainable about it because only God is; therefore only God is real and sustainable (eternal). The pairs of opposites exist in experience only because our awareness is not yet spiritually illumined. Both good and bad of any and every nature or character are unreal. They are not entities in and of their own selves. They are belief-experiences alone and can be instantly dissipated in the presence of the light of spirit. "Where the spirit of the Lord is, there is liberty." Where the presence of light is, there is no darkness but just light.

HEALING THE BODY

Even though it is hard to hear, especially as we are suffering and in pain, we have to know that it is our individual, unwittingly accepted awareness that leaves us with the experience of illness, disease, injury or accident. Equally, it is our individual, increased God awareness that frees us of the experience.

The whole of God exists and is fully embodied in and as you this moment and forever, and because God is the one power, presence and form, all power, presence and form are *with you*. One with God consciousness is a majority. No power exists outside of you and no being, presence, form or activity can control you, harm you, hinder you, make you suffer or overcome you.

Our entire experience now (from the moment of realization that God is all and that self, body and world are nothing of their own selves) is governed by our state of awareness. By the degree that we continue to believe humanity, the pairs of opposites, the personal self, the physical body and the material world, we will continue to suffer; but by the degree we fill ourselves full of God awareness each and every hour, we become free of all suffering and all its forms. Our awareness is full of light "with no darkness in it at all." We are filled "inside" and "outside" with God alone.

Never let go of God awareness—in the same way as you would never let go of a young child's hand on a busy street. Seek always to hold onto a God-state of being rather than slipping away into a material state of being. "Love the Lord thy God [the truth of being, body and world] with all thy heart, and with all thy soul, and with all thy mind, and with all thy strength." This is the key to a God-state of awareness.

Anyone can experience healing here and now because, despite appearance, the true, forever healthy, vital and incorruptible body is the only body we all have—the spiritual body *appearing to be physical* at our level of "human, physical, earthly" sense. As we know this truth and cease from attempting to heal a body that doesn't need healing, and instead make our effort to lift into and maintain a God state of being, and there rest, relax and freely receive the omnipresent light of truth, the visibility of the true body emerges through the dissipated clouds of collective belief.

It is only collective clouds of belief that have fooled us and stopped us from being, seeing and tangibly having all the freedom of truth we wish to have in every category, form and quality of life. From the moment we awaken, we are no longer fooled by appearance, and we walk free in spiritual being, body and world. The body stands in all its truth and all its health, fully real, visible and tangible. It appears to be the same body, yet is entirely new. The body of belief never was the body of truth (the "image and likeness" of God, the untainted objective sense of the spiritual body). It was the image and likeness of belief, but is now free in spirit.

From this moment on, dear friends, realize that the "personal, physical" body—which inarguably *appears to be* local and may now be suffering ill health, disease, injury or accident—has nothing to do with "you" or "yours." The entire "personal self and body" experience is that of collective belief (therefore of good and bad) and not God, truth, which is good without opposite.

THE PERFECT BODY OF SPIRIT

Only God (one) is, which is spirit, which in turn means only one body is, that body being spirit. You are spiritual being with spiritual body, and because spirit has no matter in it at all and is, therefore incorruptible, undamageable and of eternally perfect form and order, your true body, and mine, and all body, is that.

An ill, diseased, injured, decrepit or dying body is a body of belief alone. God is life eternal and does not (nor can it ever) become ill, diseased, injured, decrepit or die. Life cannot and does not die; therefore the body of life does nothing but live—vitally, freely and eternally. Do you see, therefore, that all that has to be done to heal the ailments of the belief-body is to know this truth, rest in the midst of the true body, and let its light dispel the clouds of belief? In other words, simply rest in the presence of God which is omnipresent as you, your very spiritual presence, which often feels like peace or warmth or light or love "happening" within, and let it "do the work" of dispelling the ailment of belief. This is the way of healing.

Never attempt to work on "the problem," or to heal "a reality" named illness, disease, injury, decrepitude or death. That is the way of failure. "Ye ask, and receive not, because ye ask amiss." Only God is; therefore, God is the only life, presence *and form*. And God is omnipresent and incorruptible; therefore, if we believe an appearance to be real, an actual entity with its own life and form, we are out of spiritual awareness and cannot evidence spiritual health and harmony. Never attempt to bring truth to an entity you believe needs it. Never attempt to get God to heal anything at all. If we do attempt it, we obviously believe in an entity other than God that is in desperate need of God. We have fallen down before we begin.

What we must do to keep standing in truth, and to then quickly witness truth where untruth seems to be, is to realize that *all* is God and that there is no exception to this truth. It is not wrong to want healing and health, or to want any other good whatsoever. It is right to want harmony and freedom in every department of life, but if we attempt to get God to heal or transform the various entities in our experience that we believe are something other than God, we fail. Such efforts are wasted and exhausting only because they are impossible to achieve. They are like attempting to make a rock fly. A rock cannot fly no matter how much we would like it to, and an entity other than God cannot be made God-like (whole and healthy) no matter how urgent the condition is believed to be, or how desperately God's help seems to be needed.

This "hard" truth has to be made clear; otherwise, we and others for whom we could be witnessing truth continue to needlessly suffer. All conditions that appear to lack God (good) are not entities but are a lack of God awareness. "God is light, and in Him is no darkness at all." Where dark appears to be real, we must realize it is just a lack of light, and where health and wholeness appear to be lacking, we must realize that experience is just a lack of illumined awareness—a lack of God-as-all awareness.

The solution? It is certainly not to sit and pray for light to heal our dark. If we rehearse our truth, meditate and sit in silence for God to heal our ills, all we'll get is prolonged illness. "God does not potentize the pool for a favorite few." God, principle, does not favor those who pray, meditate and sit in silence over those who do not. Nor can God be influenced, even by the Master. "I can of mine own self do nothing. . . . I seek not mine own will, but the will of the Father which has sent [is] me [and all]."

God *is,* and cannot be influenced any more than the sun can be. God is principle. Rather than attempting to influence principle to work for our collective beliefs, all we have to do is attune ourselves *to it*. Then we *have* as much of that principle and as many of its forms as we would like each day. When we know the one principle of God—which is God-*is*-all (not "will" be, or can be "made" to be, but already and forever *is*)—and then attune our awareness to *it,* we have the full and infinite measure of God as everything of our mind, body and world. We *have* the life, health, vitality, resources and limitlessness of the infinite, and all un-God-like appearance dissipates and dissolves as the non-entity or unreality it has always been.

God is the one, actual and only principle and form of all—the master principle, presence and form. God is the almighty and all-present *oneness* of existence, therefore that which is you, me and everything of earth, space and infinitely beyond. Because God is the one and the only, God is fully present, fully manifested, fully demonstrated, fully visible, fully tangible, fully real and fully practical. And every presence is God because God is the only presence. The only thing that ever presents itself to us is God. God is the *only,* the *one,* the *all-in-all* and the *all-of-all.* Do you see, therefore, that we only have to lift above what we believe, to God itself, and there we discover our whole minds, bodies and world full of God? We have to lift our awareness to God rather than hoping God will fix our belief. Light does not fix dark. Dark is a non-entity. To understand the dissipating of dark, we only have to understand what happens in the presence of light. Where the presence of light is, dark vanishes because dark is nothing but a lack of light. In this way we understand the great statement, "Where the spirit [presence] of the Lord is, there is liberty," and, equally, we understand how ill-health, disease or any discord or disharmony at all vanishes in the presence of God consciousness or a God-state of being. Where God-as-all is, there is God as all form.

This is the miracle of being and this is the purpose of being—that we reveal the glory of God (the truth of being, mind, body, world and universe). "Let your light so shine before men, that they may see your good works, and glorify your Father which is in heaven."

Every day I am grateful that we are unable to influence God. If we were able to, not only would the universe be in a state of chaos within an hour, but we would never find God itself—just as we would never find math or aerodynamics if we were able to influence them. Math itself would remain a mystery to us if we were able to influence it to benefit our need with 3 x 3 = 7, while our neighbor was able to influence it to benefit his need with 3 x 3 = 21; aerodynamics would be forever unavailable to us if we could influence it to fly our rock. The only way to discover these (or any) principles, and then live with their boundless benefits, is to lift *our awareness* to *their* reality. As soon as we have achieved that, we have the universal benefit of these principles.

Likewise, the only way we awaken to the all and unconditional good that God is and visibly and tangibly *have* its universal, all-inclusive benefit in every most practical way, is to lift our personal-self belief into the one reality of truth. It does not matter that all belief is collective and not personal. It also doesn't matter that belief is pervasively hypnotic. The one thing that matters is how individual you and I dismiss belief and its false forms as the nothingness they are and keep our awareness filled with the truth of God as all.

"One with God is a majority," so as *we* keep *ourselves* lifted in a God state of being (lifted in spiritual awareness, filled with the palpable presence and peace of God as all), we are the "window of heaven" on earth, the light which dispels the dark throughout our minds, bodies and worlds. We are "the light that lights every man that comes into the world"—the light, the truth-revealed of all worldly form, thing, amount, activity, place and condition. "Where the spirit of the Lord is, there is liberty," but where belief remains, there is discord and lack.

"God is light, and in Him is no darkness at all," and because God is all, I am that light, you are that light, all is that light. My being, mind, body and entire world—inclusive of everything in and of them—are light with no darkness, no otherness in them at all.

God is "of purer eyes [purer substance, life and form] than to behold [contain or include] evil, and canst not look on iniquity [has no awareness of iniquity, belief, non-God experience]."

The one light which is all, is too pure to contain or behold darkness or otherness of any type, name or category. God is—period; there is none other.

Belief is nothing, yet appears to be real to the believer. But in light there is nothing except light. In illumined awareness there is nothing but illumined being and form. And because the light of God is the life and body of humanity and the life and form of earth, illumined awareness is the one and incorruptible life, body and form of all being and all earth—being and earth "as it is in heaven."

God is light with no darkness in it at all. God is infinity, omnipresence, eternity with no finiteness, locality or temporality in it at all. Therefore you, I, and all are infinity, omnipresence and eternity with no finiteness, locality or temporality in us or about us at all.

I am the light of the world. I put away belief because I no longer wish to be limited and hindered by the forms, activities, amounts and conditions of disharmony, ill-health, lack and limitation. I am no longer willing to live by material sense. I am willing to live only by spiritual sense, and in that way experience the infinity, freedom, purpose and fulfillment of my being on earth.

I am the light of God as individual being, and besides the light of God, there is none else. There are no shadows, no beliefs, no pockets of darkness, no disharmony, discord, lack or limitation in mind, body or world. There is nothing but light, the one and all-inclusive light that God is as all.

If infinity included anything but the one existence of truthful being, mind, body or earth, then two gods would co-exist in conflict with each other—the good god forever battling the bad god. Orthodoxy may believe scripture to be the account of two opposing forces—a "higher" God of good opposing a "lower" god of bad—but spiritual discernment reveals one, all-present and almighty God, the God which is spirit and truth, which has "no God besides me."

God, truth, is one, and one alone. "I am the Lord, and besides me there is none else. . . . the earth is full of the goodness of the Lord." As I fill my awareness to overflowing with God-as-all, and as I continually dismiss the suggestion of anything but God as all that I am and experience, I become the presence of God which is the light—the presence and influence of truth—unto all. "Blessed are the pure in heart: for they shall see God."

"JUST LIGHT AND PEACE"

Some years ago, my attention was drawn to a lady sitting at the back of a class. She stood out. She showed no reaction to the message we were hearing, although her attention never wavered. She cautiously did not mix with the other students, nor did she say a word throughout our two days.

Then at the end of the final class, I asked if anyone would like a question answered, and this lady opened up and said, "No question, but I want to say something about what we've been hearing. I am a chemist, and in the laboratory we use electron microscopes to examine tissue and various other substances at cellular level. What we observe is light and peace no matter what the 'outer' condition suggests." She had tears in her eyes as she shared that she'd realized that the light and peace within everything was God. It was deeply touching.

No matter what we observe or experience, no matter what presents itself to us—whether human, animal, vegetable, mineral, cell, atom; animate or inanimate—it is, despite belief, God and nothing but God. Forever ignore appearance and the suggestion of belief. "Judge not by the appearance, but judge righteous judgment." Judge (realize) all to be God because the *one truth* is that God is all.

Fill yourself full of God awareness, with spirit and truth. Fill yourself to overflowing with the awareness of infinity, omnipresence and eternity, with love and grace, light and oneness.

I am, and have the light of the world. Light is all and everywhere present. Only light is, only light exists, and besides light there is none else.

I am, and have the peace of the world, and besides peace there is none else. "My peace I give unto you, not as the world gives, give I unto you"—not human, physical or material peace which is here today and gone tomorrow, but infinitely more than this; the real and one most practical and everlasting peace, give I [truthful awareness] unto you.

Peace . . . peace. My peace I give unto your awareness, your mind, your body and all in your world. My peace . . . the everlasting peace . . . the peace that heals all ills and discords by dissipating the clouds of belief in the stillness and silence of self.

Each hour—each moment!—lift into and maintain a living awareness of the oneness and omnipresence of God as all; the oneness and omnipresence of light and peace as being the very substance *and form* of all.

God (spirit, light, peace) is everywhere and equally present as all, "inner" and "outer," all-inclusive and self-inclusive, and is impossible to personalize, localize, finitize, objectify, capture or contain. God *is;* therefore, all of existence and its every appearing animate and inanimate form is that *is,* and requires no mentalization, thinking about, manipulating or coercing to be perfectly evident, real and practical as our everyday reality. Only belief clouds the one and omnipresent reality, but *God itself, reality itself,* is forever and entirely fully present and fully evident, and needs nothing *done* to make it so.

Realize forevermore that in order to personalize, objectify, finitize, localize and name any form of life whatsoever, we have to believe both we and it are separate and different from God. Then because we have belief, we have not *one,* but pairs of opposites, and because belief *is* experience, we have an experience filled with good and bad opposites, with no God to be found anywhere amongst them all.

But God, spirit, light is *indivisible and inseparable,* so by definition, if we have been dividing and separating, it has been of belief alone and not reality. Reality, peace, life, love, infinity, omnipresence, eternity—these are the *only actual reality* and are entirely indivisible and inseparable.

In *sense,* the indivisible and inseparable oneness appears to be multiplicity, but appearance has nothing to do with, nor does it change reality. Everything of sense is God, because nothing but God is. Sense molds oneness, God, spirit into sensed form. But each and every form is wholly God, therefore self-complete as God-form. No part of its entire good can ever lack. No form can ever be ill, diseased, injured, immobile, discordant, unhappy, restricted, decrepit, weak, dying or dead. As we keep our awareness filled with God—not matter, not belief—we are the light "with no darkness in it at all." Belief can no longer tempt us and convince us, can no longer draw us in and trick us into reacting and doing battle with its non-reality.

The innocence of sense is beautiful and true, and as long as we do not add belief to it, we are and have the reality of God as the reality of mind, body and world.

I am, my mind is, my body is and my world and its every form are the one light, because none but the one light exists.

I am, my mind is, my body is and my world and its every form are peace, because none but peace exists.

God is light, God is peace, and besides God there is none other. Therefore, I am that light and that peace, and all is that light and peace.

In this one truth I have nothing to save or change, heal or transform, make effort for or achieve. All is, *and I rest in that* is *and simply behold God taking place as all.*

In this way, I have attained the God-state of being, the "healing consciousness," the God consciousness or consciousness of oneness, and all is good. In a God state of being I am true and safe, and I observe the world as true and safe.

THE ONE EFFORT

We are required to make no effort in life except the *one* effort of continually lifting and maintaining our God-state of awareness. Whether it takes five minutes or one hour, five hours or even five days if needed, we make the one effort of keeping our God awareness alive.

It is sometimes (and more often is) easy, but other times it is hard—sometimes the single hardest thing we are ever required to do. But the fruits are abundant and everlasting, the fearlessness and freedom unmatched, and the happiness, purpose and fulfillment of being unequaled. God (good without opposite) becomes our reality as we "set [our] affection on things above, not on things on the earth." Good alone fills and animates our mind, body and world as we awaken to the almighty truth that "the earth [mind, body and world] is the Lord's, and the fullness thereof."

Let us give up setting our affection on, and making effort for that which appears to be—whether person, object, place, activity, amount or condition. Let us be partial to God itself and impartial to sense. If we are partial to sense we are lost in belief, and unable to have truth. But in a God-state of being, filled with spirit and light, oneness and equality, impartial to sense and its multiplicity of form, the goodness of God is our all-in-all and all-of-all. Filled with God, we can no longer be tempted by un-God-like mind, body and world. We have moved beyond our period of divided awareness and exist in a new world of oneness. Our attention and effort are "in here" in spirit, not "out there" in belief. We live open and relaxed in omnipresence, *beholding* God taking place rather than making effort for our good. "I live and move and have my being in [and as] God," and God lives and moves and has its being in and as me.

You now see that our statement "nothing local can be healed" is quite correct. Only God is; therefore, only a God-state of being (a non-local, universal, oneness-state of being) has the spiritual faculty of *seeing* and *having* the god mind, body and world. And in the God-state of being, all illness and disease (and every other form of discord, lack, pain and suffering) dissipates as naturally as dark in the presence of light.

> Finally, brethren, whatsoever things are true, whatsoever things are honest, whatsoever things are just, whatsoever things are pure, whatsoever things are lovely, whatsoever things are of good report; if there be any virtue, and if there be any praise, think on these things. Those things, which ye have both learned, and received, and heard, and seen in me, do: and the God of peace shall be with you.

Be the living light which has no darkness in it at all. Be the boundless and free spiritual being you *are,* not a being of belief doing battle with belief-form. Live free in the almighty incorporeal rather than accepting the limitations and false realities of corporeal attachment.

Realize and rely on the absolute reality and practicality of God as the one and only life. *Trust* God to be and to supply your every good, healthy, loving, harmonious, abundant and fulfilling form—freely and unconditionally. *Let* God live your life and *be* your world experience.

In this way, free of personal sense, you are the living light "that lights every man that comes into the world [into your awareness]." You free and reveal the truth of, not only every aspect of your individual experience, but that of every person and condition that touches your consciousness.

Made in the USA
Coppell, TX
03 June 2024